THE GREATEST MILITARY MISSION STORIES EVER TOLD

THE GREATEST MILITARY MISSION STORIES EVER TOLD

EDITED BY TOM McCARTHY

LYONS
PRESS

Essex, Connecticut

An imprint of The Rowman & Littlefield Publishing Group, Inc.
4501 Forbes Blvd., Ste. 200
Lanham, MD 20706
www.rowman.com

Distributed by NATIONAL BOOK NETWORK

British Library Cataloguing in Publication Information available

Library of Congress Cataloging-in-Publication Data

Names: McCarthy, Tom, 1952– editor of compilation.
Title: The greatest military mission stories ever told / edited by Tom McCarthy.
Description: Essex, Connecticut : Lyon Press, [2022] | Includes bibliographical references. |
  Summary: "A collection of stories showcasing the heroics of American forces missions of all
  kinds"—Provided by publisher.
Identifiers: LCCN 2022023586 (print) | LCCN 2022023587 (ebook) |
  ISBN 9781493066131 (paperback) | ISBN 9781493066148 (epub)
Subjects: LCSH: United States—Armed Forces—History. | United States—History, Military.
Classification: LCC E181 .G737 2022 (print) | LCC E181 (ebook) | DDC 355.00973—
  dc23/eng/20220615
LC record available at https://lccn.loc.gov/2022023586
LC ebook record available at https://lccn.loc.gov/2022023587

∞™ The paper used in this publication meets the minimum requirements of American National
Standard for Information Sciences—Permanence of Paper for Printed Library Materials, ANSI/
NISO Z39.48-1992.

Contents

INTRODUCTION

The soldiers and sailors you will encounter in this inspiring collection were not chosen for their bravery. They did not stand out from their colleagues in a challenge laid down by their officers to find the men who would excel at the task ahead. Before their missions, they had been ordinary men, normal citizens going about their normal routines. They found themselves in the military for a variety of reasons—the draft, perhaps, an urge to volunteer to help a larger purpose, maybe a desire to do something for the common good.

They were not, before these missions, extraordinary men.

Those who survived the infernos they were thrust into became something quite different afterward:

Heroes.

Courage is not the absence of fear but rather the control of it. Courage is moving ahead when every instinct in your body and mind tells you to stop and turn around.

Their orders to proceed were nothing more than an invitation to die, and usually in unpleasant ways.

But the soldiers proceeded nonetheless, because a higher cause was at stake.

This stunning collection of stories is a tribute to the courage, steely resolve, and discipline of men who accomplished daunting missions in the face of almost certain death. Nonetheless, they stepped into the breach and performed heroically.

That was their duty and they did not question. They had a mission and they accepted.

Here are ten powerful stories of American soldiers and sailors that span more than two hundred years of action with one common theme, summed up succinctly by a participant who took control of Omaha Beach on D-Day, 1944.

"We were doing the very thing that we had trained so long to do, and we were fascinated, and eagerly excited about it. We realized that any number of things might happen to us and knew too that some things we'd never dreamed of might very well be waiting for us on the beach."

From Marines taking Iwo Jima's Mount Suribachi or defending Khe San, Navy pilots taking to the air to defend Pearl Harbor after the surprise attack by the Japanese, or an outnumbered American regiment in Korea defeating the Chinese at the Battle of Chipyong-ni, courage was the common watchword, death the common consequence.

Such is the lot of soldiers everywhere.

Here is what one soldier who stormed Omaha Beach on D-Day recalled about the landing.

"The first rays of the sun turned the few clouds to crimson. It would have captured the imagination of any artist or poet. You may want to know about the two landing craft that had run aground because of the storm. The sounds of the men in pain and terror as shell after shell fell on the decks could be heard above the din of other combat. Men would jump screaming into the sea only to rise as floating corpses. One man with a flamethrower on his back disintegrated into a flaming inferno."

The same horrors could be found halfway around the world as Marines landed at Iwo Jima.

The wreckage was indescribable. For two miles the debris was so thick that there were only a few places where landing craft could still get in. The wrecked hulls of scores of landing boats testified to one price we had to pay to put our troops ashore. Tanks and half-tracks lay crippled where they had bogged down in the coarse sand. Amphibian tractors, victims of mines and well-aimed shells, lay flopped on their backs. Cranes, brought ashore to unload cargo, tilted at insane angles, and bulldozers were smashed in their own roadways.

Hellish missions were not limited to World War II. The same chaos and unbelievable bravery arose time and again in the Revolutionary War, Vietnam, the Civil War, and Korea.

Noted historian Alfred Thayer Mahan wrote about a resolute group of sailors under Benedict Arnold on Lake Champlain that repelled the British.

The little American navy on Champlain was wiped out; but never had any force, big or small, lived to better purpose or died more gloriously, for it had saved the Lake for that year.

Put yourself in Korea on a frigid winter night. Image the sight that one soldier recalled, knowing death was likely imminent.

We saw the Chinese coming from probably two miles south of George Company," said Wilburn. "And they were carrying torches of all things. I couldn't believe it, but there were so many of them, they weren't afraid of nothing. They came right across that flat ground carrying torches toward our position. You see thousands of lights coming at you like that at night and you're just a young nineteen [or] twenty-year-old man, it really shakes you up.

The Greatest Military Mission Stories Ever Told is a not-so-gentle reminder of the price of freedom—paid by American men for more than two hundred years of struggle.

One

Omaha Beach: Following General Cota

Noel F. Mehlo Jr.

On the morning of June 6, 1944, the transport USS *Charles Carroll* delivered landing craft to the western approaches of Omaha Beach. Under the command of Commander Harold Woodall Biesemeier from August 13, 1942, to June 13, 1944, this ship and her crew conducted assault landings in North Africa and in Italy, including at Sicily and Salerno, while under fire.

At 5 a.m., she stood eleven miles off the Normandy coast, rolling slightly in a wind-flecked channel swell, and at 5:20 a.m., her skipper gave the command "Away all boats!" This was the signal to disembark for all personnel headed ashore. The ship cleared its twenty landing craft over its davit falls as twenty- to thirty-foot waves threatened to smash some of them against their mothership. Through the skill of the trained crew, all were launched without damage.

After setting the landing craft into the channel, the crew of the USS *Charles Carroll* swung large cargo nets over her sides, with four each to starboard and port. The soldiers aboard, who were slated as second-wave assault troops, gathered along the ship railings to climb down the nets to the waiting craft.

General Norman Cota and the Detachment 29th Division headquarters and Headquarter Company, part of the 116th RCT, gathered amidships at Debarkation Station 11 and boarded Landing Craft 71. This designation was the official reference to General Cota's landing party. His group is also referred to as the provisional brigade headquarters for the

29th Infantry Division, the Advance Division Headquarters of the 29th Infantry Division, or, commonly, "Cota's Bastard Brigade."

First Lieutenant Jack Shea, General Cota's aide-de-camp, chronicled the entire D-Day chain of events involving General Cota in a November 1, 1944, combat narrative for Headquarters, Second Information and Historical Service, to which he was assigned as of that point in the war. Much of Cota's D-Day story derives from his report.

Landing Craft 71, crewed by an unknown ensign and coxswain Ricardo Feliciano, carried the first echelon of command troops ashore for the 29th Division.

Landing Craft 71 cleared the USS *Charles Carroll* at 6:10 a.m. (H-20) for an inshore trip of eighty-five minutes. They continued forward in conditions with three miles of good visibility.

They then reached a point four to six hundred yards offshore, where the beach landings were directed by eight stationary British Armored Motor Launches (AMLs). The AMLs' job was to efficiently direct all landing craft into the proper mine-swept lanes by use of loud-hailers. Lieutenant Shea noted that the incoming tide was about two-thirds full, having reached the band of angled-timber groin beach obstacles.

The 146th Special Underwater Demolition Battalion had yet to complete the task of blowing up these obstacles, having mislanded some two thousand yards to the east. Approximately one-third of these obstacles had Tellermines wired to the seaward face of the timbers. The US Navy's 5th Engineer Special Brigade (ESB) landed in the first wave with the mission of clearing beach defenses. These men were all heroes. As General Cota approached the beach, they were furiously attempting to accomplish their own assignments under murderous fire. Their After Action Report recorded the critical beach conditions as Cota landed.

Army and Navy doctors and Aid men worked as they could to give emergency treatment to the wounded. A surgeon of the 16th Regimental Combat Team noticed a high proportion of casualties caused by rifle bullet wounds in the head. Wounded men, lying on the exposed sand, were frequently hit a second or third time. Officer casualties were high.

Companies A, C, and D of the 116th Regimental Combat Team lost all but one officer each, and the 2nd Battalion of the same regiment lost two Company Commanders on the beach.

The confusion of the first hour of the Invasion mounted during the period from 0730 to 0830 hours. Landings continued, but men and vehicles could not move off the beach. A majority of the units piled up behind the shingle bank, where they lay in rows sometimes three deep. In many cases these units were leaderless, their officers having been killed or wounded.

The solitary craft entered its landing lane at the right western edge of Dog White Beach, located approximately seven hundred meters northeast of Vierville, when it was noticed by the coxswain that the beach was under heavy enemy fire. They altered course slightly to avoid floating mines. This craft approached the shore alone and made landfall amid the breakwaters at the Dog White and Dog Red boundary. While nearing shore, coxswain Ricardo Feliciano lost seaway and cut the throttle before beaching as they began navigating the maze of beach obstacles not previously destroyed. The craft sideslipped and was swept against an angled-timber groin by the three-knot easterly crosscurrent traversing along the face of the beach. The waves were four to six feet high and thrust Landing Craft 71 into the timber obstacle multiple times.

These collisions dislodged an attached Tellermine, which failed to explode. The coxswain gunned the motor and maneuvered the boat free, advancing closer to shore, and then Landing Craft 71 grounded on a sandbar approximately seventy-five yards from the high-water mark at 7:26 a.m. (H+56). The boat skipper dropped the ramp under heavy machine-gun, mortar, and light-cannon fire and called to the men, "Disembark!"

Between the sandbar where the ramp went down and the high-water mark at the seawall was a runnel with a varying depth of three to six feet, requiring some soldiers to swim or wade ashore. Several men found themselves immersed to their armpits. As the men emerged from the runnel, many made their way to the shelter of the tanks of the 743rd Tank Battalion.

Lieutenant Shea's report continued,

"Moderate small-arms fire was directed at the craft as the ramp was lowered. This consisted of rifle, and judging from the sound, machine-gun fire. It continued to cover the group as they made their way inland. Having landed in about two or three feet of water, it was necessary to cross a runnel (about five feet deep and thirty feet wide) which ran parallel to the high-water mark. During this phase of the landing, which necessitated wading through about 40 yards of water, Major John Sours, Regimental S4, was killed. He was hit in the chest and upper body by automatic fire, fell face down in the water. His body was later recovered as it floated in the shallows."

Two other soldiers were likewise killed in these moments. General Cota continued the advance through all of this, under the first of what would be many documented instances of threat to his life over the next thirty hours.

According to official records, all officers and men interviewed about the D-Day landings reported that there was positively no evidence of friendly aerial bombardment and little evidence of naval bombardment of the beaches. There were no craters to use for cover, and the enemy beach installations remained intact.

General Cota's party sought cover behind the nearest tank as the group moved across the beach under the cover of the tank that had engaged German antitank weapons to its near right front. The Duplex Drive amphibious tanks of Company C, 743rd Tank Battalion, were the first real cover available. The tanks landed at H-6, and there were an estimated eighteen tanks standing just above and advancing along with the rising tide. They all faced the bluffs and were spaced at intervals of approximately seventy to one hundred yards. This placed them about twenty-five feet from the seawall, from which position each of them fired at enemy positions immediately in front of each tank. Two tanks were burning to the west near the Vierville exit. One, identified as Tank "C-5," was noticeably damaged from several rounds of direct 88mm fire from the German WN 72 casemate. First Lieutenant Alfred H. Williams Jr., Company C, 743rd Tank Battalion, and his crew managed to escape that destruction.

General Cota and his men screened themselves behind a tank that was firing to its right front instead of its previously assigned target to the west: the enemy artillery positions at Pointe et Raz de la Percée. These German strongpoints were armed with two 75mm artillery pieces situated high on the bluffs and were able to fire down the beach well beyond Dog Red.

At some point during these moments, something in General Cota must have triggered his fortitude for what followed. From this moment on, he was no longer only one of many soldiers landing under fire on the beach; he rose to the occasion and led his men to a victory snatched from the jaws of imminent defeat.

An official account by Headquarters, 29th Infantry Division, recounted, "Realizing that immediate steps had to be taken to move the men from the dangerous area of the beach, General Cota, exposing himself to enemy fire, went over the seawall giving encouragement, directions and orders to those about him."

After observing the tanks in action, General Cota noticed that these tanks were not firing per operational plans, and the enemy gun positions were able to profitably employ their fire. Brigadier General Cota observed at this point that the enemy guns fired one flat trajectory shell at each landing craft just before it touched down. The Germans held fire until the point that a landing craft touched down. If they missed, they determined distance by line of sight, splash, and water ricochets. The German observers then adjusted fire within a three-second interval and fired a second shot that found its mark. Direct hits were achieved by no later than the third round.

Cota's group suffered another casualty behind the tank from machine-gun fire, and the group advanced to the seawall approximately nine hundred yards from the Vierville exit to seek better cover. This seawall was four to five feet high and had twenty- to thirty-foot-long timber-rail breakwaters seaward at about fifty-yard intervals.

By the end of D-Day, only twenty-one of fifty-one of the 743rd Tank Battalion's medium tanks would survive to continue the fight. The 743rd Tank Battalion's commander, Lieutenant Colonel John S. Upham, was wounded by machine-gun fire later in the morning.

At this point (H+60), nearly one hundred disorganized men from the Beach Brigade, 1st Battalion of the 116th RCT, Naval Aid Group men, naval fire control parties, naval beach maintenance men, 2nd Rangers, and others took shelter from enemy rifle and machine-gun fire from the bluffs above. The troops were hopelessly jumbled, unled, and firmly pinned down. No Americans had advanced past the seawall at the inland border of the beach.

As the soldiers lay pinned down by machine-gun fire, clustered in the bays formed by the seawall and breakwaters, the enemy was beginning to bring effective mortar fire to bear on those hidden behind the wall.

Sergeant Francis E. Huesser, light machine-gun squad leader, Company C, 116th Infantry, and Captain Robert J. Bedell, Company C, 116th Infantry, leader of 1st Assault Section, landed at 6:53 a.m. They described a "tremendous blossom of orange flame and black, oily smoke." Captain Bedell saw General Cota only a minute or so later.

> *They ran forward to the little wooden seawall banked with shingle. Huddled there beneath the low timber wall. It was there that they saw General Cota for the first time. All of them remembered seeing Cota, just after touching down on the beach. "He was waving a .45 around, and I figured if he could get up there so could I." [Captain Bedell] remarked that Cota came up to him, and prompted that "Well, we gotta get 'em off the beach. We've gotta get going."*

Sergeant Huesser discussed how General Cota influenced his group's actions as they blew a gap with a Bangalore torpedo. Cota "came up to us, waving that pistol around and said we had to get off the beach. That we had to get through the wire. I guess all of us figured that if he could go wandering around like that, we could, too." They snaked the pipes of the torpedo under the fencing and pulled the friction igniter. Nothing. Lieutenant Schwartz scurried over, did something to it, and took cover, and then it blew.

One critically important detail become all too apparent in the flow of events at about 7:30 a.m.: An estimated three-fourths of all radios, particularly the SCR 300s, were either destroyed by enemy fire or ruined by the salt water.

The 29th Infantry Division later reported that they believed the Germans specifically targeted radiomen either purposefully or because they mistook the backpack radios for flamethrowers.

Company H arrived in the vicinity of the breakwaters at approximately 7:30 a.m. Private First Class Arden Earll remembered seeing the first of the group of tanks working in this sector. The tank would go in reverse to the water's edge and gather up soldiers in need of cover. The tank would advance to the seawall and then fire a few rounds, allowing the wet soldiers to take cover at the seawall, and then reverse to do the dance all over. This allowed the tanks not to become stationary targets and easy picking for the Germans.

Private First Class Arden Earll, mortarman, MOS 504, Company H, 2nd Battalion, 116th Infantry, 29th Infantry Division
I got there by that tank, and I had to go around it because the tide had come in by that time, and I got right behind the tank. One enemy artillery round hit out in the water. I thought to myself: "Arden, get out of here, they are after this tank." I couldn't move, I was loaded so heavy, I couldn't move very fast. The next round came in right close to the tank. It didn't hurt the tank. But I got my first Purple Heart right there. I still got part of that artillery shell in my right wrist and hand. I wasn't hurt too bad. I had seen an American panic, before, on the way in. And I started, I began to feel, and I thought, "For God's sakes Arden, you're not hurt bad. Keep Going." So I did. Our Aid-man was a hero that day. That's all we had. We didn't have any first aid, uh, hospital, or anything like that. Now, I think there was hospital ships out there, but they couldn't get in to get us off the beach, and so, a lot of the guys just laid there. I was bleeding a little bit, but I could still walk, I could still go, I carried my load. I kept going. . . . We moved to the west down the beach to the sector General Cota landed in and was working. By the time I saw General Cota, a lot of us were hunkered down. We were waiting to see what was; we knew something was wrong, but we waited for somebody to tell us what to do next, and

that's when I saw General Cota. I do know that he walked up and down along the beach, quite a lot, and exposed himself to enemy fire at all times.

Herb Epstein, Intelligence NCO, 5th Ranger Infantry Battalion, HQ Company

As A and B were preceding us into the beach, Colonel [Max] Schneider decided to land at the Vierville Draw because the men that preceded us in the 29th Division were under murderous fire on the beach and having a hard time getting out of the boats. The fire was so intense and Colonel Schneider was observing this fire, we were in the lead boat at the time. As we got close to the shore, Schneider commanded the boat flotilla captain to swing the whole group left, parallel to the beach. So instead of landing at Dog Green according to the battle plan, we landed further to the east. As we were going parallel to the beach Schneider saw an area that wasn't too hot and ordered the flotilla commander "to get us in and get us in fast." We turned again another 90 degrees and they got us to water that wasn't very deep, at least it was reasonably dry where they landed my boat. There was a lot of artillery and mortar fire coming in and a lot of men lying on the beach.

The 5th Ranger Infantry Battalion (RIB), under the command of Lieutenant Colonel Max Schneider, had the primary mission of landing at Pointe du Hoc as a follow-up force to Lieutenant Colonel James Earl Rudder and his three companies of 2nd Ranger Infantry Battalion engaged there. After not receiving communications to land there, Schneider made his way to their secondary landing objective at Dog Green. As the battalion approached, the men witnessed the carnage that befell Companies A and B and the remnants of the 29th Infantry. Remaining calm and drawing on his experience as a former Darby's Ranger who fought in the Mediterranean, Schneider swung his flotilla of two waves of landing crafts to the east and headed in at the breakwaters where Cota and his men were.

Private First Class Randall Ching was a member of 2nd Platoon, Company B, 5th Ranger Infantry Battalion, and was in one of the westernmost bays formed by the breakwaters. He was the only Chinese

American Ranger during World War II. He was born in the States, but during the Great Depression, his family emigrated back to China. As a result, he was conscripted into the Chinese army and fought the Japanese in the late 1930s before returning to the States at the outset of US involvement in the war, and he volunteered as a Ranger.

Private First Class Randall Ching, Company B, 5th Ranger Infantry Battalion

I landed on Dog White Beach with our whole 5th Ranger Battalion. It took the Rangers five minutes to get from the beach to the seawall. I watched artillery coming up to the seawall, to the left, to the right, when I was at the seawall. It walked, it come up, because the Germans got the seawall all zeroed in. And they opened up, with three shells, Boom, Boom, Boom, all over the seawall. And I thought, oh hell, this is gonna come up pretty close to me pretty soon. It just so happened, that two landing craft landed and both ramps dropped. Both had two ramps down. So the artillery, turned their attention to those landing craft. They hit both of them. The first one was hit, was the nearest on to me, so I saw that. They hit it with three shells. People started to jump overboard because of the fire. That is the worst part of the memory in my mind. One of the persons on the landing craft was carrying a flamethrower, and the flamethrower exploded.

A vivid account of the morning of June 6, 1944, was sent in a letter to Mr. Cornelius Ryan on June 16, 1958, in response to Ryan's plea for stories associated with D-Day so that he could incorporate them into his epic *The Longest Day.* This moving account brought forth the horrors experienced and witnessed by all on that beach.

Private First Class Max D. Coleman, Company C, 5th Ranger Infantry Battalion

In your interviews with various participants of the "D" Day Operations, try to get a picture of the sky in the early dawn. I have witnessed many sunrises in my thirty-four years, but this one stayed in my mind. Apparently it was unusual not only to me, for I have asked many others about it. I am not capable of an accurate description. There was a storm of high winds, as you well know; but it was a storm with few clouds. The first rays of the sun turned the few clouds to crimson. It would have captured the imagination of any artist or poet. You may want to know about the two landing craft that had run aground because of the storm. The sounds of the men in pain and terror as shell after shell fell on the decks could be heard above the din of other combat. Men would jump screaming into the sea only to rise as floating corpses. One man with a flamethrower on his back disintegrated into a flaming inferno.

Lieutenant Colonel Harold A. Cassell, XO, 116th Infantry, was aboard Landing Craft 71 along with the alternate headquarters for the regiment. As they were on the beach in positions bracketing the vessel, Cota's men witnessed the landing as it beached and was subsequently devastated. Cassell and some fifteen men had disembarked before the blast, and the remaining survivors leapt overboard, many of them in flames. Cota's men reported that a lot of the men who did make it to shore were badly burned.

Cota worked to the west down the beach and by some accounts made it as far as half the distance to the D-1 exit near the manor, Hamel au Prêtre.

All accounts place him calmly and tactically walking in that direction, exhorting men to action. This amounted to a distance of between one-half and three-quarters of a mile. When he turned to head back to the breakwaters, he calmly walked away from these German positions. The thought of turning one's back to this amount of active firepower is astounding.

While in the vicinity of elements of Company C, 116th Infantry, General Cota happened upon a section of seawall with a low mound of earth approximately five yards beyond it. He crawled forward to reconnoiter the firing position and then personally directed the placement of a Browning Automatic Rifle there. He told the gunner to lay down suppressive fire and shoot at any enemy movement along the bluffs.

This fire was intended to cover the soldiers as they breached the wire and made their way toward the foot of the bluffs. After this, General Cota personally supervised the placement of a Bangalore torpedo in the double-apron barbed wire fence. The barbed wire in this area was standard agricultural-style barbed wire, not the heavier, squarish military concertina wire expected by the men. The wire was along the inner border of the promenade, the ten-foot-wide, asphalt-surfaced road that ran parallel with the seawall along Dog Beach.

This started elements of Companies C and D up the bluffs. During this action, Cota interacted with Lieutenant Colonel Robert Ploger, CO, 121st Engineer Combat Battalion, to secure the needed Bangalore torpedoes. The general acted above and beyond the call of duty in this instance alone at the risk of his life as he was under observation by the Germans.

Lieutenant Colonel Robert Ploger, commander,
121st Engineer Combat Battalion, 29th Division:
While I was walking west along the beach looking for some of my engineers, I ran into General Cota. He said, "Ploger, bring me some Bangalore torpedoes so we can blow this wire." I went off to look for some. A little while later I ran into General Cota again, and this time he asked me for some minefield marking tape which came in long rolls of white cloth. He wanted it to mark lanes through minefields beyond the wire and up the bluff. I immediately went off on another search.

The second wave of the 5th Ranger Infantry Battalion landed at 7:50 a.m. on the eastern edge of Dog White Beach, extending east into Dog Red Beach over a 250-yard front. Major General Raaen provided testimony regarding the Ranger landing on the beach in relation to General Cota.

Major General John C. Raaen Jr., USA (Ret.), June 6, 2018,
Witness Statement to Congress for Cota Medal of Honor Upgrade
My LCA touched down on the east edge of Omaha Dog White Beach on June 6, 1944, at 0750 British Double Daylight Time. The rest of my battalion's, the 5th Ranger Infantry Battalion, 12 boats landed to my left on Dog Red Beach. The beach was chaos. Machine gun and rifle fire poured down the beach from the enemy positions to my right. Artillery fire was concentrated on the landing craft at the water's edge. Smoke, fire, the cracking of bullets overhead, the detonation of artillery

striking Landing Craft added to the chaos. The beach was littered with burning debris from materiel destroyed by enemy fire. The dead, the dying, the wounded lay everywhere.

The situation on Dog Red Beach was desperate. The tide had reached a point about 50 to 60 yards from the wooden seawall. No troops had left the beach. Those who survived crossing the beach were piled on top of one another at the base of the four-foot seawall. Tides and wind from the storm had scattered the landing craft and many had landed as far as two miles from planned landing locations. Most troops were leaderless, no idea where they were, where they were supposed to go.

I had been on the beach no more than ten minutes, checking the men for firearms, ammunition and other equipment while awaiting orders from battalion. Several of my men called my attention to a man about 100 yards to my right moving along the edge of the beach. He was chewing on a cigar, yelling and waving at the men in the dunes and at the seawall. He was taking no action to conceal himself from the enemy, who continued to pour small-arms fire.

We thought him crazy or heroic. Everyone else was seeking cover, while this man was exposing himself not only to the enemy, but to the troops he was rallying. As he approached the bay (formed by breakwaters and the seawall) I was in, I rose to meet him. As he rounded the end of the breakwater, I saw his insignia of rank. Brigadier General!

I reported to him with a hand salute. "Sir, Captain Raaen, 5th Ranger Battalion."

He responded, "Raaen, Raaen. You must be Jack Raaen's son."

"Yes, sir."

"What's the situation here?"

"Sir, the 5th Ranger Battalion has landed intact, here and over a 250-yard front. The battalion commander has just ordered the companies to proceed by platoon infiltration to our rallying points."

"Where is your battalion commander?"

"I'll take you to him, sir," pointing out the location of Lieutenant Colonel Schneider.

"No! You remain here with your men."

As General Cota started away, he stopped and looked around, saying, "You men are Rangers. I know you won't let me down."

And with that, he was off to see Schneider. During this whole conversation, General Cota never took cover nor flinched as the bullets cracked by us and artillery detonated some 50 yards away at the waterline.

Captain Raaen was not alone in his witness of General Cota's actions over the next ten to twenty minutes. Several other 29ers and Rangers provided testimony in one form or another over the years. In many cases, the men providing the testimonials had no interaction with each other as they told their stories. The facts of their stories are in alignment in terms of General Cota's gallantry above and beyond the call of duty on the beach.

Major Richard P. Sullivan, executive officer, 5th Ranger Infantry Battalion

I watched the approach on an LCI to the beach, with troops all lined up to run down the gangway to the beach, when an artillery shell containing liquid fire (napalm?) exploded on the deck covering all with flame, causing most of the men to jump into the sea. This happened only a few yards from shore and was probably the man seen by other Rangers. He was carrying a flamethrower and took a direct hit from an artillery shell and was vaporized along with his equipment. The activities of Brigadier General Cota seemed to be stupid at the time, but it was actually nothing but the sheer heroism and dedication of a professional soldier and fine officer that prompted him to walk up and down the landing beach urging the men forward. I remember his aide-de-camp being a nervous wreck trying to get the General to stop his activities.

T/4 Lee Brown, HQ Company, 5th Ranger Infantry Battalion

We were told to keep our heads down, but I did peek up and the "zip, zip, zip" of machine-gun fire had us ducking back down quickly. Lieutenant Colonel Schneider, and I think Captain [Hugo W.] Heffelfinger, were in my LCA—the British LCA driver did a great job getting us into the beach, I did not even step into any water—I was up onto dry beach. When the ramp went down on our LCA, the lead officer off hesitated and because of that hesitation it saved many lives. The reason was because in the time of the hesitation a machine gun strafed right in front of the LCA ramp and would have cut down many of us coming right off—I was 5th, 6th, or 7th off and likely would have been cut down. The officer who hesitated and didn't charge right off, like they had been told to do, was Schneider.

He had paused to take off his Mae West and toss it down on the beach. The delay likely saved my life. I ran all the way to the sea wall as fast as I could with my M1 rifle, there really wasn't anything to hide behind until you got there. Many men fell around me on the run in to the wall. Getting to the sea wall I looked back and saw an LCT get hit and blow up.

There were bodies flying in the air—I turned to the radio man next to me and I said, "This is war!" I remember General Cota approaching us and him specifically talking to Captain John Raaen first and asking if he was Jack Raaen's son. He was then speaking with Schneider and I remember him exhorting them to lead the way on the beach. I was in awe of Cota's bravery in standing upright over them all hunkered down behind the wall and being impervious to fire.

Staff Sergeant Richard N. Hathaway Jr., Company A, 5th Ranger Infantry Battalion

Back on Omaha, I was lying on the shingle, attempting to gather my men in order to breach the concertina barbed wire on top of the beach wall when a voice behind me asked, "What outfit is this?" At the very same moment, that German machine gun, which had given us so much trouble on the way in, opened up.

I answered the voice and said, "We're the Rangers."

I got a response of, "Well, let's get off this beach!"

In a rather excited voice, I said, "We will, as soon as I blow this f-ing wire." I then turned and noticed where the voice came from. It was from a short stocky man with the stub of a cigar in his mouth, wearing a field jacket with a silver star on his shoulder, the rank of a brigadier general.

It was Brigadier General Norman Cota, the Assistant Division Commander of the Twenty-ninth Infantry Division. I couldn't help but wonder what in hell was he doing on this beach. I turned back, still looking for that German machine gun when I heard my Bangalore man yell, "Fire in the hole!" The Bangalore exploded, and with Lieutenant Charles Parker leading, we took off through the gap in the wire. I was sixth in line as we started up the bluff.

As a result of this interaction, the Rangers' official motto was born from General Cota's lips, under fire, at a time when their spirit and fighting tenacity were critically needed: "Rangers, Lead the Way!"

Lieutenant Colonel Max Schneider, CO, 5th Ranger Infantry Battalion, issued orders, the Rangers blew four gaps into the wire along their entire front, and the men began to pour through. General Cota himself moved to the Rangers of Company C at 8:07 a.m. and exhorted their advance. They moved at the double and cleared any communications trenches along the foot of the bluffs and then began the ascent in columns. The bluffs were on fire from naval shelling, and this slowed the advance but at the same time offered a smoke screen to their movements from German eyes. The Rangers were off the beach by 8:10 a.m. LCI(L) 92 came ashore at 8:10 a.m., approximately two hundred yards to the left of the Rangers' gaps in the wire and suffered the same fate as LCI(L) 91.

With the Ranger battalion on the move, General Cota turned his attention to soldiers remaining on the beach. With a gap blown in the wire in his vicinity, the first man through the wire was hit by a heavy burst of machine-gun fire and died in just minutes. Joe Balkoski tentatively identified this Stonewaller as either Private Ralph Hubbard or Private George Losey. ("Stonewaller" refers to those members of the forerunning units of the 29th Infantry Division who served under General Stonewall Jackson during the American Civil War.)

As the soldier lay dying, the others could hear his pleas: "Medic, medic, I'm hit. Help me."

He moaned and cried for a few minutes as life slipped away from him. Soldiers nearby heard the man call for his "mama" several times, and then it was over. This death demoralized these troops, and they stalled any advance to be made.

General Cota, with a desire to urge them on, stood up and charged through the gap next. Men rallied behind him, and they crossed the road unharmed and dropped into a field of marsh grass beyond. The 29ers followed a system of shallow communications trenches until they reached taller grass beyond near the base of the bluffs. No antipersonnel mines or booby traps were discovered in the trenches as the men moved. Cota's men began the ascent on a diagonal to the right, up the bluffs, through the smoke. They reached the top of the bluffs about one hundred yards to the west of a small concrete foundation positioned twenty-five yards below the bluff. This feature of the landscape remains.

Cota remained at the foot of the bluffs and then met up again at 8:30 a.m. with Colonel Canham, who had set his first CP on the bluffs near the bottom. The radiomen tried using their SC300 radios to establish contact with the 1st Infantry Division off to the east. Their attempts were unsuccessful, as the radios were damaged. As the CP began to try to function, the Germans zeroed in on it as a target and fired five or six rounds of ranged-in two-inch mortars at the group.

The fragments killed two enlisted men within three feet of the general. His radio operator, T/3 C. A. Wilson, was seriously wounded and thrown twenty to thirty feet up the bluff, while Lieutenant Shea, the general's aide, was thrown seventy-five feet down the bluff.

As a result, Colonel Canham hurriedly moved the CP up the bluff. The attack on the western portion of Omaha Beach was arrested and disorganized such that at 8:30 a.m., the commander of the 7th Naval Beach Battalion ordered a temporary halt of landings on Omaha in the face of the deteriorating situation.

Arden Earll's testimony about General Cota paints a profound picture of the courage and leadership he exhibited on the beach. The importance of this testimony is that it defines what it means to go from a near-catastrophic defeat to a heroic victory, as is often said of the US forces that assaulted Omaha Beach west on D-Day. You can see in his words the change from hopelessness to victory in action for the American infantryman—a change that was brought on by "Dutch."

Private First Class Arden Earll, mortarman, MOS 504, Company H, 2nd Battalion, 116th Infantry, 29th Infantry Division

So there the first waves were, we landed, and everybody had been told that it was going to be like a cakewalk. Just walk in, and I remember myself, when we got off of the LCVP, Sergeant Washburn was right ahead of me, and I looked around and that beach was just as flat as this tabletop, no shell craters, no nothing. We had been told we didn't need to worry about digging a fox hole, there would be so many shell craters; you could just drop into one. But there was nothing. So, why did the 29ers hunker down? Maybe I shouldn't say this, but I will. They had not been told the truth.

Maybe it wasn't General Eisenhower or General Montgomery's fault, but all the preparations for before our landing had not come to pass. So the foot troops got on there; "Hey, this isn't the way it's supposed to be!" And what did they do? Right away it affected the soldiers in their heads. They hunkered down. What do we do next? And that's the reason.

General Cota directly and positively affected this battlefield condition and caused us to overcome our fear.

We were all hunkered down behind the seawall, or whatever protection we could get, and Cota went along, prodding us on, to keep going. He said, "You're gonna die out here. It's better if you go inland to die." He did not seem to be scared of anything. He stood upright and just walked along. "Come on, keep going, keep going."

General Cota had no fear for his own safety.

General Cota was exposed to enemy sniper fire, small-arms fire, and everything they could throw at him, and it didn't seem to worry him at all. He just walked along, and said "Come on, you've got to go!" He didn't seem to be scared of anything. He could have been shot by a sniper. He could have got hit by artillery, he could have got hit by anything. He was the only high-ranking officer I witnessed do that. Everybody else was as low as they possibly could be. So he was the only one, the only physical human target that the Germans had to shoot at. Here he was, a General, and he was the target.

He said, "If you stay here, you're gonna get killed. If you go inland, you may get killed. But let's go inland and get killed. Not stay on this damn beach. The tide was coming in. Don't stop. Get the hell out of here, and get 'em."

I think that inspired a lot of people, a lot of the guys, to keep moving. They had a General tell them these things.

If it hadn't have been for a few people like him, D-Day could have very well been turned into what the British went through at Dieppe. It could have very well turned into that. It very well might have been. But General Cota thought, even if he didn't do anything, or say anything, if they just saw him, walking up and down the beach, "By God, if he could do it, we could do it!" So, that is what I think. Other men also thought, "If a General can do that, we can do it." He did these actions for his entire time on the beach.

It took courage for him to stand there in the wide open amongst all that chaos, in the midst of a lot of scared kids. General Cota probably looked like and was the age of many of their Dads. His leadership became infectious. Because when they saw the General, walking up and down and in plain sight, it inspired them to move. The General was armed only with his pistol.

Seeing General Cota gave me a lot of courage. All I could think of was, "Arden, you gotta keep going. You gotta keep going. If you're ever going to get home, there's only one way to get home, and that's to keep going." I didn't know when my time might be up. I think all of us felt that way. Our time could be up anytime, but we have to keep going.

In his first hour ashore, General Cota took what was nearly a total disaster and began an arduous journey to exert command and control over the battlespace. He reinvigorated the demoralized men. His actions during that second hour saved the remaining thousand or so men on the beach who had not already fallen as honored dead or as casualties.

The fact that so many men from so many different units and locations directly witnessed his actions on the beach is clear evidence of his movement up and down the beach during Cota's first hour in combat. Communications were nonexistent, and contact was yet to be established with the 1st Infantry Division or with General Charles Gerhardt afloat aboard the USS *Ancon*. General Bradley considered diverting the remaining follow-up forces to Utah Beach. But on the beach, now at the toe of the bluff, General Cota saw what had to be done. He had just missed his own death by mere feet after the mortar fire struck the Advance CP. He would lead the men to Vierville and beyond.

In Cota's postwar words to his grandson, "There's nothing like being shot at."

Two

Capturing San Juan Hill
with the Rough Riders

Theodore Roosevelt

On the afternoon of the 25th we moved on a couple of miles and camped in a marshy open spot close to a beautiful stream. Here we lay for several days. Captain Lee, the British attaché, spent some time with us; we had begun to regard him as almost a member of the regiment. Count von Gotzen, the German attaché, another good fellow, also visited us. General Young was struck down with the fever, and Wood took charge of the brigade. This left me in command of the regiment, of which I was very glad, for such experience as we had had is a quick teacher.

By this time the men and I knew one another, and I felt able to make them do themselves justice in march or battle. They understood that I paid no heed to where they came from; no heed to their creed, politics, or social standing; that I would care for them to the utmost of my power, but that I demanded the highest performance of duty; while in return I had seen them tested, and knew I could depend absolutely on their courage, hardihood, obedience, and individual initiative.

There was nothing like enough transportation with the army, whether in the way of wagons or mule-trains; exactly as there had been no sufficient number of landing-boats with the transports. The officers' baggage had come up, but none of us had much, and the shelter-tents proved only a partial protection against the terrific downpours of rain. These occurred almost every afternoon, and turned the camp into a tarn, and the trails into torrents and quagmires. We were not given quite the proper amount of food, and what we did get, like most of the clothing issued us, was fitter for the Klondyke than for Cuba.

We got enough salt pork and hardtack for the men, but not the full ration of coffee and sugar, and nothing else. I organized a couple of expeditions back to the seacoast, taking the strongest and best walkers and also some of the officers' horses and a stray mule or two, and brought back beans and canned tomatoes. These I got partly by great exertions on my part, and partly by the aid of Colonel Weston of the Commissary Department, a particularly energetic man whose services were of great value. A silly regulation forbade my purchasing canned vegetables, except for the officers; and I had no little difficulty in getting round this regulation, and purchasing (with my own money, of course) what I needed for the men.

One of the men I took with me on one of these trips was Sherman Bell, the former Deputy Marshal of Cripple Creek, and Wells-Fargo Express rider. In coming home with his load, through a blinding storm, he slipped and opened the old rupture. The agony was very great and one of his comrades took his load. He himself, sometimes walking, and sometimes crawling, got back to camp, where Dr. Church fixed him up with a spike bandage, but informed him that he would have to be sent back to the States when an ambulance came along.

The ambulance did not come until the next day, which was the day before we marched to San Juan. It arrived after nightfall, and as soon as Bell heard it coming, he crawled out of the hospital tent into the jungle, where he lay all night; and the ambulance went off without him. The men shielded him just as school-boys would shield a companion, carrying his gun, belt, and bedding; while Bell kept out of sight until the column started, and then staggered along behind it.

I found him the morning of the San Juan fight. He told me that he wanted to die fighting, if die he must, and I hadn't the heart to send him back. He did splendid service that day, and afterward in the trenches, and though the rupture opened twice again, and on each occasion he was within a hair's breadth of death, he escaped, and came back with us to the United States.

The army was camped along the valley, ahead of and behind us, our outposts being established on either side. From the generals to the privates all were eager to march against Santiago. At daybreak, when the tall palms began to show dimly through the rising mist, the scream of the cavalry trumpets tore the tropic dawn; and in the evening, as the bands of regiment after regiment played "The Star-Spangled Banner," all, officers and men alike, stood with heads uncovered, wherever they were, until the last strains of the anthem died away in the hot sunset air.

On landing we spent some active hours in marching our men a quarter of a mile or so inland, as boat-load by boat-load they disembarked. Meanwhile one of the men, Knoblauch, a New Yorker, who was a great athlete and a champion swimmer, by diving in the surf off the dock, recovered most of the rifles which had been lost when the boat-load of cavalry capsized. The country would have offered very great difficulties to an attacking force had there been resistance. It was little but a mass of rugged and precipitous hills, covered for the most part by dense jungle. Five hundred resolute men could have prevented the disembarkation at very little cost to themselves.

There had been about that number of Spaniards at Daiquiri that morning, but they had fled even before the ships began shelling. In their place we found hundreds of Cuban insurgents, a crew of as utter tatterdemalions as human eyes ever looked on, armed with every kind of rifle in all stages of dilapidation. It was evident, at a glance, that they would be no use in serious fighting, but it was hoped that they might be of service in scouting. From a variety of causes, however, they turned out to be nearly useless, even for this purpose, so far as the Santiago campaign was concerned.

We were camped on a dusty, brush-covered flat, with jungle on one side, and on the other a shallow, fetid pool fringed with palm-trees. Huge land-crabs scuttled noisily through the underbrush, exciting much interest among the men. Camping was a simple matter, as each man carried all he had, and the officers had nothing. I took a light mackintosh and a tooth-brush. Fortunately, that night it did not rain; and from the palm-leaves we built shelters from the sun.

General Lawton, a tall, fine-looking man, had taken the advance. A thorough soldier, he at once established outposts and pushed reconnoitering parties ahead on the trails. He had as little baggage as the rest of us. Our own Brigade-Commander, General Young, had exactly the same impedimenta that I had, namely, a mackintosh and a tooth-brush.

Next morning we were hard at work trying to get the stuff unloaded from the ship, and succeeded in getting most of it ashore, but were utterly unable to get transportation for anything but a very small quantity. The great shortcoming throughout the campaign was the utterly inadequate transportation. If we had been allowed to take our mule-train, we could have kept the whole cavalry division supplied.

In the afternoon word came to us to march. General Wheeler, a regular game-cock, was as anxious as Lawton to get first blood, and he was bent upon putting the cavalry division to the front as quickly as possible. Lawton's advance guard was in touch with the Spaniards, and there had been a skirmish between the latter and some Cubans, who were repulsed. General Wheeler made a reconnaissance in person, found out where the enemy was, and directed General Young to take our brigade and move forward so as to strike him next morning. He had the power to do this, as when General Shafter was afloat he had command ashore.

I had succeeded in finding Texas, my surviving horse, much the worse for his fortnight on the transport and his experience in getting off, but still able to carry me.

It was mid-afternoon and the tropic sun was beating fiercely down when Colonel Wood started our regiment—the First and Tenth Cavalry and some of the infantry regiments having already marched. Colonel Wood himself rode in advance, while I led my squadron, and Major Brodie followed with his. It was a hard march, the hilly jungle trail being so narrow that often we had to go in single file. We marched fast, for Wood was bound to get us ahead of the other regiments, so as to be sure of our place in the body that struck the enemy next morning. If it had not been for his energy in pushing forward, we should certainly have missed the fight. As it was, we did not halt until we were at the extreme front.

The men were not in very good shape for marching, and moreover they were really horsemen, the majority being cowboys who had never done much walking. The heat was intense and their burdens very heavy. Yet there was very little straggling. Whenever we halted they instantly took off their packs and threw themselves on their backs. Then at the word to start they would spring into place again. The captains and lieutenants tramped along, encouraging the men by example and word.

A good part of the time I was by Captain Llewellen, and was greatly pleased to see the way in which he kept his men up to their work. He never pitied or coddled his troopers, but he always looked after them. He helped them whenever he could, and took rather more than his full share of hardship and danger, so that his men naturally followed him with entire devotion. Jack Greenway was under him as lieutenant, and to him the entire march was nothing but an enjoyable outing, the chance of fight on the morrow simply adding the needed spice of excitement.

It was long after nightfall when we tramped through the darkness into the squalid coast hamlet of Siboney. As usual when we made a night camp, we simply drew the men up in column of troops, and then let each man lie down where he was. Black thunder-clouds were gathering. Before they broke the fires were made and the men cooked their coffee and pork, some frying the hardtack with the pork. The officers, of course, fared just as the men did. Hardly had we finished eating when the rain came, a regular tropic downpour. We sat about, sheltering ourselves as best we could, for the hour or two it lasted; then the fires were relighted and we closed around them, the men taking off their wet things to dry them, so far as possible, by the blaze.

Wood had gone off to see General Young, as General Wheeler had instructed General Young to hit the Spaniards, who were about four miles away, as soon after daybreak as possible. Meanwhile, I strolled over to Captain Capron's troop. He and I, with his two lieutenants, Day and Thomas, stood around the fire, together with two or three non-commissioned officers and privates; among the latter were Sergeant Hamilton Fish and Trooper Elliot Cowdin, both of New York. Cowdin, together with two other troopers, Harry Thorpe and Munro Ferguson, had been on my Oyster Bay Polo Team some years before.

Hamilton Fish had already shown himself one of the best non-commissioned officers we had. A huge fellow, of enormous strength and endurance and dauntless courage, he took naturally to a soldier's life. He never complained and never shirked any duty of any kind, while his power over his men was great. So good a sergeant had he made that Captain Capron, keen to get the best men under him, took him when he left Tampa—for Fish's troop remained behind.

As we stood around the flickering blaze that night I caught myself admiring the splendid bodily vigor of Capron and Fish—the captain and the sergeant. Their frames seemed of steel, to withstand all fatigue; they were flushed with health; in their eyes shone high resolve and fiery desire. Two finer types of the fighting man, two better representatives of the American soldier, there were not in the whole army. Capron was going over his plans for the fight when we should meet the Spaniards on the morrow, Fish occasionally asking a question. They were both filled with eager longing to show their mettle, and both were rightly confident that if they lived they would win honorable renown and would rise high in their chosen profession. Within twelve hours they both were dead.

I had lain down when toward midnight Wood returned. He had gone over the whole plan with General Young. We were to start by sunrise toward Santiago, General Young taking four troops of the Tenth and four troops of the First up the road which led through the valley; while Colonel Wood was to lead our eight troops along a hill-trail to the left, which joined the valley road about four miles on, at a point where the road went over a spur of the mountain chain and from thence went downhill toward Santiago. The Spaniards had their lines at the junction of the road and the trail.

Before describing our part in the fight, it is necessary to say a word about General Young's share, for, of course, the whole fight was under his direction, and the fight on the right wing under his immediate supervision. General Young had obtained from General Castillo, the commander of the Cuban forces, a full description of the country in front. General Castillo promised Young the aid of eight hundred Cubans, if he made a reconnaissance in force to find out exactly what the Spanish strength was. This promised Cuban aid did not, however, materialize, the Cubans, who had been beaten back by the Spaniards the day before, not appearing on the firing-line until the fight was over.

General Young had in his immediate command a squadron of the First Regular Cavalry, two hundred and forty-four strong, under the command of Major Bell, and a squadron of the Tenth Regular Cavalry, two hundred and twenty strong, under the command of Major Norvell.

He also had two Hotchkiss mountain guns, under Captain Watson of the Tenth. He started at a quarter before six in the morning, accompanied by Captain A. L. Mills, as aide. It was at half-past seven that Captain Mills, with a patrol of two men in advance, discovered the Spaniards as they lay across where the two roads came together, some of them in pits, others simply lying in the heavy jungle, while on their extreme right they occupied a big ranch.

Where General Young struck them they held a high ridge a little to the left of his front, this ridge being separated by a deep ravine from the hill-trail still farther to the left, down which the Rough Riders were advancing. That is, their forces occupied a range of high hills in the form of an obtuse angle, the salient being toward the space between the American forces, while there were advance parties along both roads. There were stone breastworks flanked by block-houses on that part of the ridge where the two trails came together. The place was called Las Guasimas, from trees of that name in the neighborhood.

General Young, who was riding a mule, carefully examined the Spanish position in person. He ordered the canteens of the troops to be filled, placed the Hotchkiss battery in concealment about nine hundred yards from the Spanish lines, and then deployed the regulars in support, having sent a Cuban guide to try to find Colonel Wood and warn him. He did not attack immediately, because he knew that Colonel Wood, having a more difficult route, would require a longer time to reach the position. During the delay General Wheeler arrived; he had been up since long before dawn, to see that everything went well. Young informed him of the dispositions and plan of attack he made. General Wheeler approved of them, and with excellent judgment left General Young a free hand to fight his battle.

So, about eight o'clock Young began the fight with his Hotchkiss guns, he himself being up on the firing-line. No sooner had the Hotchkiss one-pounders opened than the Spaniards opened fire in return, most of the time firing by volleys executed in perfect time, almost as on parade. They had a couple of light guns, which our people thought were quick firers. The denseness of the jungle and the fact that they used absolutely smokeless powder, made it exceedingly difficult to place exactly where they were, and almost immediately Young, who always liked to get as close as possible to his enemy, began to push his troops forward. They were deployed on both sides of the road in such thick jungle that it was only here and there that they could possibly see ahead, and some confusion, of course, ensued, the support gradually getting mixed with the advance.

Captain Beck took A Troop of the Tenth in on the left, next Captain Galbraith's troop of the First; two other troops of the Tenth were on the extreme right. Through the jungle ran wire fences here and there, and as the troops got to the ridge they encountered precipitous heights. They were led most gallantly, as American regular officers always lead their men; and the men followed their leaders with the splendid courage always shown by the American regular soldier. There was not a single straggler among them, and in not one instance was an attempt made by any trooper to fall out in order to assist the wounded or carry back the dead, while so cool were they and so perfect their fire discipline, that in the entire engagement the expenditure of ammunition was not over ten rounds per man.

Major Bell, who commanded the squadron, had his leg broken by a shot as he was leading his men. Captain Wainwright succeeded to the command of the squadron. Captain Knox was shot in the abdomen. He continued for some time giving orders to his troops, and refused to allow a man in the firing-line to assist him to the rear.

His First Lieutenant, Byram, was himself shot, but continued to lead his men until the wound and the heat overcame him and he fell in a faint. The advance was pushed forward under General Young's eye with the utmost energy, until the enemy's voices could be heard in the entrenchments. The Spaniards kept up a very heavy firing, but the regulars would not be denied, and as they climbed the ridges the Spaniards broke and fled.

Meanwhile, at six o'clock, the Rough Riders began their advance. We first had to climb a very steep hill. Many of the men, foot-sore and weary from their march of the preceding day, found the pace up this hill too hard, and either dropped their bundles or fell out of line, with the result that we went into action with less than five hundred men—as, in addition to the stragglers, a detachment had been left to guard the baggage on shore. At the time I was rather inclined to grumble to myself about Wood setting so fast a pace, but when the fight began I realized that it had been absolutely necessary, as otherwise we should have arrived late and the regulars would have had very hard work indeed.

Tiffany, by great exertions, had corralled a couple of mules and was using them to transport the Colt automatic guns in the rear of the regiment. The dynamite gun was not with us, as mules for it could not be obtained in time.

Captain Capron's troop was in the lead, it being chosen for the most responsible and dangerous position because of Capron's capacity. Four men, headed by Sergeant Hamilton Fish, went first; a support of twenty men followed some distance behind; and then came Capron and the rest of his troop, followed by Wood, with whom General Young had sent Lieutenants Smedburg and Rivers as aides.

I rode close behind, at the head of the other three troops of my squadron, and then came Brodie at the head of his squadron. The trail was so narrow that for the most part the men marched in single file, and it was bordered by dense, tangled jungle, through which a man could with difficulty force his way; so that to put out flankers was impossible, for they could not possibly have kept up with the march of the column. Every man had his canteen full. There was a Cuban guide at the head of the column, but he ran away as soon as the fighting began. There were also with us, at the head of the column, two men who did not run away, who, though non-combatants—newspaper correspondents—showed as much gallantry as any soldier in the field. They were Edward Marshall and Richard Harding Davis.

After reaching the top of the hill the walk was very pleasant. Now and then we came to glades or rounded hill-shoulders, whence we could look off for some distance. The tropical forest was very beautiful, and it was a delight to see the strange trees, the splendid royal palms and a tree which looked like a flat-topped acacia, and which was covered with a mass of brilliant scarlet flowers.

We heard many bird-notes, too, the cooing of doves and the call of a great brush cuckoo. Afterward we found that the Spanish guerrillas imitated these bird-calls, but the sounds we heard that morning, as we advanced through the tropic forest, were from birds, not guerrillas, until we came right up to the Spanish lines. It was very beautiful and very peaceful, and it seemed more as if we were off on some hunting excursion than as if we were about to go into a sharp and bloody little fight.

Of course, we accommodated our movements to those of the men in front. After marching for somewhat over an hour, we suddenly came to a halt, and immediately afterward Colonel Wood sent word down the line that the advance guard had come upon a Spanish outpost. Then the order was passed to fill the magazines, which was done.

The men were totally unconcerned, and I do not think they realized that any fighting was at hand; at any rate, I could hear the group nearest me discussing in low murmurs, not the Spaniards, but the conduct of a certain cow-puncher in quitting work on a ranch and starting a saloon in some New Mexican town. In another minute, however, Wood sent me orders to deploy three troops to the right of the trail, and to advance when we became engaged; while, at the same time, the other troops, under Major Brodie, were deployed to the left of the trail where the ground was more open than elsewhere—one troop being held in reserve in the center, besides the reserves on each wing. Later all the reserves were put into the firing-line.

To the right the jungle was quite thick, and we had barely begun to deploy when a crash in front announced that the fight was on. It was evidently very hot, and L Troop had its hands full; so I hurried my men up abreast of them. So thick was the jungle that it was very difficult to keep together, especially when there was no time for delay, and while I got up Llewellen's troops and Kane's platoon of K Troop, the rest of K Troop under Captain Jenkins, which, with Bucky O'Neill's troop, made up the right wing, were behind, and it was some time before they got into the fight at all.

Meanwhile, I had gone forward with Llewellen, Greenway, Kane, and their troopers until we came out on a kind of shoulder, jutting over a ravine, which separated us from a great ridge on our right. It was on this ridge that the Spaniards had some of their entrenchments, and it was just beyond this ridge that the Valley Road led, up which the regulars were at that very time pushing their attack; but, of course, at the moment we knew nothing of this.

The effect of the smokeless powder was remarkable. The air seemed full of the rustling sound of the Mauser bullets, for the Spaniards knew the trails by which we were advancing, and opened heavily on our position. Moreover, as we advanced we were, of course, exposed, and they could see us and fire. But they themselves were entirely invisible. The jungle covered everything, and not the faintest trace of smoke was to be seen in any direction to indicate from whence the bullets came. It was some time before the men fired; Llewellen, Kane, and I anxiously studying the ground to see where our opponents were, and utterly unable to find out.

We could hear the faint reports of the Hotchkiss guns and the reply of two Spanish guns, and the Mauser bullets were singing through the trees over our heads, making a noise like the humming of telephone wires; but exactly where they came from we could not tell.

The Spaniards were firing high and for the most part by volleys, and their shooting was not very good, which perhaps was not to be wondered at, as they were a long way off. Gradually, however, they began to get the range and occasionally one of our men would crumple up. In no case did the man make any outcry when hit, seeming to take it as a matter of course; at the outside, making only such a remark as: "Well, I got it that time."

With hardly an exception, there was no sign of flinching. I say with hardly an exception, for though I personally did not see an instance, and though all the men at the front behaved excellently, yet there were a very few men who lagged behind and drifted back to the trail over which we had come. The character of the fight put a premium upon such conduct, and afforded a very severe test for raw troops; because the jungle was so dense that as we advanced in open order, every man was, from time to time, left almost alone and away from the eyes of his officers.

There was unlimited opportunity for dropping out without attracting notice, while it was peculiarly hard to be exposed to the fire of an unseen foe, and to see men dropping under it, and yet to be, for some time, unable to return it, and also to be entirely ignorant of what was going on in any other part of the field.

It was Richard Harding Davis who gave us our first opportunity to shoot back with effect. He was behaving precisely like my officers, being on the extreme front of the line, and taking every opportunity to study with his glasses the ground where we thought the Spaniards were. I had tried some volley firing at points where I rather doubtfully believed the Spaniards to be, but had stopped firing and was myself studying the jungle-covered mountain ahead with my glasses, when Davis suddenly said: "There they are, Colonel; look over there; I can see their hats near that glade," pointing across the valley to our right.

In a minute I, too, made out the hats, and then pointed them out to three or four of our best shots, giving them my estimate of the range. For a minute or two no result followed, and I kept raising the range, at the same time getting more men on the firing-line. Then, evidently, the shots told, for the Spaniards suddenly sprang out of the cover through which we had seen their hats and ran to another spot; and we could now make out a large number of them.

I accordingly got all of my men up in line and began quick firing. In a very few minutes our bullets began to do damage, for the Spaniards retreated to the left into the jungle, and we lost sight of them. At the same moment a big body of men who, it afterward turned out, were Spaniards, came in sight along the glade, following the retreat of those whom we had just driven from the trenches.

We supposed that there was a large force of Cubans with General Young, not being aware that these Cubans had failed to make their appearance, and as it was impossible to tell the Cubans from the Spaniards, and as we could not decide whether these were Cubans following the Spaniards we had put to flight, or merely another troop of Spaniards retreating after the first (which was really the case), we dared not fire, and in a minute they had passed the glade and were out of sight.

At every halt we took advantage of the cover, sinking down behind any mound, bush, or tree trunk in the neighborhood. The trees, of course, furnished no protection from the Mauser bullets. Once I was standing behind a large palm with my head out to one side, very fortunately; for a bullet passed through the palm, filling my left eye and ear with the dust and splinters.

No man was allowed to drop out to help the wounded. It was hard to leave them there in the jungle, where they might not be found again until the vultures and the land-crabs came, but war is a grim game and there was no choice. One of the men shot was Harry Heffner of G Troop, who was mortally wounded through the hips. He fell without uttering a sound, and two of his companions dragged him behind a tree. Here he propped himself up and asked to be given his canteen and his rifle, which I handed to him. He then again began shooting, and continued loading and firing until the line moved forward and we left him alone, dying in the gloomy shade. When we found him again, after the fight, he was dead.

At one time, as I was out of touch with that part of my wing commanded by Jenkins and O'Neill, I sent Greenway, with Sergeant Russell, a New Yorker, and trooper Rowland, a New Mexican cow-puncher, down in the valley to find out where they were. To do this the three had to expose themselves to a very severe fire, but they were not men to whom this mattered. Russell was killed; the other two returned and reported to me the position of Jenkins and O'Neill.

They then resumed their places on the firing-line. After awhile I noticed blood coming out of Rowland's side and discovered that he had been shot, although he did not seem to be taking any notice of it. He said the wound was only slight, but as I saw he had broken a rib, I told him to go to the rear to the hospital. After some grumbling he went, but fifteen minutes later he was back on the firing-line again and said he could not find the hospital—which I doubted. However, I then let him stay until the end of the fight.

After we had driven the Spaniards off from their position to our right, the firing seemed to die away so far as we were concerned, for the bullets no longer struck around us in such a storm as before, though along the rest of the line the battle was as brisk as ever. Soon we saw troops appearing across the ravine, not very far from where we had seen the Spaniards whom we had thought might be Cubans.

Again we dared not fire, and carefully studied the new-comers with our glasses; and this time we were right, for we recognized our own cavalry-men. We were by no means sure that they recognized us, however, and were anxious that they should, but it was very difficult to find a clear spot in the jungle from which to signal; so Sergeant Lee of Troop K climbed a tree and from its summit waved the troop guidon. They waved their guidon back, and as our right wing was now in touch with the regulars, I left Jenkins and O'Neill to keep the connection, and led Llewellen's troop back to the path to join the rest of the regiment, which was evidently still in the thick of the fight.

I was still very much in the dark as to where the main body of the Spanish forces were, or exactly what lines the battle was following, and was very uncertain what I ought to do; but I knew it could not be wrong to go forward, and I thought I would find Wood and then see what he wished me to do. I was in a mood to cordially welcome guidance, for it was most bewildering to fight an enemy whom one so rarely saw.

I had not seen Wood since the beginning of the skirmish, when he hurried forward. When the firing opened some of the men began to curse. "Don't swear—shoot!" growled Wood, as he strode along the path lead-ing his horse, and everyone laughed and became cool again. The Spanish outposts were very near our advance guard, and some minutes of the hot-test kind of firing followed before they were driven back and slipped off through the jungle to their main lines in the rear.

Here, at the very outset of our active service, we suffered the loss of two as gallant men as ever wore uniform. Sergeant Hamilton Fish at the extreme front, while holding the point up to its work and fir-ing back where the Spanish advance guards lay, was shot and instantly killed; three of the men with him were likewise hit. Captain Capron, leading the advance guard in person, and displaying equal courage and coolness in the way that he handled them, was also struck, and died a few minutes afterward.

The command of the troop then devolved upon the First Lieutenant, young Thomas. Like Capron, Thomas was the fifth in line from father to son who had served in the American army, though in his case it was in the volunteer and not the regular service; the four preceding generations had furnished soldiers respectively to the Revolutionary War, the War of 1812, the Mexican War, and the Civil War. In a few minutes Thomas was shot through the leg, and the command devolved upon the Second Lieutenant, Day (a nephew of "Albemarle" Cushing, he who sunk the great Confederate ram). Day, who proved himself to be one of our most efficient officers, continued to handle the men to the best possible advantage, and brought them steadily forward. L Troop was from the Indian Territory.

Captain McClintock was hurried forward to its relief with his Troop B of Arizona men. In a few minutes he was shot through the leg and his place was taken by his First Lieutenant, Wilcox, who handled his men in the same soldierly manner that Day did.

Among the men who showed marked courage and coolness was the tall color-sergeant, Wright; the colors were shot through three times.

When I had led G Troop back to the trail I ran ahead of them, passing the dead and wounded men of L Troop, passing young Fish as he lay with glazed eyes under the rank tropic growth to one side of the trail. When I came to the front I found the men spread out in a very thin skirmish line, advancing through comparatively open ground, each man taking advantage of what cover he could, while Wood strolled about leading his horse, Brodie being close at hand.

How Wood escaped being hit, I do not see, and still less how his horse escaped. I had left mine at the beginning of the action and was only regretting that I had not left my sword with it, as it kept getting between my legs when I was tearing my way through the jungle. I never wore it again in action. Lieutenant Rivers was with Wood, also leading his horse. Smedburg had been sent off on the by no means pleasant task of establishing communications with Young.

Very soon after I reached the front, Brodie was hit, the bullet shattering one arm and whirling him around as he stood. He had kept on the extreme front all through, his presence and example keeping his men entirely steady, and he at first refused to go to the rear; but the wound was very painful, and he became so faint that he had to be sent. Thereupon,

Wood directed me to take charge of the left wing in Brodie's place, and to bring it forward; so over I went.

I now had under me Captains Luna, Muller, and Houston, and I began to take them forward, well spread out, through the high grass of a rather open forest. I noticed Goodrich, of Houston's troop, tramping along behind his men, absorbed in making them keep at good intervals from one another and fire slowly with careful aim. As I came close up to the edge of the troop, he caught a glimpse of me, mistook me for one of his own skirmishers who was crowding in too closely, and called out, "Keep your interval, sir; keep your interval, and go forward."

A perfect hail of bullets was sweeping over us as we advanced. Once I got a glimpse of some Spaniards, apparently retreating, far in the front, and to our right, and we fired a couple of rounds after them. Then I became convinced, after much anxious study, that we were being fired at from some large red-tiled buildings, part of a ranch on our front. Smoke-less powder, and the thick cover in our front, continued to puzzle us, and I more than once consulted anxiously the officers as to the exact where-abouts of our opponents. I took a rifle from a wounded man and began to try shots with it myself. It was very hot and the men were getting exhausted, though at this particular time we were not suffering heav-ily from bullets, the Spanish fire going high. As we advanced, the cover became a little thicker and I lost touch of the main body under Wood; so I halted and we fired industriously at the ranch buildings ahead of us, some five hundred yards off. Then we heard cheering on the right, and I supposed that this meant a charge on the part of Wood's men, so I sprang up and ordered the men to rush the buildings ahead of us. They came forward with a will.

There was a moment's heavy firing from the Spaniards, which all went over our heads, and then it ceased entirely. When we arrived at the buildings, panting and out of breath, they contained nothing but heaps of empty cartridge-shells and two dead Spaniards, shot through the head.

The country all around us was thickly forested, so that it was very difficult to see any distance in any direction. The firing had now died out, but I was still entirely uncertain as to exactly what had happened. I did not know whether the enemy had been driven back or whether it was merely a lull in the fight, and we might be attacked again; nor did I know what had happened in any other part of the line, while as I occupied the extreme left, I was not sure whether or not my flank was in danger.

At this moment one of our men who had dropped out arrived with the information (fortunately false) that Wood was dead. Of course, this meant that the command devolved upon me, and I hastily set about taking charge of the regiment. I had been particularly struck by the coolness and courage shown by Sergeants Dame and McIlhenny, and sent them out with small pickets to keep watch in front and to the left of the left wing.

I sent other men to fill the canteens with water, and threw the rest out in a long line in a disused sunken road, which gave them cover, putting two or three wounded men, who had hitherto kept up with the fighting-line, and a dozen men who were suffering from heat exhaustion—for the fighting and running under that blazing sun through the thick dry jungle was heart-breaking—into the ranch buildings. Then I started over toward the main body, but to my delight encountered Wood himself, who told me the fight was over and the Spaniards had retreated. He also informed me that other troops were just coming up.

The first to appear was a squadron of the Ninth Cavalry, under Major Dimick, which had hurried up to get into the fight, and was greatly disappointed to find it over. They took post in front of our lines, so that our tired men were able to get a rest, Captain McBlain, of the Ninth, good-naturedly giving us some points as to the best way to station our outposts.

Then General Chaffee, rather glum at not having been in the fight himself, rode up at the head of some of his infantry, and I marched my squadron back to where the rest of the regiment was going into camp, just where the two trails came together, and beyond—that is, on the Santiago side of—the original Spanish lines.

The Rough Riders had lost 8 men killed and 34 wounded, aside from two or three who were merely scratched and whose wounds were not reported. The First Cavalry, white, lost 7 men killed and 8 wounded; the Tenth Cavalry, 1 man killed and 10 wounded; so, out of 964 men engaged on our side, 16 were killed and 52 wounded.

The Spaniards were under General Rubin, with, as second in command, Colonel Alcarez. They had two guns, and eleven companies of about 100 men each: three belonging to the Porto Rico regiment, three to the San Fernandino, two to the Talavero, two being so-called mobilized companies from the mineral districts, and one a company of engineers; over 1,200 men in all, together with two guns.

General Rubin reported that he had repulsed the American attack, and Lieutenant Tejeiro states in his book that General Rubin forced the Americans to retreat, and enumerates the attacking force as consisting of three regular regiments of infantry, the Second Massachusetts and the Seventy-first New York (not one of which fired a gun or were anywhere near the battle), in addition to the sixteen dismounted troops of cavalry.

In other words, as the five infantry regiments each included twelve companies, he makes the attacking force consist of just five times the actual amount. As for the "repulse," our line never went back ten yards in any place, and the advance was practically steady; while an hour and a half after the fight began we were in complete possession of the entire Spanish position, and their troops were fleeing in masses down the road, our men being too exhausted to follow them.

General Rubin also reports that he lost but seven men killed. This is certainly incorrect, for Captain O'Neill and I went over the ground very carefully and counted eleven dead Spaniards, all of whom were actually buried by our burying squads. There were probably two or three men whom we missed, but I think that our official reports are incorrect in stating that forty-two dead Spaniards were found; this being based upon reports in which I think some of the Spanish dead were counted two or three times.

Indeed, I should doubt whether their loss was as heavy as ours, for they were under cover, while we advanced, often in the open, and their main lines fled long before we could get to close quarters. It was a very difficult country, and a force of good soldiers resolutely handled could have held the pass with ease against two or three times their number.

As it was, with a force half of regulars and half of volunteers, we drove out a superior number of Spanish regular troops, strongly posted, without suffering a very heavy loss. Although the Spanish fire was very heavy, it does not seem to me it was very well directed; and though they fired with great spirit while we merely stood at a distance and fired at them, they did not show much resolution, and when we advanced, always went back long before there was any chance of our coming into contact with them.

Our men behaved very well indeed. The newspaper press failed to do full justice to the regulars, in my opinion, from the simple reason that everybody knew that they would fight, whereas there had been a good deal of question as to how the Rough Riders, who were volunteer troops, and the Tenth Cavalry would behave; so there was a tendency to exalt our deeds at the expense of those of the First Regulars, whose courage and good conduct were taken for granted.

It was a trying fight beyond what the losses show, for it is hard upon raw soldiers to be pitted against an unseen foe, and to advance steadily when their comrades are falling around them, and when they can only occasionally see a chance to retaliate. Wood's experience in fighting Apaches stood him in good stead. An entirely raw man at the head of the regiment, conducting, as Wood was, what was practically an independent fight, would have been in a very trying position. The fight cleared the way toward Santiago, and we experienced no further resistance.

That afternoon we made camp and dined, subsisting chiefly on a load of beans which we found on one of the Spanish mules which had been shot. We also looked after the wounded. Dr. Church had himself gone out to the firing-line during the fight, and carried to the rear some of the worst wounded on his back or in his arms. Those who could walk had walked in to where the little field-hospital of the regiment was established on the trail.

We found all our dead and all the badly wounded. Around one of the latter the big, hideous land-crabs had gathered in a gruesome ring, waiting for life to be extinct. One of our own men and most of the Spanish dead had been found by the vultures before we got to them; and their bodies were mangled, the eyes and wounds being torn.

The Rough Rider who had been thus treated was in Bucky O'Neill's troop; and as we looked at the body, O'Neill turned to me and asked, "Colonel, isn't it Whitman who says of the vultures that 'they pluck the eyes of princes and tear the flesh of kings'?" I answered that I could not place the quotation. Just a week afterward we were shielding his own body from the birds of prey.

One of the men who fired first, and who displayed conspicuous gallantry, was a Cherokee, who was hit seven times, and of course had to go back to the States. Before he rejoined us at Montauk Point he had gone through a little private war of his own; for on his return he found that a cowboy had gone off with his sweetheart, and in the fight that ensued he shot his rival. Another man of L Troop who also showed marked gallantry was Elliot Cowdin. The men of the plains and mountains were trained by life-long habit to look on life and death with iron philosophy. As I passed by a couple of tall, lank, Oklahoma cow-punchers, I heard one say, "Well, some of the boys got it in the neck!" to which the other answered with the grim plains proverb of the South: "Many a good horse dies."

Thomas Isbell, a Cherokee in the squad under Hamilton Fish, was among the first to shoot and be shot at. He was wounded no less than seven times. The first wound was received by him two minutes after he had fired his first shot, the bullet going through his neck. The second hit him in the left thumb. The third struck near his right hip, passing entirely through the body. The fourth bullet (which was apparently from a Remington and not from a Mauser) went into his neck and lodged against the bone, being afterward cut out. The fifth bullet again hit his left hand. The sixth scraped his head and the seventh his neck. He did not receive all the wounds at the same time, over half an hour elapsing between the first and the last. Up to receiving the last wound he had declined to leave the firing-line, but by that time he had lost so much blood that he had to be sent to the rear. The man's wiry toughness was as notable as his courage.

We improvised litters and carried the more sorely wounded back to Siboney that afternoon and the next morning; the others walked. One of the men who had been most severely wounded was Edward Marshall, the correspondent, and he showed as much heroism as any soldier in the whole army. He was shot through the spine, a terrible and very painful wound, which we supposed meant that he would surely die; but he made no complaint of any kind, and while he retained consciousness persisted in dictating the story of the fight.

A very touching incident happened in the improvised open-air hospital after the fight, where the wounded were lying. They did not groan, and made no complaint, trying to help one another. One of them suddenly began to hum, "My Country, 'Tis of Thee," and one by one the others joined in the chorus, which swelled out through the tropic woods, where the victors lay in camp beside their dead.

I did not see any sign among the fighting men, whether wounded or unwounded, of the very complicated emotions assigned to their kind by some of the realistic modern novelists who have written about battles. At the front everyone behaved quite simply and took things as they came, in a matter-of-course way; but there was doubtless, as is always the case, a good deal of panic and confusion in the rear where the wounded, the stragglers, a few of the packers, and two or three newspaper correspondents were, and in consequence the first reports sent back to the coast were of a most alarming character, describing, with minute inaccuracy, how we had run into ambush.

The packers with the mules which carried the rapid-fire guns were among those who ran, and they let the mules go in the jungle; in consequence the guns were never even brought to the firing-line, and only Fred Herrig's skill as a trailer enabled us to recover them. By patient work he followed up the mules' tracks in the forest until he found the animals.

Among the wounded who walked to the temporary hospital at Siboney was the trooper, Rowland, of whom I spoke before. There the doctors examined him, and decreed that his wound was so serious that he must go back to the States. This was enough for Rowland, who waited until nightfall and then escaped, slipping out of the window and making his way back to camp with his rifle and pack, though his wound must have made all movement very painful to him. After this, we felt that he was entitled to stay, and he never left us for a day, distinguishing himself again in the fight at San Juan.

Next morning we buried seven dead Rough Riders in a grave on the summit of the trail, Chaplain Brown reading the solemn burial service of the Episcopalians, while the men stood around with bared heads and joined in singing "Rock of Ages."

Vast numbers of vultures were wheeling round and round in great circles through the blue sky overhead. There could be no more honorable burial than that of these men in a common grave—Indian and cowboy, miner, packer, and college athlete—the man of unknown ancestry from the lonely Western plains, and the man who carried on his watch the crests of the Stuyvesants and the Fishes, one in the way they had met death, just as during life they had been one in their daring and their loyalty.

THREE

Taking Mount Suribachi

Colonel Joseph H. Alexander

D-Day

Weather conditions around Iwo Jima on D-Day morning, February 19, 1945, were almost ideal. At 0645 Admiral Turner signaled: "Land the landing force!"

Shore bombardment ships did not hesitate to engage the enemy island at near-point-blank range. Battleships and cruisers steamed as close as two thousand yards to level their guns against island targets. Many of the "Old Battleships" had performed this dangerous mission in all theaters of the war. Marines came to recognize and appreciate their contributions. It seemed fitting that the old *Nevada*, raised from the muck and ruin of Pearl Harbor, should lead the bombardment force close ashore. Marines also admired the battleship *Arkansas*, built in 1912, and recently returned from the Atlantic where she had battered German positions at Pointe du Hoc at Normandy during the epic Allied landing on June 6, 1944.

Lieutenant Colonels Donald M. Weller and William W. "Bucky" Buchanan, both artillery officers, had devised a modified form of the "rolling barrage" for use by the bombarding gunships against beachfront targets just before H-hour. This concentration of naval gunfire would advance progressively as the troops landed, always remaining four hundred yards to their front. Air spotters would help regulate the pace. Such an innovation appealed to the three division commanders, each having served in France during World War I. In those days, a good rolling barrage was often the only way to break a stalemate.

The shelling was terrific. Admiral Hill would later boast that "there were no proper targets for shore bombardment remaining on Dog-Day morning." This proved to be an overstatement, yet no one could deny the unprecedented intensity of firepower Hill delivered against the areas surrounding the landing beaches. As General Kuribayashi would ruefully admit in an assessment report to Imperial General Headquarters, "we need to reconsider the power of bombardment from ships; the violence of the enemy's bombardments is far beyond description."

The amphibious task force appeared from over the horizon, the rails of the troopships crowded with combat-equipped Marines watching the spectacular fireworks. The Guadalcanal veterans among them realized a grim satisfaction watching American battleships leisurely pounding the island from just offshore. The war had come full cycle from the dark days of October 1942 when the 1st Marine Division and the Cactus Air Force endured similar shelling from Japanese battleships.

The Marines and sailors were anxious to get their first glimpse of the objective. Correspondent John P. Marquand, the Pulitzer Prize–winning writer, recorded his own first impressions of Iwo: "Its silhouette was like a sea monster, with the little dead volcano for the head, and the beach area for the neck, and all the rest of it, with its scrubby brown cliffs for the body." Lieutenant David N. Susskind, USNR, wrote down his initial thoughts from the bridge of the troopship *Mellette*: "Iwo Jima was a rude, ugly sight. . . . Only a geologist could look at it and not be repelled." As described in a subsequent letter home by US Navy Lieutenant Michael F. Keleher, a surgeon in the 25th Marines:

> *The naval bombardment had already begun, and I could see the orange-yellow flashes as the battleships, cruisers, and destroyers blasted away at the island broadside. Yes, there was Iwo—surprisingly close, just like the pictures and models we had been studying for six weeks. The volcano was to our left, then the long, flat black beaches where we were going to land, and the rough rocky plateau to our right.*

The commanders of the 4th and 5th Marine Divisions, Major Generals Clifton B. Cates and Keller E. Rockey, respectively, studied the island through binoculars from their respective ships. Each division would land two reinforced regiments abreast. From left to right, the beaches were designated Green, Red, Yellow, and Blue. The 5th Division would land the 28th Marines on the left flank, over Green Beach, the 27th Marines over Red. The 4th Division would land the 23rd Marines over Yellow Beach and the 25th Marines over Blue Beach on the right flank. General Schmidt reviewed the latest intelligence reports with growing uneasiness and requested a reassignment of reserve forces with General Smith. The 3rd Marine Division's 21st Marines would replace the 26th Marines as corps reserve, thus releasing the latter regiment to the 5th Division. Schmidt's landing plan envisioned the 28th Marines cutting the island in half, then returning to capture Suribachi, while the 25th Marines would scale the Rock Quarry and then serve as the hinge for the entire corps to swing around to the north. The 23rd Marines and 27th Marines would capture the first airfield and pivot north within their assigned zones.

General Cates was already concerned about the right flank. Blue Beach Two lay directly under the observation and fire of suspected Japanese positions in the Rock Quarry, whose steep cliffs overshadowed the right flank like Suribachi dominated the left. The 4th Marine Division figured that the 25th Marines would have the hardest objective to take on D-Day. Said Cates, "If I knew the name of the man on the extreme right of the right-hand squad, I'd recommend him for a medal before we go in."

The choreography of the landing continued to develop. Iwo Jima would represent the pinnacle of forcible amphibious assault against a heavily fortified shore, a complex art mastered painstakingly by the Fifth Fleet over many campaigns. Seventh Air Force Martin B-24 Liberator bombers flew in from the Marianas to strike the smoking island. Rocket ships moved in to saturate nearshore targets.

Then it was time for the fighter and attack squadrons from Mitscher's Task Force 58 to contribute. The Navy pilots showed their skills at bombing and strafing, but the troops naturally cheered the most at the appearance of F4U Corsairs flown by Marine Fighter Squadrons 124 and 213, led by Lieutenant Colonel William A. Millington from the fleet carrier *Essex*. Colonel Vernon E. Megee, in his shipboard capacity as air officer for General Smith's Expeditionary Troops staff, had urged Millington to put on a special show for the troops in the assault waves.

"Drag your bellies on the beach," he told Millington.

The Marine fighters made an impressive approach parallel to the island, then virtually did Megee's bidding, streaking low over the beaches, strafing furiously. The geography of the Pacific War since Bougainville had kept many of the ground Marines separated from their own air support, which had been operating in areas other than where they had been fighting, most notably the Central Pacific. "It was the first time a lot of them had ever seen a Marine fighter plane," said Megee. The troops were not disappointed.

The planes had barely disappeared when naval gunfire resumed, carpeting the beach areas with a building crescendo of high-explosive shells. The ship-to-shore movement was well under way, an easy thirty-minute run for the tracked landing vehicles (LVTs). This time there were enough LVTs to do the job: 68 LVT(A)4 armored amtracs mounting snub-nosed 75mm cannon leading the way, followed by 380 troop-laden LVT 4s and LVT 2s.

The waves crossed the line of departure on time and chugged confidently toward the smoking beaches, all the while under the climactic bombardment from the ships. Here there was no coral reef, no killer neap tides to be concerned with. The Navy and Marine frogmen had reported the approaches free of mines or tetrahedrons. There was no premature cessation of fire. The "rolling barrage" plan took effect. Hardly a vehicle was lost to the desultory enemy fire.

The massive assault waves hit the beach within two minutes of H-hour. A Japanese observer watching the drama unfold from a cave on the slopes of Suribachi reported, "At nine o'clock in the morning several hundred landing craft with amphibious tanks in the lead rushed ashore like an enormous tidal wave." Lieutenant Colonel Robert H. Williams, executive officer of the 28th Marines, recalled that "the landing was a magnificent sight to see—two divisions landing abreast; you could see the whole show from the deck of a ship." Up to this point, so far, so good.

The first obstacle came not from the Japanese but from the beach and the parallel terraces. Iwo Jima was an emerging volcano; its steep beaches dropped off sharply, producing a narrow but violent surf zone. The soft black sand immobilized all wheeled vehicles and caused some of the tracked amphibians to belly down. The boat waves that closely followed the LVTs had more trouble. Ramps would drop, a truck or jeep would attempt to drive out, only to get stuck. In short order a succession of plunging waves hit the stalled craft before they could completely unload, filling their sterns with water and sand, broaching them broadside. The beach quickly resembled a salvage yard.

The infantry, heavily laden, found its own "foot-mobility" severely restricted. In the words of Corporal Edward Hartman, a rifleman with the 4th Marine Division: "The sand was so soft it was like trying to run in loose coffee grounds." From the 28th Marines came this early, laconic report: "Resistance moderate, terrain awful."

The rolling barrage and carefully executed landing produced the desired effect, suppressing direct enemy fire, providing enough shock and distraction to enable the first assault waves to clear the beach and begin advancing inward. Within minutes six thousand Marines were ashore. Many became thwarted by increasing fire over the terraces or down from the highlands, but hundreds leapt forward to maintain assault momentum.

The 28th Marines on the left flank had rehearsed on similar volcanic terrain on the island of Hawaii. Now, despite increasing casualties among their company commanders and the usual disorganization of landing, elements of the regiment used their initiative to strike across the narrow neck of the peninsula. The going became progressively costly as more and more Japanese strongpoints along the base of Suribachi seemed to spring to life.

Within ninety minutes of the landing, however, elements of the 1st Battalion, 28th Marines, had reached the western shore, seven hundred yards across from Green Beach. Iwo Jima had been severed—"like cutting off a snake's head," in the words of one Marine. It would represent the deepest penetration of what was becoming a very long and costly day.

The other three regiments experienced difficulty leaving the black sand terraces and wheeling across toward the first airfield. The terrain was an open bowl, a shooting gallery in full view from Suribachi on the left and the rising tableland to the right. Any thoughts of a "cakewalk" quickly vanished as well-directed machine-gun fire whistled across the open ground and mortar rounds began dropping along the terraces. Despite these difficulties, the 27th Marines made good initial gains, reaching the southern and western edges of the first airfield before noon.

The 23rd Marines landed over Yellow Beach and sustained the brunt of the first round of Japanese combined arms fire. These troops crossed the second terrace only to be confronted by two huge concrete pillboxes, still lethal despite all the pounding. Overcoming these positions proved costly in casualties and time.

More fortified positions appeared in the broken ground beyond. Colonel Walter W. Wensinger's call for tank support could not be immediately honored because of congestion problems on the beach. The regiment clawed its way several hundred yards toward the eastern edge of the airstrip.

No assault units found it easy going to move inland, but the 25th Marines almost immediately ran into a buzz saw trying to move across Blue Beach. General Cates had been right in his appraisal. "That right flank was a bitch if there ever was one," he would later say. Lieutenant Colonel Hollis W. Mustain's 1st Battalion, 25th Marines, managed to scratch forward three hundred yards under heavy fire in the first half hour, but Lieutenant Colonel Chambers's 3rd Battalion, 25th Marines, took the heaviest beating of the day on the extreme right, trying to scale the cliffs leading to the Rock Quarry.

Chambers landed fifteen minutes after H-hour. "Crossing that second terrace," he recalled, "the fire from automatic weapons was coming from all over. You could've held up a cigarette and lit it on the stuff going by. I knew immediately we were in for one hell of a time."

This was simply the beginning.

While the assault forces tried to overcome the infantry weapons of the local defenders, they were naturally blind to an almost imperceptible stirring taking place among the rocks and crevices of the interior highlands. With grim anticipation, General Kuribayashi's gunners began unmasking the big guns—the heavy artillery, giant mortars, rockets, and antitank weapons held under tightest discipline for this precise moment. Kuribayashi had patiently waited until the beaches were clogged with troops and material. Gun crews knew the range and deflection to each landing beach by heart; all weapons had been preregistered on these targets long ago. At Kuribayashi's signal, these hundreds of weapons began to open fire. It was shortly after 10:00 a.m.

The ensuing bombardment was as deadly and terrifying as any the Marines had ever experienced. There was hardly any cover. Japanese artillery and mortar rounds blanketed every corner of the three-thousand-yard-wide beach. Large-caliber coast defense guns and dual-purpose antiaircraft guns firing horizontally added a deadly scissors of direct fire from the high ground on both flanks. Marines stumbling over the terraces to escape the rain of projectiles encountered the same disciplined machine-gun fire and minefields which had slowed the initial advance. Casualties mounted appallingly.

Two Marine combat veterans observing this expressed a grudging admiration for the Japanese gunners. "It was one of the worst bloodlettings of the war," said Major Karch of the 14th Marines. "They rolled those artillery barrages up and down the beach—I just didn't see how anybody could live through such heavy fire barrages."

Said Lieutenant Colonel Joseph L. Stewart, "The Japanese were superb artillerymen. . . . Somebody was getting hit every time they fired." At sea, Lieutenant Colonel Weller tried desperately to deliver naval gunfire against the Japanese gun positions shooting down at 3rd Battalion, 25th Marines, from the Rock Quarry. It would take longer to coordinate this fire: The first Japanese barrages had wiped out the 3rd Battalion, 25th Marines', entire shore fire control party.

As the Japanese firing reached a general crescendo, the four assault regiments issued dire reports to the flagship. Within a ten-minute period, these messages crackled over the command net:

> *1036: (From 25th Marines) "Catching all hell from the quarry. Heavy mortar and machine-gun fire!"*
> *1039: (From 23rd Marines) "Taking heavy casualties and can't move for the moment. Mortars killing us."*
> *1042: (From 27th Marines) "All units pinned down by artillery and mortars. Casualties heavy. Need tank support fast to move anywhere."*
> *1046: (From 28th Marines) "Taking heavy fire and forward movement stopped. Machine-gun and artillery fire heaviest ever seen."*

The landing force suffered and bled but did not panic. The profusion of combat veterans throughout the rank and file of each regiment helped the rookies focus on the objective. Communications remained effective. Keen-eyed aerial observers spotted some of the now-exposed gun positions and directed naval gunfire effectively. Carrier planes screeched in low to drop napalm canisters. The heavy Japanese fire would continue to take an awful toll throughout the first day and night, but it would never again be so murderous as that first unholy hour.

Marine Sherman tanks played hell getting into action on D-Day. Later in the battle these combat vehicles would be the most valuable weapons on the battlefield for the Marines; this day was a nightmare. The assault divisions embarked many of their tanks on board medium landing ships (LSMs), sturdy little craft that could deliver five Shermans at a time. But it was tough disembarking them on Iwo's steep beaches. The stern anchors could not hold in the loose sand; bow cables run forward to "deadmen" LVTs parted under the strain. On one occasion the lead tank stalled at the top of the ramp, blocking the other vehicles and leaving the LSM at the mercy of the rising surf. Other tanks bogged down or threw tracks in the loose sand.

Many of those that made it over the terraces were destroyed by huge horned mines or disabled by deadly accurate 47mm antitank fire from Suribachi. Other tankers kept coming. Their relative mobility, armored protection, and 75mm gunfire were most welcome to the infantry scattered among Iwo's lunar-looking, shell-pocked landscape.

Both division commanders committed their reserves early. General Rockey called in the 26th Marines shortly after noon. General Cates ordered two battalions of the 24th Marines to land at 14:00; the 3rd Battalion, 24th Marines, followed several hours later. Many of the reserve battalions suffered heavier casualties crossing the beach than the assault units, a result of Kuribayashi's punishing bombardment from all points on the island.

Mindful of the likely Japanese counterattack in the night to come—and despite the fire and confusion along the beaches—both divisions also ordered their artillery regiments ashore. This process, frustrating and costly, took much of the afternoon. The wind and surf began to pick up as the day wore on, causing more than one low-riding DUKW to swamp with its precious 105mm howitzer cargo. Getting the guns ashore was one thing; getting them up off the sand was quite another. The 75mm pack howitzers fared better than the heavier 105s. Enough Marines could readily hustle them up over the terraces, albeit at great risk. The 105s seemed to have a mind of their own in the black sand. The effort to get each single weapon off the beach was a saga in its own right.

Somehow, despite the fire and unforgiving terrain, both Colonel Louis G. DeHaven, commanding the 14th Marines, and Colonel James D. Waller, commanding the 13th Marines, managed to get batteries in place, registered, and rendering close fire support well before dark, a singular accomplishment.

Japanese fire and the plunging surf continued to make a shambles out of the beachhead. Late in the afternoon, Lieutenant Michael F. Keleher, USNR, the battalion surgeon, was ordered ashore to take over the 3rd Battalion, 25th Marines, aid station from its gravely wounded surgeon. Keleher, a veteran of three previous assault landings, was appalled by the carnage on Blue Beach as he approached: "Such a sight on that beach! Wrecked boats, bogged-down jeeps, tractors and tanks; burning vehicles; casualties scattered all over."

On the left center of the action, leading his machine-gun platoon in the 1st Battalion, 27th Marines', attack against the southern portion of the airfield, the legendary "Manila John" Basilone fell mortally wounded by a Japanese mortar shell, a loss keenly felt by all Marines on the island. Farther east, Lieutenant Colonel Robert Galer, the other Guadalcanal Medal of Honor Marine (and one of the Pacific War's earliest fighter aces), survived the afternoon's fusillade along the beaches and began reassembling his scattered radar unit in a deep shell hole near the base of Suribachi.

Late in the afternoon, Lieutenant Colonel Donn J. Robertson led his 3rd Battalion, 27th Marines, ashore over Blue Beach, disturbed at the intensity of fire still being directed on the reserve forces this late on D-Day. "They were really ready for us," he recalled. He watched with pride and wonderment as his Marines landed under fire, took casualties, and stumbled forward to clear the beach. "What impels a young guy landing on a beach in the face of fire?" he asked himself. Then it was Robertson's turn. His boat hit the beach too hard; the ramp wouldn't drop. Robertson and his command group had to roll over the gunwales into the churning surf and crawl ashore, an inauspicious start.

The bitter battle to capture the Rock Quarry cliffs on the right flank raged all day. The beachhead remained completely vulnerable to enemy direct-fire weapons from these heights; the Marines had to storm them before many more troops or supplies could be landed. In the end, it was the strength of character of Captain James Headley and Lieutenant Colonel "Jumping Joe" Chambers who led the survivors of the 3rd Battalion, 25th Marines, onto the top of the cliffs. The battalion paid an exorbitant price for this achievement, losing twenty-two officers and five hundred troops by nightfall.

The two assistant division commanders, brigadier generals Franklin A. Hart and Leo D. Hermle, of the 4th and 5th Marine Divisions, respectively, spent much of D-Day on board the control vessels, marking both ends of the Line of Departure, four thousand yards offshore. This reflected yet another lesson in amphibious techniques learned from Tarawa: Having senior officers that close to the ship-to-shore movement provided landing force decision making from the most forward vantage point.

By dusk General Leo D. Hermle opted to come ashore. At Tarawa he had spent the night of D-Day essentially out of contact at the fire-swept pier-head. This time he intended to be on the ground. Hermle had the larger operational picture in mind, knowing the corps commander's desire to force the reserves and artillery units onshore despite the carnage in order to build credible combat power. Hermle knew that whatever the night might bring, the Americans now had more troops on the island than Kuribayashi could ever muster. His presence helped his division to forget about the day's disasters and focus on preparations for the expected counterattacks.

Japanese artillery and mortar fire continued to rake the beachhead. The enormous spigot mortar shells (called "flying ashcans" by the troops) and rocket-boosted aerial bombs were particularly scary—loud, whistling projectiles, tumbling end over end. Many sailed completely over the island; those that hit along the beaches or the south runways invariably caused dozens of casualties with each impact. Few Marines could dig a proper foxhole in the granular sand ("like trying to dig a hole in a barrel of wheat"). Among urgent calls to the control ship for plasma, stretchers, and mortar shells came repeated cries for sandbags.

Veteran Marine combat correspondent Lieutenant Cyril P. Zurlinden, soon to become a casualty himself, described that first night ashore:

> *At Tarawa, Saipan, and Tinian, I saw Marines killed and wounded in a shocking manner, but I saw nothing like the ghastliness that hung over the Iwo beachhead. Nothing any of us had ever known could compare with the utter anguish, frustration, and constant inner battle to maintain some semblance of sanity.*

Personnel accounting was a nightmare under those conditions, but the assault divisions eventually reported the combined loss of 2,420 men to General Schmidt (501 killed, 1,755 wounded, 47 dead of wounds, 18 missing, and 99 combat fatigue). These were sobering statistics, but Schmidt now had 30,000 Marines ashore. The casualty rate of 8 percent left the landing force in relatively better condition than at the first days at Tarawa or Saipan. The miracle was that the casualties had not been twice as high. General Kuribayashi had possibly waited a little too long to open up with his big guns.

The first night on Iwo was ghostly. Sulfuric mists spiraled out of the earth. The Marines, used to the tropics, shivered in the cold, waiting for Kuribayashi's warriors to come screaming down from the hills. They would learn that this Japanese commander was different. There would be no wasteful, vainglorious banzai attacks, this night or any other. Instead, small teams of infiltrators, which Kuribayashi termed "Prowling Wolves," probed the lines, gathering intelligence. A barge full of Japanese special landing forces tried a small counter landing on the western beaches and died to the man under the alert guns of the 28th Marines and its supporting LVT crews.

Otherwise, the night was one of continuing waves of indirect fire from the highlands. One high velocity round landed directly in the hole occupied by the 1st Battalion, 23rd Marines', commander, Lieutenant

Colonel Ralph Haas, killing him instantly. The Marines took casualties throughout the night. But with the first streaks of dawn, the veteran landing force stirred. Five infantry regiments looked north; a sixth turned to the business at hand in the south: Mount Suribachi.

SURIBACHI

The Japanese called the dormant volcano Suribachi-yama; the Marines dubbed it "Hotrocks." From the start the Marines knew their drive north would never succeed without first seizing that hulking rock dominating the southern plain. "Suribachi seemed to take on a life of its own, to be watching these men, looming over them," recalled one observer, adding, "the mountain represented to these Marines a thing more evil than the Japanese."

Colonel Kanehiko Atsuchi commanded the two thousand soldiers and sailors of the Suribachi garrison. The Japanese had honeycombed the mountain with gun positions, machine-gun nests, observation sites, and tunnels, but Atsuchi had lost many of his large-caliber guns in the direct naval bombardment of the preceding three days. General Kuribayashi considered Atsuchi's command to be semiautonomous, realizing the invaders would soon cut communications across the island's narrow southern tip. Kuribayashi nevertheless hoped Suribachi could hold out for ten days, maybe two weeks.

Some of Suribachi's stoutest defenses existed down low, around the rubble-strewn base. Here nearly seventy camouflaged concrete blockhouses protected the approaches to the mountain; another fifty bulged from the slopes within the first hundred feet of elevation. Then came the caves, the first of hundreds the Marines would face on Iwo Jima.

The 28th Marines had suffered nearly four hundred casualties in cutting across the neck of the island on D-Day. On D+1, in a cold rain, they prepared to assault the mountain. Lieutenant Colonel Chandler Johnson, commanding the 2nd Battalion, 28th Marines, set the tone for the morning as he deployed his tired troops forward: "It's going to be a hell of a day in a hell of a place to fight the damned war!" Some of the 105mm batteries of the 13th Marines opened up in support, firing directly overhead. Gun crews fired from positions hastily dug in the black sand directly next to the 28th Marines command post. Regimental executive officer Lieutenant Colonel Robert H. Williams watched the cannoneers fire at Suribachi "eight hundred yards away over open sights."

As the Marines would learn during their drive north, even 105mm howitzers would hardly shiver the concrete pillboxes of the enemy. As the prep fire lifted, the infantry leapt forward, only to run immediately into very heavy machine-gun and mortar fire. Colonel Harry B. "Harry the Horse" Liversedge bellowed for his tanks. But the 5th Tank Battalion was already having a frustrating morning. The tankers sought a defilade spot in which to rearm and refuel for the day's assault. Such a location did not exist on Iwo Jima those first days. Every time the tanks congregated to service their vehicles they were hit hard by Japanese mortar and artillery fire from virtually the entire island. Getting sufficient vehicles serviced to join the assault took most of the morning. Hereafter the tankers would maintain and reequip their vehicles at night.

This day's slow start led to more setbacks for the tankers; Japanese antitank gunners hiding in the jumbled boulders knocked out the first approaching Shermans. Assault momentum slowed further. The 28th Marines overran forty strongpoints and gained roughly two hundred yards all day. They lost a Marine for every yard gained. The tankers unknowingly redeemed themselves when one of their final 75mm rounds caught Colonel Atsuchi as he peered out of a cave entrance, killing him instantly.

Elsewhere, the morning light on D+1 revealed the discouraging sights of the chaos created along the beaches by the combination of Iwo Jima's wicked surf and Kuribayashi's unrelenting barrages. In the words of one dismayed observer:

> *The wreckage was indescribable. For two miles the debris was so thick that there were only a few places where landing craft could still get in. The wrecked hulls of scores of landing boats testified to one price we had to pay to put our troops ashore. Tanks and half-tracks lay crippled where they had bogged down in the coarse sand. Amphibian tractors, victims of mines and well-aimed shells, lay flopped on their backs. Cranes, brought ashore to unload cargo, tilted at insane angles, and bulldozers were smashed in their own roadways.*

Bad weather set in, further compounding the problems of general unloading. Strong winds whipped sea swells into a nasty chop; the surf turned uglier. These were the conditions faced by Lieutenant Colonel Carl A. Youngdale in trying to land the 105mm-howitzer batteries of his 4th Battalion, 14th Marines. All twelve of these guns were preloaded in DUKWs, one to a vehicle. Added to the amphibious trucks' problems of marginal seaworthiness with that payload was contaminated fuel. As Youngdale watched in horror, eight DUKWs suffered engine failures, swamped, and sank, with great loss of life. Two more DUKWs broached in the surf zone, spilling their invaluable guns into deep water. At length Youngdale managed to get his remaining two guns ashore and into firing position.

General Schmidt also committed one battery of 155mm howitzers of the corps artillery to the narrow beachhead on D+1. Somehow these weapons managed to reach the beach intact, but it then took hours to get tractors to drag the heavy guns up over the terraces. These, too, commenced firing before dark, their deep bark a welcome sound to the infantry.

Concern with the heavy casualties in the first twenty-four hours led Schmidt to commit the 21st Marines from corps reserve. The seas proved to be too rough. The troops had harrowing experiences trying to debark down cargo nets into the small boats bobbing violently alongside the transports; several fell into the water. The boating process took hours. Once afloat, the troops circled endlessly in their small Higgins boats, waiting for the call to land. Wiser heads prevailed. After six hours of awful seasickness, the 21st Marines returned to its ships for the night.

Even the larger landing craft, the LCTs and LSMs, had great difficulty beaching. Sea anchors needed to maintain the craft perpendicular to the breakers rarely held fast in the steep, soft bottom. "Dropping those stern anchors was like dropping a spoon in a bowl of mush," said Admiral Hill.

Hill contributed significantly to the development of amphibious expertise in the Pacific War. For Iwo Jima, he and his staff developed armored bulldozers to land in the assault waves. They also experimented with hinged Marston matting, used for expeditionary airfields, as a temporary roadway to get wheeled vehicles over soft sand. On the beach at Iwo, the bulldozers proved to be worth their weight in gold. The

Marston matting was only partially successful—LVTs kept chewing it up in passage—but all hands could see its potential.

Admiral Hill also worked with the Naval Construction Battalion (NCB) personnel—Seabees, as they were called—in an attempt to bring supply-laden causeways and pontoon barges ashore. Again, the surf prevailed, broaching the craft, spilling the cargo. In desperation, Hill's beach masters turned to round-the-clock use of DUKWs and LVTs to keep combat cargo flowing.

Once the DUKWs got free of the crippling load of 105mm howitzers, they did fine. LVTs were probably better, because they could cross the soft beach without assistance and conduct resupply or medevac missions directly along the front lines. Both vehicles suffered from inexperienced LST crews in the transport area who too often would not lower their bow ramps to accommodate LVTs or DUKWs approaching after dark. In too many cases, vehicles loaded with wounded Marines thus rejected became lost in the darkness, ran out of gas, and sank. The amphibian tractor battalions lost 148 LVTs at Iwo Jima. Unlike Tarawa, Japanese gunfire and mines accounted for less than 20 percent of this total. Thirty-four LVTs fell victim to Iwo's crushing surf; eighty-eight sank in deep water, mostly at night.

Once ashore and clear of the loose sand along the beaches, the tanks, half-tracks, and armored bulldozers of the landing force ran into the strongest minefield defenses yet encountered in the Pacific War. Under General Kuribayashi's direction, Japanese engineers had planted irregular rows of antitank mines and the now-familiar horned antiboat mines along all possible exits from both beaches. The Japanese supplemented these weapons by rigging enormous makeshift explosives from five-hundred-pound aerial bombs, depth charges, and torpedo heads, each triggered by an accompanying pressure mine. Worse, Iwo's loose soil retained enough metallic characteristics to render the standard mine detectors unreliable. The Marines were reduced to using their own engineers on their hands and knees out in front of the tanks, probing for mines with bayonets and wooden sticks.

While the 28th Marines fought to encircle Suribachi and the beach masters and shore party attempted to clear the wreckage from the beaches, the remaining assault units of the VAC resumed their collective assault against Airfield No. 1. In the 5th Marine Division's zone, the relatively fresh troops of the 1st Battalion, 26th Marines, and the 3rd Battalion, 27th Marines, quickly became bloodied in forcing their way across the western runways, taking heavy casualties from time-fuzed air bursts fired by Japanese dual-purpose antiaircraft guns zeroed along the exposed ground. In the adjacent 4th Division zone, the 23rd Marines completed the capture of the airstrip, advancing eight hundred yards, but sustaining high losses.

Some of the bitterest fighting in the initial phase of the landing continued to occur along the high ground above the Rock Quarry on the right flank. Here the 25th Marines, reinforced by the 1st Battalion, 24th Marines, engaged in literally the fight of its life. The Marines found the landscape, and the Japanese embedded in it, unreal.

The second day of the battle had proven unsatisfactory on virtually every front. To cap off the frustration, when the 1st Battalion, 24th Marines, finally managed a breakthrough along the cliffs late in the day, their only reward was two back-to-back cases of "friendly fire." An American air strike inflicted eleven casualties; misguided salvos from an unidentified gunfire support ship took down ninety more. Nothing seemed to be going right.

The morning of the third day, D+2, seemed to promise more of the same frustrations. Marines shivered in the cold wind and rain; Admiral Hill twice had to close the beach due to high surf and dangerous undertows. But during one of the grace periods, the 3rd Division's 21st Marines managed to come ashore, all of it extremely glad to be free of the heaving small boats. General Schmidt assigned it to the 4th Marine Division at first.

The 28th Marines resumed its assault on the base of Suribachi—more slow, bloody fighting, seemingly boulder by boulder. On the west coast, the 1st Battalion, 28th Marines, made the most of field artillery and naval gunfire support to reach the shoulder of the mountain. Elsewhere, murderous Japanese fire restricted any progress to a matter of yards. Enemy mortar fire from all over the volcano rained down on the 2nd Battalion, 28th Marines, trying to advance along the eastern shore. Recalled rifleman Richard Wheeler of the experience, "It was terrible, the worst I can remember us taking."

That night the amphibious task force experienced the only significant air attack of the battle. Fifty kamikaze pilots from the 22nd Mitate special attack unit left Katori Airbase near Yokosuka and flung themselves against the ships on the outer perimeter of Iwo Jima. In desperate action that would serve as a prelude to Okinawa's fiery engagements, the kamikazes sank the escort carrier *Bismarck Sea* with heavy loss of life and damaged several other ships, including the veteran *Saratoga*, finally knocked out of the war. All fifty Japanese planes were expended.

It rained even harder on the fourth morning, D+3. Marines scampering forward under fire would hit the deck, roll, attempt to return fire—only to discover that the loose volcanic grit had combined with the rain to jam their weapons. The 21st Marines, as the vanguard of the 3rd Marine Division, hoped for good fortune in its initial commitment after relieving the 23rd Marines. The regiment instead ran headlong into an intricate series of Japanese emplacements which marked the southeastern end of the main Japanese defenses. The newcomers fought hard all day to scratch and claw an advance of two hundred net yards. Casualties were disproportionate.

On the right flank, Lieutenant Colonel Chambers continued to rally the 3rd Battalion, 25th Marines, through the rough pinnacles above the Rock Quarry. As he strode about directing the advance of his decimated companies that afternoon, a Japanese gunner shot him through the chest. Chambers went down hard, thinking it was all over: "I started fading in and out. I don't remember too much about it except the frothy blood gushing out of my mouth.... Then somebody started kicking the hell out of my feet. It was [Captain James] Headley, saying, "Get up; you were hurt worse on Tulagi!'"

Captain Headley knew Chambers's sucking chest wound portended a grave injury. He sought to reduce his commander's shock until they could get him out of the line of fire. This took doing. Lieutenant Michael F. Keleher, USNR, now the battalion surgeon, crawled forward with one of his corpsmen. Willing hands lifted Chambers on a stretcher. Keleher and several others, bent double against the fire, carried him down the cliffs to the aid station, and eventually on board a DUKW, making the evening's last run out to the hospital ships.

All three battalion commanders in the 25th Marines had now become casualties. Chambers would survive to receive the Medal of Honor; Captain Headley would command the shot-up 3rd Battalion, 25th Marines, for the duration of the battle. By contrast, the 28th Marines on D+3 made commendable progress against Suribachi, reaching the shoulder at all points. Late in the day, combat patrols from the 1st Battalion, 28th Marines, and the 2nd Battalion, 28th Marines, linked up at Tobiishi Point at the southern tip of the island. Recon patrols returned to tell Lieutenant Colonel Johnson that they found few signs of live Japanese along the mountain's upper slopes on the north side.

At sundown Admiral Spruance authorized Task Force 58 to strike Honshu and Okinawa, then retire to Ulithi to prepare for the Ryukyuan campaign. All eight Marine Corps fighter squadrons thus left the Iwo Jima area for good. Navy pilots flying off the ten remaining escort carriers would pick up the slack. Without slighting the skill and valor of these pilots, the quality of close air support to the troops fighting ashore dropped off after this date. The escort carriers, for one thing, had too many competing missions, namely combat air patrols, antisubmarine sweeps, searches for downed aviators, and harassing strikes against neighboring Chichi Jima. Marines on Iwo Jima complained of slow response time to air-support requests, light payloads (rarely greater than one-hundred-pound bombs), and high delivery altitudes (rarely below 1,500 feet). The Navy pilots did deliver a number of napalm bombs. Many of these failed to detonate, although this was not the fault of the aviators; the early napalm "bombs" were simply old wing-tanks filled with the mixture, activated by unreliable detonators. The Marines also grew concerned about these notoriously inaccurate area weapons being dropped from high altitudes.

By Friday, February 23 (D+4), the 28th Marines stood poised to complete the capture of Mount Suribachi. The honor went to the 3rd Platoon (reinforced), Company E, 2nd Battalion, 28th Marines, under the command of First Lieutenant Harold G. Schrier, the company executive officer. Lieutenant Colonel Johnson ordered Schrier to scale the summit, secure the crater, and raise a fifty-four-by-twenty-eight-inch American flag for all to see. Schrier led his forty-man patrol forward at 08:00.

The regiment had done its job, blasting the dozens of pillboxes with flame and demolitions, rooting out snipers, knocking out the masked batteries. The combined-arms pounding by planes, field pieces, and naval guns the past week had likewise taken its toll on the defenders. Those who remained popped out of holes and caves to resist Schrier's advance, only to be cut down. The Marines worked warily up the steep northern slope, sometimes resorting to crawling on hands and knees.

Part of the enduring drama of the Suribachi flag-raising was the fact that it was observed by so many people. Marines all over the island could track the progress of the tiny column of troops during its ascent. ("Those guys oughta be getting flight pay," said one wag.) Likewise, hundreds of binoculars from the ships offshore watched Schrier's Marines climbing ever upward. Finally, they reached the top and momentarily disappeared from view. Those closest to the volcano could hear distant gunfire. Then, at 10:20, there was movement on the summit; suddenly the Stars and Stripes fluttered bravely.

Lusty cheers rang out from all over the southern end of the island. The ships sounded their sirens and whistles. Wounded men propped themselves up on their litters to glimpse the sight. Strong men wept unashamedly. Navy Secretary Forrestal, thrilled by the sight, turned to Holland Smith and said, "The raising of that flag means a Marine Corps for another five hundred years."

Three hours later an even larger flag went up to more cheers. Few would know that Associated Press photographer Joe Rosenthal had just captured the embodiment of the American warfighting spirit on film. *Leatherneck* magazine photographer Staff Sergeant Lou Lowery had taken a picture of the first flag-raising and almost immediately got in a firefight with a couple of enraged Japanese. His photograph would become a valued collector's item. But Rosenthal's would enthrall the free world.

Captain Thomas M. Fields, commanding officer of Company D, 2nd Battalion, 26th Marines, heard his men yell "Look up there!" and turned in time to see the first flag go. His first thought dealt with the battle still at hand: "Thank God the Japs won't be shooting us down from behind anymore."

The 28th Marines took Suribachi in three days at the cost of more than five hundred troops (added to its D-Day losses of four hundred men). Colonel Liversedge began to reorient his regiment for operations in the opposite direction, northward. Unknown to all, the battle still had another month to run its bloody course.

Four

Supplying the Embattled Marines at Khe Sanh

Captain Moyers S. Shore II, USMC

"Attention to Colors."

The order having been given, Captain William H. Dabney, a product of the Virginia Military Institute, snapped to attention, faced the jerry-rigged flagpole, and saluted, as did every other man in Company I, 3rd Battalion, 26th Marines. The ceremony might well have been at any one of a hundred military installations around the world except for a few glaring irregularities. The parade ground was a battle-scarred hilltop to the west of Khe Sanh and the men in the formation stood half submerged in trenches or foxholes. Instead of crisply starched utilities, razor sharp creases, and gleaming brass, these Marines sported scraggly beards, ragged trousers, and rotted helmet liner straps.

The only man in the company who could play a bugle, Second Lieutenant Owen S. Matthews, lifted the pock-marked instrument to his lips and spat out a choppy version of "To the Colors" while two enlisted men raced to the RC-292 radio antenna which served as the flagpole and gingerly attached the Stars and Stripes. As the mast with its shredded banner came upright, the Marines could hear the ominous "thunk," "thunk," "thunk," to the southwest of their position, which meant that North Vietnamese 120mm mortar rounds had left their tubes. They also knew that in twenty-one seconds those "thunks" would be replaced by much louder, closer sounds, but no one budged until Old Glory waved high over the hill.

When Lieutenant Matthews sharply cut off the last note of his piece, Company I disappeared; men dropped into trenches, dived headlong into foxholes, or scrambled into bunkers. The area which moments before had been bristling with humanity was suddenly a ghost town. Seconds later explosions walked across the hilltop spewing black smoke, dirt, and debris into the air. Rocks, splinters, and spent shell fragments rained on the flattened Marines but, as usual, no one was hurt. As quickly as the attack came, it was over.

While the smoke lazily drifted away, a much smaller banner rose from the Marines' positions. A pole adorned with a pair of red silk panties—Maggie's Drawers—was waved back and forth above one trenchline to inform the enemy that he had missed again. A few men stood up and jeered or cursed at the distant gunners; others simply saluted with an appropriate obscene gesture. The daily flag-raising ceremony on Hill 881 South was over.

This episode was just one obscure incident that coupled with hundreds of others made up the battle for Khe Sanh. The ceremony carried with it no particular political overtones but was intended solely as an open show of defiance toward the Communists as well as a morale booster for the troops. The jaunty courage, quiet determination, and macabre humor of the men on Hill 881S exemplified the spirit of the US and South Vietnamese defenders who not only defied the enemy but, in a classic seventy-seven-day struggle, destroyed him.

The Khe Sanh Combat Base (KSCB) sat atop a plateau in the shadow of Dong Tri Mountain and overlooked a tributary of the Quang Tri River. The base had a small dirt airstrip, which had been surfaced by a US Navy Mobile Construction Battalion (Seabees) in the summer of 1966; the field could accommodate helicopters and fixed-wing transport aircraft. Artillery support was provided by Battery F. The Khe Sanh area of operations was also within range of the 175mm guns of the US Army's 2nd Battalion, 94th Artillery, at Camp Carroll and the Rockpile. In addition, there was a Marine Combined Action Company (CAC) and a Regional Forces company located in the village of Khe Sanh, approximately 3,500 meters south of the base.

The enemy had much to gain by taking Khe Sanh. If the garrison fell, the defeat might well turn out to be the coup de grace to American participation in the war. At first, the Marines anticipated a major pitched battle, similar to the one in 1967, but the enemy continued to bide his time and the battle at Khe Sanh settled into one of supporting arms.

At Khe Sanh, the periodic showers of enemy artillery shells were, quite naturally, a major source of concern to Commanding Officer Colonel David E. Lownds, who placed a high priority on the construction of stout fortifications. Understandably, not every newcomer to Khe Sanh immediately moved into a thick bunker or a six-foot trench with overhead cover. The colonel had spent most of his tour with a one-battalion regiment and had prepared positions for that battalion; then, almost overnight, his command swelled to five battalions. The new units simply had to build their own bunkers as quickly as they could.

The average bunker usually started as an eight-by-eight-foot dugout with one six-by-six-inch timber inserted in each corner and the center for support. The overhead consisted of planks, a strip of runway matting, sandbags, loose dirt, and more sandbags. Some enterprising Marines piled on more loose dirt, then took discarded 105mm casings and drove them into the top of the bunker like nails. These casings often caused predetonation of the heavier-caliber rounds. The combat engineers attached to the 26th Marines could build one of these bunkers in three or four days; the average infantrymen took longer.

The Marines were also faced with another question concerning their defenses: "How large an artillery round could you defend against and still remain within the realm of practicality?" Since the 26th Marines was supplied solely by air, building material was a prime consideration. Matting and sandbags were easy enough to come by, but lumber was at a premium. Fortifications which could withstand a hit from an 82mm mortar were a must because the North Vietnamese had an ample supply of these weapons, but the base was also being pounded, to a lesser degree, by heavier-caliber guns. With the material available to the 26th Marines, it was virtually impossible to construct a shelter that was thick enough or deep enough to stop the heavy stuff.

Colonel Lownds decided to build a new regimental CP bunker. The engineers supplied the specifications for an overhead that would withstand a 122mm rocket; to be on the safe side, the colonel doubled the thickness of the roof. The day before the CP was to be occupied, a 152mm round landed squarely on top of the bunker and penetrated both layers.

The massing of enemy artillery made the hill outposts that much more important. Had they been able to knock the Marines from those summits, the North Vietnamese would have been able to fire right down the throats of the base defenders and make their position untenable. As it was, the companies on Hills 881S, 861, 861A, and 558 not only denied the enemy an unobstructed firing platform from which to pound the installation, they also served as the eyes for the rest of the regiment in the valley, which was relatively blind to enemy movement.

While the 60mm and 82mm mortars were scattered around in proximity of the combat base, the NVA rocket sites and artillery pieces were located well to the west, southwest, and northwest, outside of friendly counterbattery range. One particularly awesome and effective weapon was the Soviet-built 122mm rocket. When fired, the projectile was fairly accurate in deflection but, because it was powered by a propellant, the biggest margin of error was in range. The North Vietnamese preferred to position their launching sites so its gunners could track along the long axis of a given target; longs and shorts would land "in the ballpark."

The KSCB hugged the airstrip and was roughly in the shape of a rectangle with the long axis running east and west. This made the optimum firing positions for the 122mm rocket either to the east or west of the base in line with the runway. To the west, Hill 881S or 861 would have been ideal locations because in clear weather those vantage points provided an excellent view of Khe Sanh and were almost directly on line with the airstrip.

Unfortunately for the NVA, the Marines had squatters' rights on those pieces of real estate and were rather hostile to claim jumpers. As an alternative, the North Vietnamese decided on 881N, but this choice had one drawback, since the line of sight between that northern peak and the combat base was masked by the top of Hill 861.

Because of their greater range, the enemy's 130mm and 152mm artillery batteries were located even further to the west. These guns were cleverly concealed in two main firing positions. One was on Co Roc Mountain, which was southwest of where Route 9 crossed the Laotian border; the other area was 305, so called because it was on a bearing of 305 degrees (west-northwest) from Hill 881S at a range of about ten thousand meters. While the heavy caliber artillery rounds which periodically ripped into the base were usually referred to as originating from Co Roc, 305 was the source of about 60 to 70 percent of this fire, probably because it was adjacent to a main supply artery. Both sites were vulnerable only to air attack and were extremely difficult to pinpoint because of the enemy's masterful job of camouflage, his cautious employment, and the extreme distance from friendly observation posts. The NVA gunners fired only a few rounds every hour so that continuous muzzle flashes did not betray their positions and, after each round, quickly scurried out to cover the guns with protective nets and screens. Some pieces, mounted on tracks, were wheeled out of caves in Co Roc Mountain, fired, and returned immediately. Though never used in as great a quantity as the rockets and mortars, these shells wreaked havoc at Khe Sanh because there was very little that they could not penetrate; even duds went about four feet into the ground.

At the base the Marines had devised a crude but effective early warning system for such attacks. Motor transport personnel had mounted a horn from a two-and-a-half-ton truck in the top of a tree, and the lead wires were attached to two beer can lids. When a message was received from 881S, a Marine, who monitored the radio, pressed the two lids together and the blaring horn gave advanced warning of the incoming artillery rounds. The radio operator relayed the message over the regimental net and then dived into a hole. Men in the open usually had from five to eighteen seconds to find cover or just hit the deck before "all hell broke loose." When poor visibility obscured the view between 881S and the base, the radio operator usually picked himself up, dusted off, and jokingly passed a three-word message to Company I which indicated that the rounds had arrived on schedule—"Roger India . . . Splash."

The firing position which plagued the Marines the most was located to the southwest of the hill in a U-shaped draw known as "the Horse-shoe." There were at least two NVA 120mm mortars in this area which, in spite of an avalanche of American bombs and artillery shells, were either never knocked out or were frequently replaced. These tubes were registered on the hill and harassed Company I constantly. Anyone caught aboveground when one of the 120s crashed into the perimeter was almost certain to become a casualty because the explosion produced an extremely large fragmentation pattern.

The only thing that the Marines had going for them was that they could frequently spot a telltale flash of an artillery piece or hear the "thunk" when a mortar round left the tube, but the heavy shells took their toll. On Hill 881S alone, 40 Marines were killed throughout the siege and over 150 were wounded at least once.

Considering the sheer weight of the bombardment, enemy shells caused a relatively small number of fatalities at the base. Besides the solid fortifications, there were two factors which kept casualties to a minimum. The first was the flak jacket—a specially designed nylon vest reinforced with overlapping fiberglass plates. The jacket would not stop a high-velocity bullet, but it did protect a man's torso and most vital organs against shell fragments. The bulky vest was not particularly popular in hot weather when the Marines were on patrol, but in a static, defensive position the jacket was ideal. The second factor was the high quality of leadership at platoon and company level. Junior officers and staff non-commissioned officers (NCOs) constantly moved up and down the lines to supervise the younger, inexperienced Marines, many of whom had only recently arrived in Vietnam.

The veteran staff NCOs, long known as the "backbone of the Corps," knew from experience that troops had to be kept busy. A man who was left to ponder his problems often developed a fatalistic attitude that could increase his reaction time and decrease his lifetime. The crusty NCOs did not put much stock in the old cliche: "If a round has your name on it, there's nothing you can do." Consequently, the Marines worked; they dug trenches, filled sandbags, ran for cover, and returned to fill more sandbags.

Morale remained high and casualties, under the circumstances, were surprisingly low.

Although the NVA encircled the KSCB and applied constant pressure, the defenders were never restricted entirely to the confines of the perimeter. The term "siege," in the strictest sense of the word, was somewhat of a misnomer because the Allies conducted a number of daily patrols, often as far as five hundred meters from their own lines.

One vital area was the drop zone. When the weather turned bad in February, the KSCB was supplied primarily by parachute drops. Colonel Lownds set up his original zone inside the FOB-3 compound but later moved it several hundred meters west of Red Sector because he was afraid that the falling pallets might injure someone.

The fight on Hill 861A was extremely bitter. At 0305 the North Vietnamese opened up on American positions with a tremendous 82mm mortar barrage. This was followed by continuous volleys of RPG rounds which knocked out several Marine crew-served weapons and shielded the advance of the NVA sappers and assault troops. The North Vietnamese blew lanes through the barbed wire along the northern perimeter and slammed into the Company E lines. Second Lieutenant Donald E. Shanley's 1st Platoon bore the brunt of the attack and reeled back to supplementary positions. Quickly the word filtered back to the company CP that the enemy was inside the wire, and Captain Earle G. Breeding ordered that all units employ tear gas in defense, but the North Vietnamese were obviously "hopped up" on some type of narcotic, and the searing fumes had very little effect. Following the initial assault there was a brief lull in the fighting. The NVA soldiers apparently felt that, having secured the northernmost trenchline, they owned the entire objective and stopped to sift through the Marine positions for souvenirs. Magazines and paperbacks were the most popular. Meanwhile, the temporary reversal only served to enrage the Marines. Following a shower of grenades, Lieutenant Shanley and his men charged back into their original positions and swarmed all over the surprised enemy troops.

The counterattack quickly deteriorated into a melee that resembled a bloody, waterfront barroom brawl—a style of fighting not completely alien to most Marines. Because the darkness and ground fog drastically reduced visibility, hand-to-hand combat was a necessity. Using their knives, bayonets, rifle butts, and fists, the men of the 1st Platoon ripped into the hapless North Vietnamese with a vengeance. Captain Breeding, a veteran of the Korean conflict who had worked his way up through the ranks, admitted that, at first, he was concerned over how his younger, inexperienced Marines would react in their first fight. As it turned out, they were magnificent.

The captain saw one of his men come face-to-face with a North Vietnamese in the inky darkness; the young American all but decapitated his adversary with a crushing, roundhouse right to the face, then leaped on the flattened soldier and finished the job with a knife.

Another man was jumped from behind by a North Vietnamese who grabbed him around the neck and was just about to slit his throat when one of the Marine's buddies jabbed the muzzle of his M-16 between the two combatants. With his selector on full automatic, he fired off a full magazine; the burst tore huge chunks from the back of the embattled Marine's flak jacket but it also cut the North Vietnamese in half. Since the fighting was at such close quarters, both sides used hand grenades at extremely short range. The Marines had the advantage because of their armored vests, and they would throw a grenade then turn away from the blast, hunch up, and absorb the fragments in their flak jackets and the backs of their legs. On several occasions, Captain Breeding's men used this technique and "blew away" enemy soldiers at less than ten meters.

No one engaged in the donnybrook was exactly sure just how long it lasted—all were too busy fighting to check their watches. More than likely, the enemy was inside the wire less than a half hour. During the fighting, Captain Breeding fed fire team–sized elements from the 2nd and 3rd Platoons into the fray from both flanks of the penetration. The newcomers appeared to be afraid that they might miss all the action and tore into the enemy as if they were making up for lost time. Even though the E/2/26 company commander was no newcomer to blood and gore, he was awed by the ferocity of the attack. Captain Breeding later said: "It was like watching a World War II movie. Charlie didn't know how to cope with it . . . we walked all over them." Those dazed NVA soldiers who survived the vicious onslaught retreated into another meat grinder; as they ran from the hill, they were blasted by recoilless rifle fire from 2/26, which was located on Hill 558.

At approximately 0610, the North Vietnamese officers rallied the battered remnants and tried again, but the second effort was also stopped cold. By this time, Captain Breeding, who was busier than the proverbial one-armed paper hanger, was assisting in the coordination of fire support from five separate sources.

The Marines of Captain Dabney's I/3/26, located on Hill 881S, provided extremely effective and enthusiastic support throughout the attack. In three hours, Captain Dabney's men pumped out close to 1,100 rounds from only three 81mm mortars, and the tubes became so hot that they actually glowed in the dark. Again, the bulk of the heavy artillery fire, along with radar-controlled bombing missions, was placed on the northern avenues leading to the hill positions. The enemy units, held in reserve, were thus shredded by the bombardment as they moved up to continue the attack.

After the second assault fizzled out, the North Vietnamese withdrew, but enemy gunners shelled the base and outposts throughout the day. At 1430, replacements from 2/26 were helilifted to Hill 861A. Captain Breeding had lost seven men, most of whom were killed in the opening barrage, and another thirty-five were medevaced, so the new arrivals brought E/2/26 back up to normal strength.

On the other hand, the NVA suffered 109 known dead; many still remained in the 1st Platoon area where they had been shot, slashed, or bludgeoned to death. As near as Captain Breeding could tell, he did not lose a single man during the fierce hand-to-hand struggle; all American deaths were apparently the result of the enemy's mortar barrage and supporting fire. The Marines never knew how many other members of the North Vietnamese had fallen as a result of the heavy artillery and air strikes, but the number was undoubtedly high. All in all, it had been a bad day for the Communists.

The North Vietnamese took their revenge in the early morning hours of 7 February; their victims were the defenders of the Special Forces camp at Lang Vei. At 0042, an American advisor reported that the installation was under heavy attack by enemy tanks. This was the first time that the NVA had employed its armor in the south and, within thirteen minutes, nine PT-76 Soviet-built tanks churned through the defensive wire, rumbled over the antipersonnel minefields, and bulled their way into the heart of the compound.

A North Vietnamese battalion, equipped with satchel charges, tear gas, and flamethrowers, followed with an aggressive infantry assault that was coordinated with heavy attacks by fire on the 26th Marines. Colonel Lownds placed the base on Red Alert and called in immediate artillery and air in support. Although the Marines responded quickly, the defensive fires had little effect because, by that time, the enemy had overrun the camp. The defenders who survived buttoned themselves up in bunkers and, at 0243, called for artillery fire to dust off their own positions.

Part of Colonel Lownds's mission as coordinator of all friendly forces in the Khe Sanh area was to provide artillery support for Lang Vei and, if possible, to reinforce the camp in case of attack. Under the circumstances, a relief in strength was out of the question. Any column moving down the road, especially at night, would undoubtedly have been ambushed. If the Marines went directly over the mountains, they would have to hack through the dense growth and waste precious hours. A large-scale heliborne effort was ruled out because the North Vietnamese apparently anticipated such a move and withdrew their tanks to the only landing zones near the camp which were suitable for such an operation. Even with tactical aircraft providing suppressive fire, a helo assault into the teeth of enemy armor was ill-advised. The most important factor, however, was that NVA units in the area greatly outnumbered any force Colonel Lownds could commit.

Since a relief in force was undesirable, plans for a hit-and-run rescue attempt were quickly drawn up. Major General Norman J. Anderson, commanding the 1st MAW, and Colonel Jonathan F. Ladd of the US Army Special Forces worked out the details. Two major points agreed upon were that the helicopters employed in the operation would be those which were not essential to the 26th Marines at the moment and that Marine fixed-wing support would be provided.

As soon as it was light, the survivors of the Lang Vei garrison managed to break out of their bunkers and work their way to the site of an older camp some four to five hundred meters to the east. Later that same day, a raiding party boarded Quang Tri–based MAG-helicopters and took off for Lang Vei. A flight of Huey gunships, led by Lieutenant Colonel William J. White, Commanding Officer of Marine Observation Squadron 6, as well as jet aircraft escorted the transport choppers. While the jets and Hueys covered their approach, the helicopters swooped into a small strip at the old camp and took on survivors, including fifteen Americans. In spite of the heavy suppressive fire provided by the escorts, three transport helos suffered battle damage during the evacuation. One overloaded chopper, flown by Captain Robert J. Richards of Marine Medium Helicopter Squadron 262, had to make the return trip to Khe Sanh at treetop level because the excess weight prevented the pilot from gaining altitude.

There was a large number of indigenous personnel—both military and civilian—who could not get out on the helicopters and had to move overland to Khe Sanh. A portion of these were members of the Laotian Volunteer Battalion 33, which on 23 January had been overrun at Ban Houei San, Laos (near the Laotian–South Vietnam border), by three NVA battalions. The remnants fled across the border and took refuge at Lang Vei, and when the Special Forces camp fell, the Laotians continued their trek to the east with a host of other refugees. At 0800 on the 8th, about three thousand approached the southern perimeter at Khe Sanh and requested admittance. Colonel Lownds, fearing that NVA infiltrators were in their midst, denied them entrance until each was searched and processed. This took place near the FOB-3 compound, after which some of the refugees were evacuated. The Laotians were eventually returned to their own country.

Also on the morning of 8 February, the North Vietnamese launched the first daylight attack against the 26th Marines. At 0420, a reinforced battalion hit the 1st Platoon, A/1/9, which occupied Hill 64 some five hundred meters west of the 1/9 perimeter. Following their usual pattern, the North Vietnamese tried to disrupt the Marines' artillery support with simultaneous bombardment of the base. To prevent friendly reinforcements from reaching the small hill, the enemy also shelled the platoon's parent unit and, during the fight, some 350 mortar and artillery rounds fell on the 1/9 positions. North Vietnamese assault troops launched a two-pronged attack against the northwestern and southwestern corners of the A/1/9 outpost and either blew the barbed wire with Bangalore torpedoes or threw canvas on top of the obstacles and rolled over them. The enemy soldiers poured into the trenchline and attacked the bunkers with RPGs and satchel charges. They also emplaced machine guns at the edge of the penetrations and pinned down those Marines in the eastern half of the perimeter who were trying to cross over the hill and reinforce their comrades.

The men in the northeastern sector, led by the platoon commander, Second Lieutenant Terence R. Roach Jr., counterattacked down the trenchline and became engaged in savage hand-to-hand fighting. While rallying his troops and directing fire from atop an exposed bunker, Lieutenant Roach was mortally wounded. From sheer weight of numbers, the North Vietnamese gradually pushed the Marines back until the enemy owned the western half of the outpost. At that point, neither side was able to press the advantage. Pre-registered mortar barrages from 1/9 and artillery fire from the KSCB had isolated the NVA assault units from any reinforcements, but at the same time the depleted 1st Platoon was not strong enough to dislodge the enemy.

One Marine had an extremely close call during the fight but lived to tell about it. On the northern side of the perimeter, Private First Class Michael A. Barry of the 1st Squad was engaged in a furious hand grenade duel with the NVA soldiers when a ChiCom grenade hit him on top of the helmet and landed at the young Marine's feet. PFC Barry quickly picked it up and drew back to throw, but the grenade went off in his hand. Had it been an American M-26 grenade, the private would undoubtedly have been blown to bits, but ChiCom grenades frequently produced an uneven frag pattern. In this case, the bulk of the blast went down and away from the Marine's body; Barry had the back of his right arm, his back, and his right leg peppered with metal fragments, but he did not lose any fingers and continued to function for the rest of the battle.

In another section of the trenchline, Lance Corporal Robert L. Wiley had an equally hair-raising experience. Wiley, a shell-shock victim, lay flat on his back in one of the bunkers which had been overrun by the enemy. His eardrums had burst, he was temporarily paralyzed, and his glazed eyes were fixed in a corpse-like stare, but the Marine was alive and fully aware of what was going on around him.

Thinking that Wiley was dead, the North Vietnamese were only interested in rummaging through his personal effects for souvenirs. One NVA soldier found the Marine's wallet and took out several pictures, including a snapshot of his family gathered around a Christmas tree. After pocketing their booty, the North Vietnamese moved on; Lance Corporal Wiley was later rescued by the relief column.

At 0730, Lieutenant Colonel Mitchell committed a second platoon, headed by the Company A commander, Captain Henry J. M. Radcliffe, to the action. By 0900, the relief force had made its way to the eastern slope of the small hill and established contact with the trapped platoon. During the advance, Companies B and D, along with one section of tanks, delivered murderous direct fire to the flanks and front of Captain Radcliffe's column, breaking up any attempt by the enemy to interdict the linkup. After several flights of strike aircraft had pasted the reverse slope of the hill, the company commander led his combined forces in a frontal assault over the crest and, within fifteen minutes, drove the North Vietnamese from the outpost.

Automatic weapons chopped down many North Vietnamese as they fled from the hill. The battered remnants of the enemy force retreated to the west and, once in the open, were also taken under fire by the rest of the Marine battalion. In addition, the artillery batteries at KSCB contributed to the slaughter and, when the smoke cleared, 150 North Vietnamese were dead. Although the platoon lines were restored, Colonel Lownds decided to abandon the position and, at 1200, the two units withdrew with their casualties. Marine losses that morning on the outpost were 21 killed and 26 wounded; at the base, 5 were killed and 6 wounded.

During the next two weeks, the NVA mounted no major ground attack but continued to apply pressure on the KSCB. There were daily clashes along the Marine lines, but these were limited to small fire fights, sniping incidents, and probes against the wire. A decrease in activity along the various infiltration routes indicated that the enemy had completed his initial buildup and was busily consolidating positions from which to launch an all-out effort. The Allies continued to improve their defenses and by mid-February most units occupied positions with three or four layers of barbed wire, dense minefields, special detection devices, deep trenches, and mortar-proof bunkers. The battle reverted to a contest of supporting arms, and the North Vietnamese stepped up their shelling of the base, especially with direct fire weapons. Attempts to silence the enemy guns were often frustrated because the Marines were fighting two battles during February—one with the NVA, the other with the weather.

The weather at Khe Sanh throughout February could be characterized in one word—miserable. The northeast monsoons had long since spilled over into the Khe Sanh Valley, and every morning the base was shrouded with ground fog and low scud layers which dissipated around 1000 or 1100. When the sun finally managed to burn through, the cloud ceiling retreated slightly but still hovered low enough to prevent the unrestricted use of airborne artillery spotters and strike aircraft. It was during these periods, when the overcast was between one hundred and five hundred feet, that enemy artillery, rocket, and mortar fire was the heaviest. North Vietnamese forward observers, perched along the lower slopes of the surrounding hills, called in and adjusted barrages with little fear of retaliation against their own gun positions. Later in the afternoon, when the fog rolled in again and obscured the enemy's view, the incoming tapered off.

The Marines adjusted their schedule accordingly. They usually worked under the cover of the haze in the morning, went underground during the midday shelling, and returned to their duties later in the afternoon. While the extremely low cloud cover occasionally befriended the men at the base, it constantly plagued the pilots whose mission was to resupply the 26th Marines.

The job of transporting enough "bullets, beans, and bandages" to sustain the 6,680 Khe Sanh defenders fell to the C-130s of Marine Aerial Refueler Transport Squadron 152 and the US Air Force 834th Air Division; the C-123s of the 315th Air Commando Wing; the UH-34, CH-46, and UH-1E helicopters of Marine Aircraft Group 36 (MAG-36); and the CH-53 choppers of MAG-16.

Even under ideal circumstances, the airlift would have been a massive undertaking. The difficulties, however, were compounded by the poor visibility, which was below minimum for airfield operations 40 percent of the time, and the heavy volume of antiaircraft and artillery fire directed at the incoming transports. The North Vietnamese had moved several antiaircraft units into the hills east of the airstrip, forcing the C-130 Hercules, the C-123 Providers, and the helicopters to run the gauntlet during their final approach. Under cover of the heavy fog, some audacious North Vietnamese gun crews positioned their antiaircraft weapons just off the eastern threshold of the runway and fired in the blind whenever they heard the drone of incoming planes. Several aircraft were hit while on GCA final and completely in the soup. Immediately after touchdown, the aircraft were subjected to intense mortar and rocket fire; in fact, the incoming was so closely synchronized with their arrival, the fixed-wing transports were nicknamed "mortar magnets" by the Marines.

The key to survival for the pilots was a steep approach through the eastern corridor, a short roll-out, and a speedy turnaround after landing. A small ramp paralleled the western end of the strip, which the transport crews used as an unloading point. After roll-out, the pilot turned off the runway onto the easternmost taxiway, then wheeled onto the ramp while the loadmasters shoved the pallets of supplies out the back. All outgoing passengers were loaded on the double, because the 76 planes rarely stopped rolling. The pilot completed the loop by turning back onto the runway via the western taxiway and took off in the opposite direction from which he landed. It was not uncommon for the entire circuit to be completed within three minutes; even then, the planes were tracked by exploding mortar rounds.

On 10 February, a tragedy occurred which resulted in a drastic alteration of the unloading process. A Marine C-130, heavily laden with bladders of fuel for the 26th Marines, was making its approach to the field under intense fire. Just before the giant bird touched down, the cockpit and fuel bags were riddled by enemy bullets. With flames licking at one side, the stricken craft careened off the runway 3,100 feet from the approach end, spun around, and was rocked by several muffled explosions.

The C-130 then began to burn furiously. Crash crews rushed to the plane and started spraying it with foam.

The pilot, Chief Warrant Officer Henry Wildfang, and his copilot suffered minor burns as they scrambled out the overhead hatch in the cockpit. Firefighters in specially designed heat suits dashed into the flaming debris and pulled several injured crewmen and passengers to safety—rescue attempts came too late for six others. One of those killed in the crash, Lieutenant Colonel Carl E. Peterson, the 1st MAW Engineer Officer, was a reserve officer who only a few months before had volunteered for active duty. As a result of this accident and damage sustained by other transports while on the ground, C-130 landings at Khe Sanh were suspended.

With the field closed to C-130s, a US Air Force innovation—the Low Altitude Parachute Extraction System, or LAPES—was put into effect. This self-contained system, which had been used extensively during the renovation of the airstrip in the fall of 1967, enabled the aircraft to unload their cargo without landing. When making a LAPES run, the Hercules pilot made his approach from the east, during which he opened the tail ramp and deployed a reefed cargo parachute.

Prior to touchdown, he added just enough power to hold the aircraft about five feet above the ground. As the plane skimmed over the runway and approached the intended extraction point, the pilot electrically opened the streaming chute, which was attached to the roller-mounted cargo pallets. The sudden jolt of the blossoming chute snatched the cargo from the rear hatch, and the pallets came to a skidding halt on the runway. The pilot then jammed the throttles to the firewall, eased back on the yoke, and executed a high-angle, westerly pullout to avoid ground fire while the Marines moved onto the runway with forklifts and quickly gathered in the supplies.

The system was quite ingenious and allowed the aircraft to pass through the V-ring in a matter of seconds. Even though the airmen could not control the skidding pallets after release, some pilots perfected their individual technique and were able to place the cargo on a twenty-five-meter square with consistency. On one occasion, however, an extraction chute malfunctioned and the cargo rocketed off the western end of the runway; the eight-ton pallet of lumber smashed into a mess hall located near the end of the strip and crushed three Marines to death.

Another technique—the Ground Proximity Extraction System or GPES—was also used but to a lesser degree than the LAPES (fifteen GPES deliveries during the siege as compared to fifty-two LAPES). Both utilized the low approach, but with GPES the cargo was extracted by a hook extended from a boom at the rear of the aircraft. As the C-130 swooped low over the runway, the pilot tried to snag an arresting cable similar to the one used on aircraft carriers; only his hook was attached to the cargo bundles and not the plane. Upon engagement, the pallets were jerked from the rear hatch and came to a dead stop on the runway. With the GPES, the chance of a pallet skidding out of control or overturning was greatly reduced. The only problem that occurred was not with the system itself but with faulty installation.

The Marines who initially emplaced the GPES were frequently chased away from their work by incoming mortar rounds and, as a result of the periodic interruptions, the cable was not anchored properly. The first C-130 that snagged the wire ripped the arresting gear out by the roots. After the initial bugs were remedied, the system worked so successfully that, on one pass, a load containing thirty dozen eggs was extracted without a single eggshell being cracked.

Most of the time, however, the low overcast precluded the use of either extraction system, and the preponderance of supplies was delivered by paradrops. This technique called for close air/ground coordination, and the C-130 pilots relied on the Marine Air Traffic Control Unit (MATCU) at Khe Sanh to guide them into the drop zones. The Marine ground controller lined the aircraft up on the long axis of the runway for a normal instrument approach, and when the Hercules passed a certain point over the eastern threshold of the field, the controller called "Ready, Ready, Mark." At "Mark," the pilot pushed a stopwatch, activated his Doppler navigational system, turned to a predetermined heading, and maintained an altitude of between five hundred and six hundred feet.

The Doppler device indicated any deviation from the desired track to the drop zone, which was west of Red Sector, and the release point was calculated by using the stopwatch—twenty to twenty-six seconds from

"Mark," depending on the winds. At the computed release point, the pilot pulled the C-130 into an eight-degree nose-up attitude, and sixteen parachute bundles, containing fifteen tons of supplies, slid from the rear of the aircraft and floated through the overcast into the three-hundred-meter-square drop zone. Under Visual Flight Rules (VFR), the average computed error for the drops was only ninety-five meters. Even when these missions were executed completely under Instrument Flight Rules (IFR), the average distance that the bundles landed from the intended impact point was 133 meters—well inside the drop zone. On a few occasions, however, the parachute bundles missed the zone and drifted far enough away from the base to preclude a safe recovery. In these rare instances, friendly artillery and air strikes were brought to bear on the wayward containers to keep them from falling into the hands of the enemy. During the siege, Air Force C-130 crews conducted a total of 496 paradrops at Khe Sanh.

Although the paradrops were sufficient for bulk commodities such as rations and ammunition, there were certain items which had to be delivered or picked up personally. Medical supplies, special ammunition, and other delicate cargo would not withstand the jolt of a parachute landing. In addition, there were replacements to be shuttled into the base and casualties to be evacuated. With the cancellation of all C-130 landings, this job was left up to the sturdy C-123 Providers of the 315th Air Commando Wing, as well as MAG-36 and MAG-16 helicopters.

The choppers could maneuver around areas of heavy ground fire, land, unload, take on medevacs, and depart very quickly, but their payloads were limited. On the other hand, the C-123s had a larger cargo capacity but were restricted to a more rigid approach and provided better targets both in the pattern and on the ground. The Providers, however, required much less runway from which to operate than the C-130s and could land and take off using only 1,400 feet of the 3,900-foot strip. This saving feature enabled the pilots to make a steep approach, short roll-out, and rapid turnaround. The crews still had to undergo those frantic moments on the ground when the geysers of dirty-black smoke bracketed their aircraft. Nevertheless, the dauntless C-123 crews continued their perilous missions throughout the siege with great success.

No discussion of the airlift would be complete without mention of the MAG-36 and MAG-16 helicopter pilots who flew in and out of Khe Sanh daily delivering supplies, delicate cargo, reinforcements, and evacuating casualties. The chopper crews were faced with the same problems that plagued the fixed-wing transports—low ceilings and enemy ground fire—but to a greater degree because of their slow speed and vulnerability. MAG-36s operated primarily from Quang Tri and Dong Ha, and were reinforced from the group's main base at Phu Bai. These valiant pilots and crewmen in their Huey gunships, CH-46 transports, and UH-34s flew long hours, day and night, in all kinds of weather to sustain the Marines in and around Khe Sanh. The CH-53s of Da Nang–based MAG-16, with their heavier payload, also made a sizeable contribution to this effort.

The resupply of the hill outposts was a particularly hazardous aspect of the overall mission. Approximately 20 percent of Colonel Lownds's personnel occupied these redoubts and, for all practical purposes, were cut off from the rest of the garrison. The road north of the base was not secure, and the perimeters atop the hills were too small and irregular for parachute drops; the only way that the isolated posts could be sustained was by helicopter. When the dense monsoon clouds rolled into the valley, the mountaintops were the first to become submerged and, as the overcast lifted, the last to reappear. During February, several of the outposts were completely obscured for more than a week and resupply was impossible.

During these periods, the North Vietnamese took advantage of the reduced visibility and emplaced heavy automatic weapons along the neighboring peaks and waited for the ceiling to lift, which invariably heralded the arrival of helicopters. As a result, the UH-1Es, UH-34s, and CH-46s were subjected to a hail of enemy bullets during each mission.

When the helicopters proceeded to the hills singly or in small groups, each mission was a hair-raising experience for both the chopper crews and the men on the ground. A good example of what often transpired during those frantic moments occurred early in the siege on Hill 881S when Captain Dabney called for a chopper to evacuate a badly wounded Marine.

One corporal was assigned as a stretcher bearer because he had a badly impacted wisdom tooth and, once aboard, he could ride out on the helicopter and have the tooth extracted at the main base. Because of the 120mm mortars located in the Horseshoe and the antiaircraft guns which ringed the hill, the men on 881S had to employ a variety of diversions to keep the enemy gunners from getting the range of the incoming choppers. In this instance, they threw a smoke grenade a good distance away from the actual landing zone in hopes that the gunners would register on the smoke and the helicopter would be in and out before the North Vietnamese could readjust. This meant that the helo had about nineteen seconds to get off the ground.

The ruse did not come off as planned. The stretcher bearers had barely loaded the wounded man aboard the helicopter, a CH-46, when 120mm mortar rounds bracketed the aircraft and spurred the pilot to action. The helo lurched into the air, and the sudden jolt rolled the corporal with the bad tooth over the edge of the tail ramp; he held on desperately for a few seconds but finally let go and fell about twenty feet to the ground. Cursing to himself, the young man limped back to his trench and waited for another chance.

Later that day, a UH-34 swooped in to pick up another casualty, and the prospective dental patient quickly scrambled aboard. This trip also covered about twenty feet—ten feet up and ten feet down—because the tail rotor of the UH-34 was literally sawed off by a burst from an enemy machine gun just after the bird became airborne. After the swirling craft came to rest, the passengers and the three-man crew quickly clamored out the hatch and dived into a nearby trench. A heavy mortar barrage ensued, during which several more men were hit.

By the time another CH-46 arrived on the scene, the passenger list had grown to fourteen, including ten casualties, the crew of the downed helo, and the original dental case. Because of the heavy concentration of enemy fire in the original zone, the Marines had blasted out another landing site on the opposite side of the hill. The chopper touched down, and thirteen of the fourteen Marines boarded before the crew chief stated emphatically that the aircraft was full. As luck would have it, the young Marine with the swollen jaw was the fourteenth man. Thoroughly indignant, the three-time loser returned to his position and mumbled that he would rather suffer from a toothache than try and get off the hill by helicopter.

It was the consensus of both the ground commanders and pilots alike that the problem of getting helicopters to and from the hills was becoming critical. The technique then employed was resulting in casualties among both the air crews and the infantry units, as well as a rapid rise in the attrition of MAG-36 helicopters. The Huey gunships, though putting forth a valiant effort, did not possess the heavy volume of fire required to keep the approach lanes open. As a result, the 1st MAW adopted another system which provided more muscle.

The solution was basically a page out of the *Fleet Marine Force Manual for Helicopter Support Operations*. All helicopter flights to the hill outposts were to be escorted by strike aircraft, which would provide suppressive fire. The A-4 Skyhawks of Chu Lai–based MAG-12 were selected as the fixed-wing escorts, and the little jet was perfect for the job. Affectionately referred to as "Scooters" by their pilots, the A-4 was a highly maneuverable attack aircraft; its accuracy, dependability, and varied ordnance load had made it the workhorse of Marine close air support for many years.

The operation went into effect on 24 February. Because of the large number of aircraft utilized in each mission—twelve A-4s, one TA-4, twelve CH-46s, and four UH-1E gunships—the overall effort was nicknamed the Super Gaggle by its planners. The difficulty in execution was primarily one of coordination and control because of the various agencies involved. Additional factors that had to be considered were departure weather, destination weather, and coordination of friendly artillery and air strikes around Khe Sanh. Lieutenant Colonel Carey, the 1st MAW Operations Officer and one of the planners, later described the mechanics of the Super Gaggle:

> *Success of the effort was predicated on timing, coordination, and often-times luck. Luck, as used, refers to the ability to guess whether the weather would hold long enough to complete an effort once it got under way. The effort began with the TA-4 on station determining if sufficient ceiling existed for the "Scooters" of MAG-12 to provide sufficient suppressive fires to assure success. . . . Once the TA-4 called all conditions go, an "H" hour was set and the Super Gaggle began. Twelve A-4s would launch from Chu Lai while simultaneously, one hundred miles to the north,*

twelve to sixteen helos would launch from the Quang Tri helo base and proceed to the Dong Ha LSA (Logistics Support Area) for supply pickup. The object was for all aircraft to arrive in the objective area on a precise schedule. So the operation generally consisted as follows: (1) Softening up known enemy positions by four A-4s, generally armed with napalm and bombs; (2) Two A-4s armed with CS (tear gas) tanks saturate enemy antiaircraft and automatic weapons positions; (3) thirty to forty seconds prior to final run in by the helos two A-4s lay a smoke screen along selected avenues of approach. . . . (4) While helos make final run into the target, four A-4s with bombs, rockets, and 20mm guns provide close-in fire suppression. . . . Once the helos commenced their descent the factors of weather, their four-thousand-pound externally carried load, and the terrain would not permit a second chance. If an enemy gun was not suppressed there was no alternative for the helos but to continue. They (the transport pilots) were strengthened with the knowledge that following close on their heels were their gunships, ready to pick them up if they survived being shot down. Fortunately, these tactics were so successful that during the entire period of the Super Gaggle, only two CH-46s were downed en route to the hill positions. The crews were rescued immediately by escorting Huey gunships.

These missions, however, looked much more orderly on paper than they did in the air, and the operation lived up to its name. Only those who have experienced the hazards of monsoon flying can fully appreciate the veritable madhouse that often exists when large numbers of aircraft are confined to the restricted space beneath a low-hanging overcast.

Coupled with this was the fact that the fluffy looking clouds around Khe Sanh housed mountains which ran up to three thousand feet. No doubt, the aircrews involved in the Gaggle were mindful of the standard warning issued to fledgling aviators: "Keep your eyes out of the cockpit; a midair collision could ruin your whole day."

Even though the missions were well-coordinated and executed with a high degree of professionalism, it often appeared that confusion reigned because planes were everywhere. A-4s bore in on the flanks of the approach lanes, blasting enemy gun positions and spewing protective smoke; CH-46s groped through the haze trying to find the landing zones; the hornet-like UH-1E gunships darted in from the rear in case someone was shot down; and the lone 87TA-4 circled overhead trying to keep his flock from running amuck. During the missions to 881S, the men of India and Mike, 3/26, added to the hullabaloo with a little twist of their own. When the CH-46s settled over the hill, the Marines on the ground tossed out a few dozen smoke grenades for added cover and then every man in the perimeter fired a full magazine at anything on the surrounding slopes which appeared hostile. With some 350 men hosing down the countryside at the same time, the din was terrific.

Neither the deluge of lead from 881S nor the suppressive fire of the jets and gunships kept the NVA completely quiet. The 120mm mortar crews in the Horseshoe were especially active during the resupply runs to 881S and always lobbed some rounds onto the hill in hopes of knocking down a helicopter. These tubes had been previously registered on the LZs, and the smoke screens had little effect on their fire; as a result, the Marines frequently shifted landing zones.

The smoke did block the view of the North Vietnamese machine gunners, and they were forced to fire blindly through the haze—if they dared fire at all. The choppers still took hits but nowhere near as many as before the Gaggle was initiated. The CH-46 pilots, poised precariously above the LZs during the few agonizing seconds it took to unload their cargo, often heard the sickening smack which meant that a bullet had torn into the fuselage of their thin-skinned helos.

The members of the two-man Helicopter Support Teams (HST), 3rd Shore Party Battalion, who were attached to the rifle companies were also prime targets. These men had to stand up while they guided the choppers into the LZs and, every few days, they had to attach bundles of cargo nets, which accumulated from previous missions, for the return trip to Dong Ha. This was dangerous for the aircrews as well as the HST men because, during the hookup, the pilots had to hold their aircraft in a vulnerable position a few feet above the ground with the nose cocked up and the belly exposed to fire from the front. While they attached the bundles, the ground support personnel could hear the machine-gun rounds zing a few inches over their heads and slap into the soft underside of the suspended helicopter. Not all the bullets and shell fragments passed overhead; on 881S, the defenders were operating with their fourth HST when the siege ended.

In spite of the seriousness of the situation, the Gaggle was not without its lighter episodes. In one instance, an HST man attached to I/3/26 hooked up an outgoing load and gave the pilot the "thumbs-up" when he discovered that he had become entangled in the pile of nets. The CH-46 surged into the air with the startled Marine dangling helplessly from the bottom of the net by one foot. But for the quick reaction of his comrade on the ground who informed the pilot by radio that the chopper had taken on more than the prescribed load, the young cargo handler would have had a rather interesting trip to Dong Ha.

The CH-46 crews also provided a human touch during these missions. When the Sea Knights swept over the hills, it was not uncommon to see a machine gunner on board quit his weapon for a second, nonchalantly pitch a case of soda pop out the hatch, and then quickly return to blaze away at the enemy positions.

At 1st MAW Headquarters, Lieutenant Colonel Carey, who had been an infantryman in Korea before he went to flight school and who sympathized with the men on the outposts, felt that a small gesture acknowledging their continued outstanding performance was in order. Special efforts were made to obtain quantities of dry ice for packing, and one day, without notice, hundreds of Dixie cups of ice cream were delivered to the men on the hills as part of the regular resupply. This effort was dubbed Operation COOL IT. The only hitch developed on 881S, where the Marines, unaware of the contents, allowed the cargo to remain in the LZ until after dark, when it was safe to venture out of the trenchline. The ice cream was a little sloppy but edible and greatly appreciated.

The introduction of the Super Gaggle was a turning point in the resupply effort. Prior to its conception, the Marines on the outposts dreaded the thought of leaving their positions to retrieve cargo—even when it included mail—because of the heavy shelling. With a dozen Skyhawks pasting the surrounding hills during each mission, this threat was alleviated to a large degree and casualties tapered off. The Company I, 3/26, commander later stated: "If it weren't for the Gaggle, most of us probably wouldn't be here today."

The helicopter pilots, knowing that their jet jockey compatriots were close at hand, were also able to do their job more effectively. In the past, the transport crew chiefs occasionally had to jettison their external load prematurely when the pilot took evasive action to avoid ground fire. When this occurred, the cargo nets usually slammed into the perimeter and splattered containers all over the hilltop. With the Super Gaggle, the pilots had less enemy fire to contend with and did not bomb the hills with the cargo pallets as much; as a result more supplies arrived intact. In addition, the system greatly facilitated the picking up of wounded personnel.

The Marine helicopters continued their flights to and from Khe Sanh throughout the siege. In spite of the obstacles, the chopper pilots crammed enough sorties into those days with flyable weather to haul 465 tons of supplies to the base during February. When the weather later cleared, this amount was increased to approximately forty tons a day. While supporting Operation SCOTLAND, MAG-36 and MAG-16 flew 9,109 sorties, transported 14,562 passengers, and delivered 4,661 tons of cargo.

Colonel Lownds was more than satisfied with the airborne pipeline which kept his cupboard full, and he had quite a cupboard. The daily requirement for the 26th Marines to maintain normal operations had jumped from sixty tons in mid-January to roughly 185 tons when all five battalions were in place. While the defenders didn't live high off the hog on this amount, at no time were they desperately lacking the essentials for combat. There were periods on the hills when the Marines either stretched their rations and water or went without, but they never ran short of ammunition.

Understandably, ammunition had the highest priority—even higher than food and water. A man might not be able to eat a hand grenade, but neither could he defend himself very effectively with a can of fruit cocktail. This did not mean that the men of the 26th Marines went hungry. On the average, the troops at the base received two C-Ration meals a day, and this fare was occasionally supplemented with juice, pastry, hot soup, or fresh fruit. The men on the hills subsisted almost entirely on C-Rations, and the time between meals varied, depending on the weather.

Within the compound, water was rationed only when the pump was out of commission, and that was a rare occurrence. Lieutenant Colonel Heath's position on Hill 558 was flanked by two streams so 2/26 was well supplied, but the Marines on the other four outposts depended on helilifts for water; it was used sparingly for drinking and cooking. Besides the essentials, the 26th Marines also required tons of other supplies such as fortification material, fuel, tires, barbed wire, and spare parts—to name a few. PX items were on the bottom of the bottom of the priority totem pole because, as Colonel Lownds remarked: "If you have to, you can live without those." On the other hand, mail had a priority second only to ammunition and rations. The men at Khe Sanh received over forty-three tons of mail during the worst month of the siege.

One portion of the airlift which affected morale as much as the arrival of mail was the swift departure of casualties. A man's efficiency was greatly improved by the knowledge that if he were hit, he could expect immediate medical attention and, when necessary, a speedy evacuation. Those with minor wounds were usually treated at the various battalion aid stations and returned to duty; the more seriously injured were taken to Company C, 3rd Medical Battalion. Charley Med, as this detachment was called, was located just south of and adjacent to the aircraft loading ramp. There, US Navy doctors and corpsmen treated the walking wounded, performed surgery, and prepared the litter cases for medevac. From Charley Med, it was a short, but often nerve-racking trip to a waiting aircraft and a hospital at Phu Bai. During the siege, the courageous men of Charley Med, often working under heavy enemy fire, treated and evacuated 852 wounded personnel.

Thus the Marine and US Air Force transport pilots, helicopter crews, loadmasters, and ground personnel kept open the giant umbilical cord which meant life for the combat base. Without their efforts, the story of Khe Sanh would undoubtedly have been an abbreviated edition with a not-too-happy ending. On the other hand, accounts of the heroism, inge-nuity, and skill demonstrated by these men would fill a book. But there were other things besides manna falling from the heavens at Khe Sanh, and the vital role of the transports was frequently eclipsed by the efforts of air crews who carried a much deadlier cargo.

FIVE

Doolittle Hits Tokyo

Colonel Robert Barr Smith (Ret.) and Laurence J. Yadon

The spring of 1942 was not a happy time for the United States and her allies. America had lost the Philippines; Britain had lost Malaya and was falling back in Burma; Holland had lost her possessions in the Dutch East Indies. Naval losses for all three nations had been heavy, and many people were deeply concerned with the vital short-term need to salvage whatever could be saved from the ruin. And all of these nations had Hitler's rampant Germany to contend with, plus her arrogant ally, Italy, in addition to Japan.

But some of those same people already had their thoughts and dreams focused on something else, something far more satisfying: revenge. Admiral Yamamoto, the able architect of Japan's aggression in the Pacific, had put it perfectly in responding to congratulations on Japan's successful attack on the Hawaiian Islands.

"I fear," he said, "that all we have done is awaken a sleeping giant."

He was, as most Americans would say, right on the money.

President Roosevelt was one of those intent on striking back, and the sooner the better. And so, just two weeks after the sneak attack on Pearl Harbor, in a meeting with the Joint Chiefs of Staff at the White House, he voiced his notion that the United States should bomb Japan as soon as possible, in order to boost American morale. Planning began immediately.

Since there was no base close enough to Japan from which to fly off bombers against the home islands of Imperial Japan, it became obvious that the raiders would have to come by sea. Taking off from one of the Navy's carriers might just be possible, with some modifications of the bombers and a lot of luck. The raiders would have to be multi-engined bombers, and those belonged to the Army Air Corps. The Navy's aircraft carriers would have to sail deep into the Pacific, dangerously close to Japan's home waters, if the Army's bombers were to carry a decent bomb load and have any chance of flying from their targets on to some place of reasonable safety where the crews might survive.

For the bombers could not return to the carrier from which they had been launched, even if they could manage a carrier landing, a problematical possibility itself. The carriers would have to clear out at high speed once they had launched the strike. Waters that close to Japan were far too dangerous, and America's small carrier force was far too precious to risk by loitering for most of a day so near Japan. In order to reach Japan from any distance with a decent load of bombs—a half ton per plane was the goal—the multi-engined Army aircraft had to be capable of taking off from a carrier flight deck.

No four-engined bomber would even fit on a carrier flight deck, let alone take off from one. So it would have to be a medium bomber, and the planners carefully looked over the available aircraft. Two types were rejected because their wingspan was too broad for the carrier; in the end the planners settled on the B-25 Mitchell. It was twice tested, and both times took off successfully from USS *Hornet*.

Work began immediately on major modifications. The interior changes to the plane were mostly to accommodate extra gas tanks to almost double the bomber's regular fuel capacity, but there were more. The treasured Norden bombsight was replaced by a crude device dreamed up by one of the pilots, called the "Mark Twain" and costing a whole twenty cents. The belly turret and one radio were removed to save weight, and a pair of dummy guns were added to the stern of each B-25.

Starting on the 1st of March, the crews began rehearsals in Florida, flying at night and over water, practicing low-altitude bombing and take-offs from a section of runway painted in the shape and size of a carrier deck. And on the 1st of April, 1942, sixteen modified bombers were loaded on *Hornet* at Alameda Naval Air Station on San Francisco Bay.

Each aircraft had a crew of five, and a two-hundred-man maintenance and support detachment went to sea with them.

Next day the task force sailed out into the broad Pacific: *Hornet*, sister-ship *Enterprise*—providing fighter cover for the little task force—and three heavy and one light cruiser, eight destroyers, and two fleet oilers. On April 17th the oilers refueled everybody, and then they and the destroyers turned for home. The carriers and cruisers pushed on at high speed for their launching point in the dangerous seas east of Japan.

They were unobserved most of the way, but on the morning of April 18, the little fleet ran into a Japanese picket boat, *Nitto Maru*. Light cruiser *Nashville* promptly sent *Nitto Maru* to the bottom, but she had gotten off a radio signal before she sank. On the correct assumption that the presence of American ships was now known by the Japanese naval command, Captain (later Admiral) Mark Mitscher of *Hornet* made a hard but wise decision. He would launch the strike immediately, although the task force was still some 170 nautical miles short of the planned launch point, and ten hours ahead of schedule.

All sixteen B-25s got into the air in everybody's first real carrier take-off. Each bomber carried three 250-pound bombs and a bundle of incendiaries, rigged to break apart and scatter over a broad area once they were dropped. Several bombs had medals attached to them, Japanese "friendship medals" given to Americans in a less hostile time. Now they would be returned . . . with interest.

Flying in at "zero feet," Doolittle's men arrived over Japan and split up, their coming apparently a complete surprise to the Japanese defenders in spite of the little picket boat's radio warning. There was some light antiaircraft fire and attacks by a few fighters as the bombers struck at ten targets in Tokyo, two more in Yokohoma, and one each in Nagoya, Kobe, Yokosuka, and Osaka. Only one B-25 was damaged, and gunners on *Hara Karier* got two Japanese fighters; *Whirling Dervish* shot down another one. The bombers' nose gunners sprayed everything in sight, and the force was gone into the west as suddenly as it had come.

The raid's planners had laid out a course southwest across the East China Sea that would bring the aircraft over China in about twelve hours. There were bases there that could receive them, primarily at a place called Zhuzhou, for which fifteen of the bombers headed. The sixteenth aircraft was gobbling gasoline at a frightening rate, and its commander wisely elected to turn for the closer Soviet Union, landing near Vladivostok. The Russians had a problem: At the time they had a nonaggression pact with Japan, so they decided they could not honor a request from the United States to release the crew. The American crew was therefore interned; well-treated, but still not free. That is, until they were moved to a town near the Iranian border.

There the plane commander managed to bribe a man he thought was a smuggler, who got the Americans across the border into sanctuary at a British consulate. It much later developed that the providential "smuggling" was in fact the work of the Soviets' NKVD law enforcement agency, achieving clandestinely what their government could not legally do in the cold light of day.

The other crews either bailed out or crash-landed in China. They got much unselfish help from the Chinese, soldiers and civilians alike, and also from an American missionary. Sixty-nine men escaped the Japanese; three were killed in action when their B-25 crashed, and a fourth died when he fell from a cliff after bailing out. Two crews were missing and unaccounted for until, in August, the Swiss consul in Shanghai advised that two crew members had drowned after their aircraft landed at sea, and the other eight were prisoners of the Japanese.

In August the Japanese announced that all eight had been "tried" and sentenced to death, although several sentences had been commuted, they said, to life in prison. In fact, three Americans were shot by firing squad. The rest were imprisoned on starvation rations. One man died; the remaining emaciated aircrew were freed by American troops in August 1945. Remarkably, one of those four, Corporal Jacob DeShazer, later returned to Japan as a missionary, and served there for more than thirty years. Greater love hath no man.

The raid was a tremendous psychological blow to Japan, although, as predicted, the material damage was relatively light. Until now the holy home islands were thought to be safe from the inferior Westerners. By contrast, the delight in America overflowed, a bright ray of sunshine for a country deeply angry at the nation that smiled and talked peace even while its carriers were steaming into position to strike at Pearl Harbor.

One of the authors still remembers his father's comment when the news of the raid on Japan broke: "Take that, you bastards!"

Not only in Japan, but all across America, people asked, "Where did the American bombers come from?"

Why, from Shangri-La, said President Roosevelt, using the name of the hidden mountain paradise created in James Hilton's classic novel *Lost Horizon*. The Japanese navy tried hard to find the American ships from which they knew the raid was launched, but they only managed to add to their embarrassment. Even though they used five carriers and a multitude of other ships, they still failed to find the American task force, let alone attack it, adding to the great shame of allowing the enemy to penetrate so deeply into the holy waters of Imperial Japan in the first place.

The dark side of the raid was the predictable Japanese reaction in China, especially in the eastern coastal provinces that could harbor American airmen as they did the Doolittle raiders. Operation *Seigo* did its evil best to ensure that no Chinese who helped the American raiders would ever do so again. The generally accepted civilian death toll from Japanese reprisals was ten thousand. Other estimates run as high as a quarter of a million.

There was an unexpected consequence, too. There is a suggestion that the strike on Japan may have reinforced Admiral Isoroku Yamamoto's decision to strike at Midway Island, or at least forced his hand on timing, setting the stage for the US Navy's decisive whipping of the Japanese in June of 1942. Midway was a startling, massive American victory, gutting Japan's carrier force and, maybe more importantly, destroying much of her cadre of experienced carrier pilots.

America rejoiced at the daring raid on the Japanese homeland. Jimmie Doolittle, who thought he might be court-martialed for losing his entire command, instead received the Congressional Medal of Honor and was promoted two grades to brigadier general.

The bombs didn't do much damage; nobody expected them to. But while Japan was deeply ashamed and could never feel secure again, America smiled. And one small step had been taken toward the far-off day of complete retribution. Japan had sowed the wind at Pearl Harbor. Four years later, a big, sleek bomber named *Enola Gay* would bring the very fires of hell to the islands of Japan.

Six

How the *Merrimac* Was Sunk in Cuba

Rupert S. Holland

The Spanish fleet was mounting an assault in the Cuban harbor of Santiago. It would be an easy sail into the Caribbean for a surprise attack on the Americans. Or so they thought.

A heroic crew on a secret and audacious mission and an iconic old ship would change Spanish plans. In the small hours of the morning of June 3, 1898, the *Merrimac*, a vessel that had once been a collier in the United States Navy, slipped away from the warships of the American fleet that lay off the coast of Cuba and headed toward the harbor of Santiago.

The moon was almost full, and there was scarcely a cloud in the sky. To the northwest lay the *Brooklyn*, her great mass almost white in the reflected light. On the northeast the *Texas* loomed dark and warlike, and farther away lay a ring of other ships, dim and ghostly in the distance. Ahead was the coast of Cuba, with an outline of mountains rising in a half circle beyond the harbor.

Five miles across the water, Morro Castle guarded the entrance to the harbor, in which lay a fleet of the Spanish admiral Cervera. To steer directly for Morro Castle would be to keep the *Merrimac* full in the moon's path, and to avoid this she stood to the eastward of the course and stole along at a slow rate of speed. The small crew on board, a commander and seven men, were stripped to their underclothes and wore life preservers and revolver belts. Each man had taken his life in his hands when he volunteered for this night's work.

They wanted to sink the *Merrimac* at a narrow point in the harbor and bottle up the Spanish fleet beyond it. As they neared the great looming fortress of the Morro, it was impossible to keep the ship hidden; the sentries on the castle must see the dark object now and wonder what she intended. The *Merrimac* gave up its oblique course and steered straight ahead.

The order "Full speed!" went from Lieutenant Hobson, a naval constructor in command, to the engineer. Foam dashed over the bows, and the long shape shot for the harbor entrance, regardless of what the enemy might think or do. Soon the Morro stood up high above them, the moon clearly revealing the great central battery that crowned the fortress top. The Spanish guns were only five hundred yards away, and yet the enemy had given no sign of having seen the *Merrimac*.

Then suddenly a light flashed from near the water's edge on the left side of the entrance, and a roar followed. The *Merrimac* did not quiver. The shot must have fallen astern. Again there was a flash, and this time the crew could hear the splash of water as the projectile struck back of them. Through their night glasses, they saw a picket boat with rapid-fire guns lying close in the shadows of the shore. Her guns had probably been aimed at the *Merrimac*'s rudder, but so far they had missed their aim. With a rapid-fire gun to reply, the *Merrimac* might have demolished the other boat in half a minute, but she had no such equipment. She would have to pass within a ship's length of this picket. There was nothing to do but pay no heed to her aim at the *Merrimac*'s rudder and steer for the high wall off Morro Castle, where the deepwater channel ran close inshore.

"A touch of port helm!" was the order.

"A touch of port helm, sir," came the answer, and the vessel stood toward the wall.

There came a crash from the port side.

"The western battery has opened on us, sir!" reported the man on the bridge to Hobson.

"Very well; pay no attention to it," was the answer.

The commander knew he must take the *Merrimac* at least another ship's length forward and wondered if the enemy would give him that much grace. A shot crossed the bridge and struck. No one was hurt. They had almost reached the point where they were to stop. Another moment or two, and over the engine telegraph went the order, "Stop!"

The engineer obeyed. The *Merrimac* slowed off Morro rock. A high rocket shot across the channel entrance. From each side came the firing of batteries. Hobson and his men were too busy to heed them. The *Merrimac*, still swinging under her own headway, brought her bow within thirty feet of the rock before she righted. Another ship's length, and she would be at the point where her commander had planned to take her; then the steering gear stopped working, and she was left at the mercy of the current.

The ship must be sunk before the current could carry her out of the course. This was done by exploding torpedoes on the outside of the vessel. Hobson gave the order, and the first torpedo went off, blowing out the collision bulkhead. There was no reply from the second or third torpedoes.

Hobson crossed the bridge and shouted, "Fire all torpedoes!"

In the roar of the Spanish batteries, his voice could hardly be heard. Meantime the guns on the shores back of the harbor were pouring their shot at the black target in the moonlight, and the din was terrific. Word came to Hobson that some of the torpedoes could not be fired, as their cells had been broken. The order was given to fire the others, and the fifth exploded promptly, but the remaining ones had been shattered by Spanish fire and were useless.

The commander knew that under these circumstances, it would take some time for the *Merrimac* to sink. The important point was to keep the ship in the center of the harbor, but the stern anchor had already been cut away. Hobson watched the bow move against the shoreline. There was nothing to do but wait and see where the tide would swing them. The crew now gathered on deck. One of them, Kelly, had been dazed by an exploding shell. When he had picked himself up, he started down the engine-room hatch but found the water rising.

Then he remembered the *Merrimac*'s purpose and tried to reach the torpedo of which he had charge. The torpedo was useless, and he headed back to the deck, climbing up on all fours. It was a strange sight to see him stealing up, and Hobson and some of the others drew their revolvers, thinking for the moment that he must be an enemy who had boarded the ship.

Fortunately they recognized him almost immediately. The tide was bearing them to the center of the channel when there came a blasting noise and shock. A mine had exploded beneath them.

"Lads, they're helping us!" cried the commander.

But the mine did not break the deck, and the ship only settled a little lower. For a moment it seemed as if the coal might have closed the breach made by the explosion, but just as the crew feared that they were to be carried past the point chosen for sinking, the current from the opposite shore caught them, and the *Merrimac* settled crosswise. It was now only a matter of time before she would sink in the harbor. The crew could now turn their attention to themselves.

Hobson said to them:

"We will remain here, lads, till the moon sets. When it is dark, we will go down the after hatch to the coal, where her stern will be left out of water. We will remain inside all day and tonight at ebb tide try to make our way to the squadron. If the enemy comes on board, we will remain quiet until he finds us and will repel him. If he then turns artillery on the place where we are, we will swim out to points farther forward."

He started toward the bow to reconnoiter but was persuaded not to expose himself to the enemy's fire. One of the men discovered a break in the bulwarks that gave a good view, and Hobson stood there. The moon was bright, though now low, and the muzzles of the Spanish guns were very near them. The crew, however, remained safely hidden behind the rail. From all sides came the firing, and the Americans, lying full length on the *Merrimac*'s deck, felt the continual shock of projectiles striking around them.

Some of the crew suggested that they should take to the small boat, but the commander knew that this would be certain destruction and ordered them to remain. Presently a shot struck the boiler, and a rush of steam came up the deck near where they lay. A canteen was passed from hand to hand. Hobson, having no pockets, carried some tourniquets around his left arm and a roll of antiseptic lint in his left hand, ready in case any of his crew was wounded.

Looking through the hole in the bulwarks, the commander saw that the *Merrimac* was again moving. Sunk deep though she was, the tide was carrying her on and might bear her some distance. There seemed to be no way in which they could make her sink where she was. Two more mines exploded but missed the ship, and as she floated on, it became evident that they could not block the channel completely. But shortly the *Merrimac* gave a lurch forward and settled to the port side. Now the Spanish *Reina Mercedes* was near at hand, and the *Pluton* was coming close inboard, but their guns and torpedoes did not hasten the sinking of the collier. She plunged again and settled in the channel.

A rush of water came up the gangway, and the crew were thrown against the bulwarks and then into the sea. The life preservers helped to keep them afloat, but when they looked for the lifeboat, they found that it had been carried away. A catamaran was the largest piece of floating wreckage, and they swam to this. The firing had now stopped.

The wreckage began to drift away, and the crew were left swimming about the catamaran, apparently unseen by the enemy. The men were ordered to cling to this rude craft, their bodies in the water, their heads hidden by the boards, and to keep quiet, as Spanish boats were passing close to them. All the crew were safe, and Hobson expected that in time some Spanish officers would come out to reconnoiter the channel.

He knew that his men could not swim against the tide to the harbor entrance, and even had they been able to do so, it would have been too dangerous a risk, as the banks were now lined with soldiers and the water patrolled by small boats. Their hope lay in surrendering before they were fired upon. The moon had now nearly set, and the shadow of the high banks fell across the water. Boats rowed by Spanish sailors pulled close to the catamaran, but acting under orders from their commander, the crew of the *Merrimac* kept well out of sight.

The sun rose, and a new day came.

Soon the crew could see the line of distant mountains and the steep slopes leading to Morro Castle. A Spanish torpedo destroyer was heading up the harbor, and a bugle at one of the batteries could be heard across the waters. Still the Americans clung to the catamaran, although their teeth were chattering and they had to work their arms and legs to keep warm.

Presently one of the men said, "A steam launch is heading for us, sir!"

The commander looked about and saw a large launch, the curtains aft drawn down, coming from around a point of land straight toward the catamaran. As it drew near, the launch swerved to the left. When it was about thirty yards away, Hobson hailed it. The boat instantly stopped and began to back, while some riflemen appeared on the deck and took position for firing. No shot followed, however.

Hobson called out again, asking whether there were any officers on the boat and adding that if there were, he was ready to surrender himself and his American sailors as prisoners of war. The curtain at the stern was lowered, a Spanish officer gave an order, and the rifles dropped.

The American commander swam to the launch and climbed on board, being helped up by the Spanish officer, who turned out later to be no other than Admiral Cervera himself. Hobson surrendered for himself and his crew. The launch then drew close to the catamaran, and the sailors clinging to it were pulled on board. Although the Spaniards knew that the *Merrimac*'s men had bottled up their warships in the harbor, they could not help praising their bravery. The Spanish launch took them to the *Reina Mercedes*. There the men were given dry clothes and food. Although all were scratched and bruised, only one was wounded, and his wound, though painful, was not serious.

The American officer was invited to join the Spaniards at breakfast and was treated with as much courtesy as if he had been an honored guest. Afterward Hobson wrote a note to Admiral Sampson, who was in command of the American fleet.

The note read:

"Sir: I have the honor to report that the *Merrimac* is sunk in the channel. No loss, only bruises. We are prisoners of war, being well cared for."

He asked that this should be sent under a flag of truce. Later in the day, the Americans were taken from the warship in a launch and carried across the harbor to Morro Castle. This course brought them within a short distance of where the *Merrimac* had sunk, and as Hobson noted the position, he concluded that the plan had only partly succeeded and that the channel was not completely blocked.

Landing at a small wharf, the Americans were marched up a steep hill that led to the Morro from the rear. The fortress stood out like one of the medieval castles of Europe, commanding a wide view of sea and shore. The road brought them to the bridge that crossed the moat. They marched under the portcullis and entered a vaulted passage. The American officer was shown into the guard room, while the crew were led on.

A few minutes later Admiral Cervera came into the guard room and held out his hand to Hobson. The admiral said that he would have liked to send the American's note under a flag of truce to his fleet but that this had been refused by the general in command. He added, however, that some word should be sent to inform their friends of the safe escape of the *Merrimac*'s men.

Hobson was then led to a cell in the tower of the castle. As the jailer stopped to unlock the door, Hobson had a view of the sea and made out the line of the American battleships moving in two columns. He was told to enter the cell, which was a bare and ill-looking place, but a few minutes later, a Spanish captain arrived with apologies, saying that he hoped soon to provide the Americans with better quarters.

A little later furniture was brought to the cell and food, cigars, cigarettes, and a bottle of brandy provided for the American officer. In fact, he and his men fared as well as the Spanish officers and soldiers themselves. The governor of the fortress sent a note to ask what he could do to improve Hobson's comfort. Officers of all ranks called to shake hands with him and express their admiration for his courage.

That first night in the castle, after the sentries had made their rounds, Hobson climbed up on his cot-bed and looked through a small window at the top of the cell. The full moon showed a steep slope from the fortress to the water, then the wide sweep of the harbor, with a picket boat on duty as it had been the night before, and beyond the boat the great Spanish warships and still farther off the batteries of Socapa.

It was hard to believe that only twenty-four hours before, the center of that quiet moonlit water had been ablaze with fire aimed at the small collier Hobson had commanded. As he studied the situation, he decided that the *Merrimac* probably blocked the channel.

The enemy would hesitate a long time before they would try to take their fleet past the sunken vessel, and that delay would give Admiral Sampson time to gather his ships. Even if the channel were not entirely blocked, the Spanish ships could only leave the harbor in single line and with the most skillful steering. Therefore, he concluded that his perilous expedition had been successful. Next morning a Spanish officer brought him news that a flag of truce had been carried to Admiral Sampson with word of the crew's escape and that the messengers had been given a box for Hobson and bags of clothes, some money, and other articles for him and his crew.

The men, now dressed again in the uniform of American Marines, were treated as prisoners of war and lived almost as comfortably as their captors. While Hobson was having his coffee on the morning of June 6th, he heard the whiz and crash of an exploding shell, then another, and another and knew that a general bombardment of the fortress had begun. He hastily examined the cell to see what protection it would offer from bricks and mortar falling from the walls and roof. At the first shot, the sentry on guard had bolted the door and left.

The American pulled the table and washstand in front of the door and stood the galvanized iron box that had been sent him against the end of the table; this he thought would catch splinters and stones, which would probably be more dangerous than actual shells. He lay down under the protection of this cover. He knew that the gunners of the American fleet were good shots and figured that they could easily demolish all that part of the Morro in which his cell was situated.

One shell after another against the walls of the fortress made the whole structure tremble, and it seemed as if part of the walls would be blown away. Fortunately, however, the firing soon turned in another direction, and Hobson could come from his shelter and, standing on his cot-bed, look through the window at the battle. Several times he took shelter again under the table and several times returned to watch the cannonade. The shells screamed through the air, plowed through shrubs and earthworks, knocked bricks and mortar from the Morro, and set fire to some of the Spanish ships.

But no serious damage was done, and the bombardment ended in a standoff between the two sides. The American officer had no desire to pass through such a cannonade again, and he wrote to the Spanish governor to ask that his crew and himself be transferred to safer quarters. Next day an officer arrived with orders to take all the prisoners to the city of Santiago. So, after a four days' stay in Morro Castle, the little party set out on an inland march, guarded by some thirty Spanish soldiers.

It was not far to Santiago, and there the Americans were housed in the regular army barracks. These quarters were much better than those in the fortress, and the British consul secured many comforts and delicacies for the Americans. The men of the *Merrimac* stayed in Santiago during the siege of that city.

On July 5th arrangements were made to exchange Hobson and his men. In the afternoon they were blindfolded and guided out of the city. Half a mile or more beyond the entrenchments, they were told that they might remove the handkerchiefs and found themselves facing their own troops on a distant ridge. Soon they were being welcomed by their own men, who told them of the recent victories won by fleet and army.

Not long afterward they reached their ships and were received on board the *New York* by the officers and men who had watched them set out on their dangerous mission on that moonlit night of June 3rd. They gave a royal welcome to the small crew who had brought the collier into the very heart of the Spanish lines and sunk her, taking their chances of escape. They were the heroes of a desperate adventure, from which every man returned unharmed.

SEVEN

Benedict Arnold's Navy

Captain Alfred Thayer Mahan

At the time when hostilities began between Great Britain and her American Colonies, the fact was realized generally, being evident to reason and taught by experience, that control of the water, both ocean and inland, would have a preponderant effect upon the contest. It was clear to reason, for there was a long seaboard with numerous interior navigable watercourses, and at the same time scanty and indifferent communications by land.

Critical portions of the territory involved were yet an unimproved wilderness.

Experience, the rude but efficient schoolmaster of that large portion of mankind which gains knowledge only by hard knocks, had confirmed through the preceding French wars the inferences of the thoughtful. Therefore, conscious of the great superiority of the British Navy, which, however, had not then attained the unchallenged supremacy of a later day, the American leaders early sought the alliance of the Bourbon kingdoms, France and Spain, the hereditary enemies of Great Britain. There alone could be found the counterpoise to a power which, if unchecked, must ultimately prevail.

Nearly three years elapsed before the colonists accomplished this object, by giving a demonstration of their strength in the enforced surrender of Burgoyne's army at Saratoga. This event has merited the epithet "decisive" because, and only because, it decided the intervention of France.

It may be affirmed, with little hesitation, that this victory of the colonists was directly the result of naval force—that of the colonists themselves.

It was the cause that naval force from abroad, entering into the contest, transformed it from a local to a universal war, and assured the independence of the Colonies. That the Americans were strong enough to impose the capitulation of Saratoga was due to the invaluable year of delay secured to them by their little navy on Lake Champlain, created by the indomitable energy, and handled with the indomitable courage, of the traitor, Benedict Arnold.

That the war spread from America to Europe, from the English Channel to the Baltic, from the Bay of Biscay to the Mediterranean, from the West Indies to the Mississippi, and ultimately involved the waters of the remote peninsula of Hindustan, is traceable, through Saratoga, to the rude flotilla which in 1776 anticipated its enemy in the possession of Lake Champlain. The events which thus culminated merit therefore a clearer understanding, and a fuller treatment, than their intrinsic importance and petty scale would justify otherwise.

In 1775, only fifteen years had elapsed since the expulsion of the French from the North American continent. The concentration of their power, during its continuance, in the valley of the St. Lawrence had given direction to the local conflict, and had impressed upon men's minds the importance of Lake Champlain, of its tributary Lake George, and of the Hudson River, as forming a consecutive, though not continuous, water line of communications from the St. Lawrence to New York. The strength of Canada against attack by land lay in its remoteness, in the wilderness to be traversed before it was reached, and in the strength of the line of the St. Lawrence, with the fortified posts of Montreal and Quebec on its northern bank.

The wilderness, it is true, interposed its passive resistance to attacks from Canada as well as to attacks upon it; but when it had been traversed, there were to the southward no such strong natural positions confronting the assailant. Attacks from the south fell upon the front, or at best upon the flank, of the line of the St. Lawrence. Attacks from Canada took New York and its dependencies in the rear.

LAKE CHAMPLAIN AND CONNECTED WATERS

These elements of natural strength, in the military conditions of the North, were impressed upon the minds of the Americans by the prolonged resistance of Canada to the greatly superior numbers of the British colonists in the previous wars. Regarded, therefore, as a base for attacks, of a kind with which they were painfully familiar, but to be undergone now under disadvantages of numbers and power never before experienced, it was desirable to gain possession of the St. Lawrence and its posts before they were strengthened and garrisoned. At this outset of hostilities, the American insurgents, knowing clearly their own minds, possessed the advantage of the initiative over the British government, which still hesitated to use against those whom it styled rebels the preventive measures it would have taken at once against a recognized enemy.

Under these circumstances, in May 1775, a body of 270 Americans, led by Ethan Allen and Benedict Arnold, seized the posts of Ticonderoga and Crown Point, which were inadequately garrisoned. These are on the upper waters of Lake Champlain, where it is less than a third of a mile wide; Ticonderoga being on a peninsula formed by the lake and the inlet from Lake George, Crown Point on a promontory twelve miles lower down. They were positions of recognized importance, and had been advanced posts of the British in previous wars. A schooner being found there, Arnold, who had been a seaman, embarked in her and hurried to the foot of the lake.

The wind failed him when still thirty miles from St. John's, another fortified post on the lower narrows, where the lake gradually tapers down to the Richelieu River, its outlet to the St. Lawrence. Unable to advance otherwise, Arnold took to his boats with thirty men, pulled through the night, and at six o'clock on the following morning surprised the post, in which were only a sergeant and a dozen men. He reaped the rewards of celerity. The prisoners informed him that a considerable body of troops was expected from Canada, on its way to Ticonderoga; and this force in fact reached St. John's on the next day.

When it arrived, Arnold was gone, having carried off a sloop which he found there and destroyed everything else that could float. By such trifling means two active officers had secured the temporary control of the lake itself and of the approaches to it from the south. There being no roads, the British, debarred from the waterline, were unable to advance. Sir Guy Carleton, Governor and Commander-in-Chief in Canada, strengthened the works at St. John's and built a schooner; but his force was inadequate to meet that of the Americans.

The seizure of the two posts, being an act of offensive war, was not at once pleasing to the American Congress, which still clung to the hope of reconciliation; but events were marching rapidly, and ere summer was over the invasion of Canada was ordered. General Montgomery, appointed to that enterprise, embarked at Crown Point with two thousand men on September 4th, and soon afterward appeared before St. John's, which after prolonged operations capitulated on the 3rd of November.

On the 13th Montgomery entered Montreal, and thence pressed down the St. Lawrence to Pointe aux Trembles, twenty miles above Quebec. There he joined Arnold, who in the month of October had crossed the northern wilderness, between the headwaters of the Kennebec River and St. Lawrence. On the way he had endured immense privations, losing five hundred men of the twelve hundred with whom he started; and upon arriving opposite Quebec, on the 10th of November, three days had been unavoidably spent in collecting boats to pass the river.

Crossing on the night of the 13th, this adventurous soldier and his little command climbed the Heights of Abraham by the same path that had served Wolfe so well sixteen years before. With characteristic audacity he summoned the place. The demand of course was refused; but that Carleton did not fall at once upon the little band of seven hundred that bearded him shows by how feeble a tenure Great Britain then held Canada.

Immediately after the junction Montgomery advanced on Quebec, where he appeared on the 5th of December. Winter having already begun, and neither his numbers nor his equipments being adequate to regular siege operations, he very properly decided to try the desperate chance of an assault upon the strongest fortress in America. This was made on the night of December 31st, 1775. Whatever possibility of success there may have been vanished with the death of Montgomery, who fell at the head of his men.

The American army retired three miles up the river, went into winter-quarters, and established a land blockade of Quebec, which was cut off from the sea by the ice.

"For five months," wrote Carleton to the Secretary for War, on the 14th of May, 1776, "this town has been closely invested by the rebels."

From this unpleasant position it was relieved on the 6th of May, when signals were exchanged between it and the *Surprise*, the advance ship of a squadron under Captain Charles Douglas, which had sailed from England on the 11th of March. Arriving off the mouth of the St. Lawrence on the morning of April 12th, Douglas found ice extending nearly twenty miles to sea, and packed too closely to admit of working through it by dexterous steering.

The urgency of the case not admitting delay, he ran his ship, the *Isis*, with a speed of five knots, against a large piece of ice about ten or twelve feet thick, to test the effect. The ice, probably softened by salt water and salt air, went to pieces.

"Encouraged by this experiment," continues Douglas, somewhat magnificently, "we thought it an enterprise worthy an English ship of the line in our King and country's sacred cause, and an effort due to the gallant defenders of Quebec, to make the attempt of pressing her by force of sail, through the thick, broad, and closely connected fields of ice, to which we saw no bounds toward the western part of our horizon.

"Before night (when blowing a snowstorm, we brought-to, or rather stopped), we had penetrated about eight leagues into it, describing our path all the way with bits of the sheathing of the ship's bottom, and sometimes pieces of the cutwater, but none of the oak plank; and it was pleasant enough at times, when we stuck fast, to see Lord Petersham exercising his troops on the crusted surface of that fluid through which the ship had so recently sailed."

It took nine days of this work to reach Anticosti Island, after which the ice seems to have given no more trouble; but further delay was occasioned by fogs, calms, and headwinds.

Upon the arrival of the ships of war, the Americans at once retreated. During the winter, though reinforcements must have been received from time to time, they had wasted from exposure, and from smallpox, which ravaged the camp. On the 1st of May the returns showed nineteen hundred men present, of whom only a thousand were fit for duty. There were then on hand but three days' provisions, and none other nearer than St. John's. The inhabitants would of course render no further assistance to the Americans after the ships arrived. The Navy had again decided the fate of Canada, and was soon also to determine that of Lake Champlain.

When two hundred troops had landed from the ships, Carleton marched out, "to see," he said, "what these mighty boasters were about."

The sneer was unworthy a man of his generous character, for the boasters had endured much for faint chances of success; and the smallness of the reinforcement which encouraged him to act shows either an extreme prudence on his part or the narrow margin by which Quebec escaped. He found the enemy busy with preparations for retreat, and upon his appearance they abandoned their camp. Their forces on the two sides of the river being now separated by the enemy's shipping, the Americans retired first to Sorel, where the Richelieu enters the St. Lawrence, and thence continued to fall back by gradual stages. It was not until June 15th that Arnold quitted Montreal; and at the end of June the united force was still on the Canadian side of the present border line. On the 3rd of July it reached Crown Point, in a pitiable state from smallpox and destitution.

Both parties began at once to prepare for a contest upon Lake Champlain.

The Americans, small as their flotilla was, still kept the superiority obtained for them by Arnold's promptitude a year before. On the 25th of June the American General Schuyler, commanding the Northern Department, wrote: "We have happily such a naval superiority on Lake Champlain, that I have a confident hope the enemy will not appear upon it this campaign, especially as our force is increasing by the addition of gondolas, two nearly finished.

Arnold, however, "whose technical knowledge caused him to be entrusted with the naval preparations, says that 300 carpenters should be employed and a large number of gondolas, row-galleys, be built, twenty or thirty at least. There is great difficulty in getting the carpenters needed."

Arnold's ideas were indeed on a scale worthy of the momentous issues at stake.

"To augment our navy on the lake appears to me of the utmost importance. There is water between Crown Point and Pointe au Fer for vessels of the largest size. I am of opinion that row-galleys are the best construction and cheapest for this lake. Perhaps it may be well to have one frigate of 36 guns. She may carry 18-pounders on the Lake, and be superior to any vessel that can be built or floated from St. John's."

Unfortunately for the Americans, their resources in men and means were far inferior to those of their opponents, who were able eventually to carry out, though on a somewhat smaller scale, Arnold's idea of a sailing ship, strictly so called, of force as yet unknown in inland waters.

Such a ship, aided as she was by two consorts of somewhat similar character, dominated the Lake as soon as she was afloat, reversing all the conditions. To place and equip her, however, required time, invaluable time, during which Arnold's two schooners exercised control.

Baron Riedesel, the commander of the German contingent with Carleton, after examining the American position at Ticonderoga, wrote, "If we could have begun our expedition four weeks earlier, I am satisfied that everything would have been ended this year (1776); but, not having shelter nor other necessary things, we were unable to remain at the other [southern] end of Champlain."

So delay favors the defense, and changes issues. What would have been the effect upon the American cause if, simultaneously with the loss of New York, August 20th–September 15th, had come news of the fall of Ticonderoga, the repute of which for strength stood high? Nor was this all; for in that event, the plan which was wrecked in 1777 by Sir William Howe's ill-conceived expedition to the Chesapeake would doubtless have been carried out in 1776.

In a contemporary English paper occurs the following significant item: "London, September 26th, 1776. Advices have been received here from Canada, dated August 12th, that General Burgoyne's army has found it impracticable to get across the lakes this season. The naval force of the Provincials is too great for them to contend with at present. They must build larger vessels for this purpose, and these cannot be ready before next summer. The design *was* that the two armies commanded by Generals Howe and Burgoyne should cooperate; that they should both be on the Hudson River at the same time; that they should join about Albany, and thereby cut off all communication between the northern and southern Colonies."

As Arnold's more ambitious scheme could not be realized, he had to content himself with gondolas and galleys, for the force he was to command as well as to build. The precise difference between the two kinds of rowing vessels thus distinguished by name, the writer has not been able to ascertain.

The gondola was a flat-bottomed boat, and inferior in nautical qualities—speed, handiness, and seaworthiness—to the galleys, which probably were keeled. The latter certainly carried sails, and may have been capable of beating to windward. Arnold preferred them, and stopped the building of gondolas.

"The galleys," he wrote, "are quick moving, which will give us a great advantage in the open lake."

The complements of the galleys were eighty men, of the gondolas forty-five; from which, and from their batteries, it may be inferred that the latter were between one-third and one-half the size of the former. The armaments of the two were alike in character, but those of the gondolas much lighter. American accounts agree with Captain Douglas's report of one galley captured by the British. In the bows, an 18- and a 12-pounder; in the stern, two 9s; in broadside, from four to six 6s. There is in this a somewhat droll reminder of the disputed merits of bow, stern, and broadside fire in a modern ironclad; and the practical conclusion is much the same. The gondolas had one 12-pounder and two 6s. All the vessels of both parties carried a number of swivel guns.

Amid the many difficulties which lack of resources imposed upon all American undertakings, Arnold succeeded in getting afloat with three schooners, a sloop, and five gondolas on the 20th of August. He cruised at the upper end of Champlain till the 1st of September, when he moved rapidly north, and on the 3rd anchored in the lower narrows, twenty-five miles above St. John's, stretching his line from shore to shore.

Scouts had kept him informed of the progress of the British naval preparations so that he knew that there was no immediate danger; while an advanced position, maintained with a bold front, would certainly prevent reconnaissances by water, and possibly might impose somewhat upon the enemy. The latter, however, erected batteries on each side of the anchorage, compelling Arnold to fall back to the broader lake. He then had soundings taken about Valcour Island, and between it and the western shore; that being the position in which he intended to make a stand. He retired thither on the 23rd of September.

The British on their side had contended with no less obstacles than their adversaries, though of a somewhat different character. To get carpenters and materials to build, and seamen to man, were the chief difficulties of the Americans, the necessities of the seaboard conceding but partially the demands made upon it; but their vessels were built upon the shores of the Lake and launched into navigable waters. A large fleet of transports and ships of war in the St. Lawrence supplied the British with adequate resources, which were utilized judiciously and energetically by Captain Douglas; but to get these to the Lake was a long and arduous task.

A great part of the Richelieu River was shoal, and obstructed by rapids. The point where lake navigation began was at St. John's, to which the nearest approach by a hundred-ton schooner from the St. Lawrence was Chambly, ten miles below. Flatboats and longboats could be dragged upstream, but vessels of any size had to be transported by land; and the engineers found the roadbed too soft in places to bear the weight of a hundred tons.

Under Douglas's directions, the planking and frames of two schooners were taken down at Chambly and carried round by road to St. John's, where they were again put together. At Quebec he found building a new hull, of 180 tons. This he took apart nearly to the keel, shipping the frames in thirty longboats, which the transport captains consented to surrender, together with their carpenters, for service on the Lake.

Drafts from the ships of war, and volunteers from the transports, furnished a body of seven hundred seamen for the same employment—a force to which the Americans could oppose nothing equal, commanded as it was by regular naval officers. The largest vessel was ship-rigged and had a battery of eighteen 12-pounders; she was called the *Inflexible* and was commanded by Lieutenant John Schanck.

The two schooners, *Maria*, Lieutenant Starke, and *Carleton*, Lieutenant James Richard Dacres, carried respectively fourteen and twelve 6-pounders. These were the backbone of the British flotilla. There were also a radeau, the *Thunderer*, and a large gondola, the *Loyal Convert*, both heavily armed; but, being equally heavy of movement, they do not appear to have played any important part. Besides these, when the expedition started, there were twenty gunboats, each carrying one fieldpiece, from 24s to 9-pounders or, in some cases, howitzers.

"By all these means," wrote Douglas on July 21st, "our acquiring an absolute dominion over Lake Champlain is not doubted of." The expectation was perfectly sound. With a working breeze, the *Inflexible* alone could sweep the Lake clear of all that floated on it. But the element of time remained. From the day of this writing till that on which he saw the *Inflexible* leave St. John's, October 4th, was over ten weeks; and it was not until the 9th that Carleton was ready to advance with the squadron. By that time the American troops at the head of the Lake had increased to eight or ten thousand. The British land force is reported as thirteen thousand, of which six thousand were in garrison at St. John's and elsewhere.

Arnold's last reinforcements reached him at Valcour on the 6th of October. On that day, and in the action of the 11th, he had with him all the American vessels on the Lake except one schooner and one galley. His force, thus, was two schooners and a sloop, broadside vessels, besides four galleys and eight gondolas, which may be assumed reasonably to have depended on their bow guns; there, at least, was their heaviest fire. Thus reckoned, his flotilla, disposed to the best advantage, could bring into action at one time, two 18s, thirteen 12s, one 9, two 6s, twelve 4s, and two 2-pounders, independent of swivels; total thirty-two guns, out of eighty-four that were mounted in fifteen vessels.

To this the British had to oppose, in three broadside vessels, nine 12s and thirteen 6s, and in twenty gunboats, twenty other brass guns, "from twenty-four to nines, some with howitzers;" total forty-two guns. In this statement the radeau and gondola have not been included because of their unmanageableness. Included as broadside vessels, they would raise the British armament—by three 24s, three 12s, four 9s, and a howitzer—to a total of fifty-three guns. Actually, they could be brought into action only under exceptional circumstances, and are more properly omitted.

These minutiae are necessary for the proper appreciation of what Captain Douglas justly called "a momentous event." It was a strife of pigmies for the prize of a continent, and the leaders are entitled to full credit both for their antecedent energy and for their dispositions in the contest; not least the unhappy man who, having done so much to save his country, afterward blasted his name by a treason unsurpassed in modern war.

Energy and audacity had so far preserved the Lake to the Americans; Arnold determined to have one more try of the chances. He did not know the full force of the enemy, but he expected that "it would be very formidable, if not equal to ours." The season, however, was so near its end that a severe check would equal a defeat, and would postpone Carleton's further advance to the next spring. Besides, what was the worth of such a force as the American, such a flotilla, under the guns of Ticonderoga, the Lake being lost? It was eminently a case for taking chances, even if the detachment should be sacrificed, as it was.

Arnold's original purpose had been to fight under way; and it was from this point of view that he valued the galleys, because of their mobility. It is uncertain when he first learned of the rig and battery of the *Inflexible*; but a good lookout was kept, and the British squadron was sighted from Valcour when it quitted the narrows. It may have been seen even earlier; for Carleton had been informed, erroneously, that the Americans were near Grand Island, which led him to incline to that side, and so open out Valcour sooner. The British anchored for the night of October 10th, between Grand and Long Islands.

Getting under way next morning, they stood up the Lake with a strong northeast wind, keeping along Grand Island, upon which their attention doubtless was fastened by the intelligence which they had received; but it was a singular negligence thus to run to leeward with a fair wind, without thorough scouting on both hands. The consequence was that the American flotilla was not discovered until Valcour Island, which is from 120 to 180 feet high throughout its two miles of length, was so far passed that the attack had to be made from the south—from leeward.

When the British were first made out, Arnold's second in command, Waterbury, urged that in view of the enemy's superiority the flotilla should get under way at once, and fight them "on a retreat in the main lake;" the harbor being disadvantageous "to fight a number so much superior, and the enemy being able to surround us on every side, we lying between an island and the main."

Waterbury's advice evidently found its origin in that fruitful source of military errors of design, which reckons the preservation of a force first of objects, making the results of its action secondary. With sounder judgment, Arnold decided to hold on. A retreat before square-rigged sailing vessels having a fair wind, by a heterogeneous force like his own, of unequal speeds and batteries, could result only in disaster. Concerted fire and successful escape were alike improbable; and besides, escape, if feasible, was but throwing up the game.

Better trust to a steady, well-ordered position, developing the utmost fire. If the enemy discovered him, and came in by the northern entrance, there was a five-foot knoll in mid-channel which might fetch the biggest of them up; if, as proved to be the case, the island should be passed, and the attack should be made from leeward, it probably would be partial and in disorder, as also happened. The correctness of Arnold's decision not to chance a retreat was shown in the retreat of two days later.

Valcour is on the west side of the Lake, about three-quarters of a mile from the main; but a peninsula projecting from the island at mid-length narrows this interval to a half mile. From the accounts, it is clear that the American flotilla lay south of this peninsula. Arnold therefore had a reasonable hope that it might be passed undetected.

Writing to Gates, the Commander-in-Chief at Ticonderoga, he said: "There is a good harbour, and if the enemy venture up the Lake it will be impossible for them to take advantage of our situation. If we succeed in our attack upon them, it will be impossible for any to escape. If we are worsted, our retreat is open and free. In case of wind, which generally blows fresh at this season, our craft will make good weather, while theirs cannot keep the Lake."

It is apparent from this, written three weeks before the battle, that he then was not expecting a force materially different from his own. Later, he describes his position as being "in a small bay on the west side of the island, as near together as possible, and in such a form that few vessels can attack us at the same time, and those will be exposed to the fire of the whole fleet." Though he unfortunately gives no details, he evidently had sound tactical ideas. The formation of the anchored vessels is described by the British officers as a half-moon.

When the British discovered the enemy, they hauled up for them. Arnold ordered one of his schooners, the *Royal Savage*, and the four galleys, to get under way; the two other schooners and the eight gondolas remaining at their anchors. The *Royal Savage*, dropping to leeward—by bad management, Arnold says—came, apparently unsupported, under the distant fire of the *Inflexible* as she drew under the lee of Valcour at 11 a.m., followed by the *Carleton*, and at greater distance by the *Maria* and the gunboats.

Three shots from the ship's 12-pounders struck the *Royal Savage*, which then ran ashore on the southern point of the island. The *Inflexible*, followed closely by the *Carleton*, continued on, but fired only occasionally; showing that Arnold was keeping his galleys in hand, at long bowls—as small vessels with one 18 should be kept when confronted with a broadside of nine guns.

Between the island and the main the northeast wind doubtless drew more northerly, adverse to the ship's approach; but, a flaw off the cliffs taking the fore and aft sails of the *Carleton*, she fetched "nearly into the middle of the rebel half-moon, where Lieutenant J. R. Dacres intrepidly anchored with a spring on her cable."

The *Maria*, on board which was Carleton, together with Commander Thomas Pringle, commanding the flotilla, was to leeward when the chase began, and could not get into close action that day. By this time, seventeen of the twenty gunboats had come up and, after silencing the *Royal Savage*, pulled up to within point-blank range of the American flotilla.

"The cannonade was tremendous," wrote Baron Riedesel. Lieutenant Edward Longcroft, of the radeau *Thunderer*, not being able to get his raft into action, went with a boat's crew on board the *Royal Savage*, and for a time turned her guns upon her former friends; but the fire of the latter forced him again to abandon her, and it seemed so likely that she might be retaken that she was set on fire by Lieutenant Starke of the *Maria*, when already "two rebel boats were very near her. She soon after blew up."

The American guns converging on the *Carleton* in her central position, she suffered severely. Her commander, Lieutenant Dacres, was knocked senseless; another officer lost an arm; only Mr. Edward Pellew, afterward Lord Exmouth, remained fit for duty. The spring being shot away, she swung bows on to the enemy, and her fire was thus silenced. Captain Pringle signaled to her to withdraw; but she was unable to obey.

To pay her head off the right way, Pellew himself had to get out on the bowsprit under a heavy fire of musketry to bear the jib over to windward; but to make sail seems to have been impossible. Two artillery boats were sent to her assistance, "which towed her off through a very thick fire, until out of farther reach, much to the honor of Mr. John Curling and Mr. Patrick Carnegy, master's mate and midshipman of the *Isis*, who conducted them; and of Mr. Edward Pellew, mate of the *Blonde*, who threw the towrope from the *Carleton*'s bowsprit."

This service on board the *Carleton* started Pellew on his road to fortune; but, singularly enough, the lieutenancy promised him in consequence, by both the First Lord and Lord Howe, was delayed by the fact that he stayed at the front instead of going to the rear, where he would have been "within their jurisdiction." The *Carleton* had two feet of water in the hold, and had lost eight killed and six wounded—about half her crew—when she anchored out of fire.

In this small but stirring business, the Americans, in addition to the *Royal Savage*, had lost one gondola. Besides the injuries to the *Carleton*, a British artillery boat, commanded by a German lieutenant, was sunk. Toward evening the *Inflexible* got within point-blank shot of the Americans, "when five broadsides," wrote Douglas, "silenced their whole line." One fresh ship, with scantling for seagoing, and a concentrated battery, has an unquestioned advantage over a dozen light-built craft, carrying one or two guns each, and already several hours engaged.

At nightfall the *Inflexible* dropped out of range, and the British squadron anchored in line of battle across the southern end of the passage between the island and the main; some vessels were extended also to the eastward, into the open Lake.

"The best part of my intelligence," wrote Burgoyne next day from St. John's, to Douglas at Quebec, "is that our whole fleet was formed in line above the enemy, and consequently they must have surrendered this morning, or given us battle on our own terms. The Indians and light troops are abreast with the fleet; they cannot, therefore, escape by land."

The British squadron sharing this confidence, a proper lookout was not kept. The American leader immediately held a conference with his officers and decided to attempt a retreat, "which was done with such secrecy," writes Waterbury, "that we went through them entirely undiscovered."

The movement began at 7 p.m., a galley leading, the gondolas and schooners following, and Arnold and his second bringing up the rear in the two heaviest galleys. This delicate operation was favored by a heavy fog, which did not clear till next morning at eight. As the Americans stole by, they could not see any of the hostile ships.

By daylight they were out of sight of the British. Riedesel, speaking of this event, says, "The ships anchored, secure of the enemy, who stole off during the night, and sailing round the left wing, aided by a favorable wind, escaped under darkness." The astonishment next morning, he continues, was great, as was Carleton's rage. The latter started to pursue in such a hurry that he forgot to leave orders for the troops which had been landed; but, failing to discover the fugitives, he returned and remained at Valcour till nightfall, when scouts brought word that the enemy were at Schuyler's Island, eight miles above.

The retreat of the Americans had been embarrassed by their injuries, and by the wind coming out ahead. They were obliged to anchor on the 12th to repair damages, both hulls and sails having suffered severely. Arnold took the precaution to write to Crown Point for bateaux, to tow in case of a southerly wind; but time did not allow these to arrive. Two gondolas had to be sunk on account of their injuries, making three of that class so far lost.

The retreat was resumed at 2 p.m., but the breeze was fresh from the southward, and the gondolas made very little way. At evening the British chased again. That night the wind moderated, and at daybreak the American flotilla was twenty-eight miles from Crown Point—fourteen from Valcour—having still five miles' start.

Later, however, by Arnold's report, "the wind again breezed up to the southward, so that we gained very little either by beating or rowing. At the same time the enemy took a fresh breeze from northeast, and, by the time we had reached Split Rock, were alongside of us."

The galleys of Arnold and Waterbury, the *Congress* and the *Washington*, had throughout kept in the rear, and now received the brunt of the attack made by the *Inflexible* and the two schooners, which had entirely distanced their sluggish consorts. This fight was in the upper narrows, where the Lake is from one to three miles wide; and it lasted, by Arnold's report, for five glasses (two hours and a half), the Americans continually retreating until about ten miles from Crown Point.

There, the *Washington* having struck some time before, and final escape being impossible, Arnold ran the *Congress* and four gondolas ashore in a small creek on the east side; pulling to windward, with the cool judgment that had marked all his conduct, so that the enemy could not follow him—except in small boats with which he could deal. There he set his vessels on fire, and stood by them until assured that they would blow up with their flags flying. He then retreated to Crown Point through the woods, "despite the savages"; a phrase which concludes this singular aquatic contest with a quaint touch of local color.

In three days of fighting and retreating, the Americans had lost one schooner, two galleys, and seven gondolas—in all, ten vessels out of fifteen. The killed and wounded amounted to over eighty, twenty odd of whom were in Arnold's galley. The original force, numbering seven hundred, had been decimated. Considering its raw material and the recency of its organization, words can scarcely exaggerate the heroism of the resistance, which undoubtedly depended chiefly upon the personal military qualities of the leader. The British loss in killed and wounded did not exceed forty.

The little American navy on Champlain was wiped out; but never had any force, big or small, lived to better purpose or died more gloriously, for it had saved the Lake for that year.

Whatever deductions may be made for blunders, and for circumstances of every character which made the British campaign of 1777 abortive and disastrous, thus leading directly to the American alliance with France in 1778, the delay, with all that it involved, was obtained by the Lake campaign of 1776.

On October 15th, two days after Arnold's final defeat, Carleton dated a letter to Douglas from before Crown Point, whence the American garrison was withdrawn. A week later Riedesel arrived, and wrote that "were our whole army here it would be an easy matter to drive the enemy from their entrenchments," at Ticonderoga, and—as has been quoted already—four weeks sooner would have ensured its fall. It is but a coincidence that just four weeks had been required to set up the *Inflexible* at St. John's; but it typifies the whole story.

Save for Arnold's flotilla, the two British schooners would have settled the business. "Upon the whole, Sir," wrote Douglas in his final letter from Quebec before sailing for England.

"I scruple not to say, that had not General Carleton authorized me to take the extraordinary measure of sending up the *Inflexible* from Quebec, things could not this year have been brought to so glorious a conclusion on Lake Champlain."

Douglas further showed the importance attached to this success by men of that day by sending a special message to the British ambassador at Madrid, "presuming that the early knowledge of this great event in the southern parts of Europe may be of advantage to His Majesty's service."

That the opinion of the government was similar may be inferred from the numerous rewards bestowed. Carleton was made a Knight of the Bath, and Douglas a baronet.

The gallantry shown by both sides upon Lake Champlain in 1776 is evident from the foregoing narrative. With regard to the direction of movements—the skill of the two leaders—the same equal credit cannot be assigned. It was a very serious blunder, on October 11th, to run to leeward, passing a concealed enemy, undetected, upon waters so perfectly well known as those of Champlain were; it having been the scene of frequent British operations in previous wars.

Owing to this, "the *Maria*, because of her distant situation (from which the *Inflexible* and *Carleton* had chased by signal) when the rebels were first discovered, and baffling winds, could not get into close action." For the same reason the *Inflexible* could not support the *Carleton*.

The Americans, in the aggregate distinctly inferior, were thus permitted a concentration of superior force upon part of their enemies.

It is needless to enlarge upon the mortifying incident of Arnold's escape that evening. To liken small things to great—always profitable in military analysis—it resembled Hood's slipping away from de Grasse at St. Kitts.

BENEDICT ARNOLD

In conduct and courage, Arnold's behavior was excellent throughout. Without enlarging upon the energy which created the flotilla, and the breadth of view which suggested preparations that he could not enforce, admiration is due to his recognition of the fact—implicit in deed, if unexpressed in word—that the one use of the Navy was to contest the control of the water; to impose delay, even if it could not secure ultimate victory.

No words could say more clearly than do his actions that, under the existing conditions, the Navy was useless, except as it contributed to that end; valueless, if buried in port. Upon this rests the merit of his bold advance into the lower narrows; upon this his choice of the strong defensive position of Valcour; upon this his refusal to retreat, as urged by Waterbury, when the full force of the enemy was disclosed—a decision justified, or rather, illustrated, by the advantages which the accidents of the day threw into his hands.

His personal gallantry was conspicuous there as at all times of his life.

"His countrymen," said a generous enemy of that day, "chiefly gloried in the dangerous attention which he paid to a nice point of honor, in keeping his flag flying, and not quitting his galley till she was in flames, lest the enemy should have boarded and struck it."

It is not the least of the injuries done to his nation in after years, that he should have silenced this boast and effaced this glorious record by so black an infamy.

With the destruction of the flotilla ends the naval story of the Lakes during the War of the American Revolution. Satisfied that it was too late to proceed against Ticonderoga that year, Carleton withdrew to St. John's and went into winter-quarters. The following year the enterprise was resumed under General Burgoyne; but Sir William Howe, instead of cooperating by an advance up the Hudson, which was the plan of 1776, carried his army to Chesapeake Bay, to act thence against Philadelphia.

Burgoyne took Ticonderoga and forced his way as far as Saratoga, sixty miles from Ticonderoga and thirty from Albany, where Howe should have met him. There he was brought to a stand by the army which the Americans had collected, found himself unable to advance or to retreat, and was forced to lay down his arms on October 17th, 1777.

The garrison left by him at Ticonderoga and Crown Point retired to Canada, and the posts were reoccupied by the Americans. No further contest took place on the Lake, though the British vessels remained in control of it, and showed themselves from time to time up to 1781. With the outbreak of war between Great Britain and France, in 1778, the scene of maritime interest shifted to salt water, and there remained till the end.

Eight

Raiding Union Commerce
with Rafael Semmes

Albert M. Goodrich

In the decade preceding the Civil War in America, the carrying trade of the United States had grown into a vast industry. The hardy seamen of New England had flung out the Stars and Stripes to every breeze and cast anchor in the most remote regions where a paying cargo might be found. Up to October 1862, they hardly felt that they had more at stake in the War of the Rebellion than any other loyal citizens.

But in that month the news swept along the seaboard that the Confederate Commerce Raider Rafael Semmes's *Alabama* lay within a few days' sail of their harbors, dealing out swift vengeance upon all Northern vessels which came in her way.

Captain Rafael Semmes was a typical representative of Southern chivalry. He was an ardent admirer of the South and a firm believer in her peculiar "institution." His memoirs, written after the war, breathe secession in every line. He was born in Charles County, Maryland, September 27, 1809. At the age of seventeen he received an appointment as midshipman but did not enter active service until six years later, meanwhile adding the study of law to his naval studies. In 1834, at the end of his first cruise, he was admitted to the bar. In 1837 he was made a lieutenant and commanded the United States brig *Somers*, which assisted in blockading the Mexican coast during the war with that country. While in chase of another vessel a terrific gale arose. The *Somers* was foundered and most of her crew were drowned. A court-martial acquitted Semmes of any fault in this matter, and in 1855 he was promoted to the rank of commander.

In February 1861, he was a member of the Lighthouse Board, of which body he had been secretary for several years.

The provisional government of the Confederacy was not yet a fortnight old when he was summoned to Montgomery. Hastily resigning his Federal commission, he met Jefferson Davis in that city, and was soon speeding northward on an important mission.

Semmes entered the Confederate navy with the rank of commander, the same which he had held in the Federal service. He was promoted to captain about the time he took command of the *Alabama*, and near the close of the war was again promoted, to rear admiral.

The *Alabama* was 220 feet long, 32 feet in breadth of beam, and 18 feet from deck to keel. She carried two horizontal engines of 300 horsepower each, and had bunkers for 350 tons of coal, sufficient for eighteen days' continuous steaming. Captain Semmes was, however, very economical with his coal supply and only used the engines for emergencies. The *Alabama* proved to be a good sailor under canvas, and the greater number of her prizes were taken simply under sail. This enabled the vessel to keep at sea three or four months at a time, and to strike Northern commerce at the most unexpected places, while only once did a Federal war vessel succeed in getting a glimpse of her against the will of her commander.

Whether or not the decline of American shipping is principally due to unwise legislation, certain it is that its downfall dates from the appearance in the mid-Atlantic of this awful scourge of the seas. Northern newspapers called the craft a pirate, and no other word seemed to the New England sea captains adequate to describe the ruthless destroyer.

Although regularly commissioned by the Confederate government, she never entered a Confederate port from the time she left the stocks until she tried conclusions with the *Kearsarge* off the coast of France; and this, together with the further fact that her crew was chiefly of European origin—largely English—was used as an argument that she could not be considered as a legitimate vessel of war. None of the great nations of the world adopted this view, however, and she was everywhere accorded the same treatment that was extended to war vessels of the United States.

DODGING THE *SAN JACINTO*

To his surprise Captain Semmes found the whole town expecting him, although this was the first port he had entered since leaving Terceira two months previous. The *Agrippina* had been in this port a week, and her master, Captain McQueen, had not been able to resist the temptation to boast of his connection with the *Alabama* and aver that his cargo of coal was intended for her bunkers.

It had, moreover, been whispered about that the *Agrippina* had guns and ammunition under the coal, which were intended for the Confederate cruiser, and also that Captain McQueen had stated that he expected to receive some further instructions as to his movements from the British consul, Mr. Lawless.

Diplomatic relations between Great Britain and the United States were very much strained at this time, and the consul was much incensed because his name had been connected with the *Alabama* in this public manner. When cross-questioned by the consul, McQueen became frightened and denied that his cargo was for the *Alabama*, but admitted that he had said that he took a cargo to Terceira for her, and also that he expected to receive a letter from the owners of the *Agrippina* in care of the consul. Mr. Lawless warned him against engaging in such illegal traffic under the British flag, and having satisfied himself that the *Agrippina's* cargo was really intended for the Confederate cruiser and that the *Alabama* might soon be expected in port, he laid the whole matter before the governor of the island. That official did not seem at all surprised, took the matter very coolly, and stated that if the *Alabama* came in she would receive the ordinary courtesies accorded to belligerent cruisers in French ports.

When the *Alabama* did come in and Captain Semmes became acquainted with the real state of affairs, Captain McQueen spent a bad quarter of an hour in his presence, and the same day the *Agrippina* hastily got up her anchor and went to sea. Seven days was long enough for McQueen's chatter to be wafted many a league even without the aid of the telegraph, and the United States consul, Mr. John Campbell, had not been idle.

Captain Semmes applied to the governor for permission to land his prisoners, consisting of Captain Lincoln and family, of the *T. B. Wales*, ex-Consul Fairfield and family, Captain Mellen, of the *Levi Starbuck*, and forty-three seamen belonging to the two vessels. No objection being offered, the prisoners went ashore and sought the friendly offices of the United States consul to assist them in reaching their own country.

It was just a year since Captain Semmes, then in command of the *Sumter*, had been blockaded in this very port by the United States gunboat *Iroquois*, and had adroitly given the latter the slip. Now, in a much better vessel than the *Sumter*, he felt able to defy foes like the *Iroquois*.

But a surprise was brewing for him between decks.

After dark George Forrest swam ashore and bribed a boatman to put him aboard his vessel again with five gallons of a vile brand of whisky. His fellow conspirators pulled him and his purchase in through a berth deck port, and the crew proceeded to hold high carnival. When the watch below was called, the boatswain was knocked down with a belaying pin and an officer who tried to quell the disturbance was saluted with oaths and every kind of missile within reach.

The captain was immediately notified and ordered a beat to quarters. The officers appeared armed and charged forward, assisted by the sober portion of the crew, and after a sharp fight succeeded in securing the worst of the mutineers. Captain Semmes had the drunken sailors drenched with buckets of cold water until they begged for mercy. Forrest was identified by a guard from the shore as the man who bought the liquor, and he was placed in double irons and under guard.

Captain Semmes had said to people on shore that the *Alabama* would go to sea during the night. But she did not go, and early the next morning the Stars and Stripes were floating outside the harbor at the masthead of the steam sloop *San Jacinto*, mounting fourteen guns.

"We paid no sort of attention to the arrival of this old wagon of a ship," writes Semmes in his memoirs. Nevertheless, it must be recorded that he beat to quarters and kept the *Alabama* close under the guns of the French fort in the harbor. He might be able to outsail the *San Jacinto*, but he knew very well that one or two of her broadsides would be very apt to send the *Alabama* to the bottom, in case Captain Ronckendorff should take it into his head to violate the neutrality of a French port. Moreover, his crew were hardly in a condition either of mind or body to meet a determined enemy.

The captain of the *San Jacinto* refused to receive a pilot or come to an anchor, because his vessel would then come within the twenty-four-hour rule, and the *Alabama* would be permitted that length of time to get out of reach when she chose to depart, before the *San Jacinto*, according to international law governing neutral ports, would be permitted to follow her.

During the day Governor Candé sent a letter to Captain Ronckendorff warning him that he must either come to anchor and submit to the twenty-four-hour rule or keep three miles outside the points which formed the entrance to the harbor. Being well aware that the governor had correctly stated the law governing the case, Captain Ronckendorff readily promised acquiescence.

Public sentiment in Martinique among the white population was almost unanimously favorable to the South, and while the law was thus enforced to the letter as against the Federals, practically every white person in the port stood ready to give Captain Semmes any assistance which might enable him to escape from his ponderous adversary. The crew of the *Alabama* spent the 19th of November in various stages of recovery from the debauch and fight of the previous night, and repairing and painting occupied the time of some of them.

In the afternoon a French naval officer went on board and furnished Captain Semmes with an accurate chart of the harbor. Toward night the captain of the *Hampden*, an American merchant ship lying in the harbor near the *Alabama*, in company with Captain Mellen, were rowed out to the *San Jacinto*, bearing a letter from the United States consul to Captain Ronckendorff, informing him in regard to the situation ashore.

The news of their departure was not long in reaching the *Alabama*. Suspecting that some code of signals was being arranged, Captain Semmes determined to take time by the forelock. He asked for a government pilot, who was promptly furnished, and just at dusk the *Alabama* hoisted anchor and steamed toward the inner harbor. The evening was cloudy. Darkness came on early, and rain began to fall. All lights on board were extinguished or covered, and having passed out of sight of the

Hampden, the course was altered and the *Alabama* ran out through the most southerly channel.

When the captain of the *Hampden* returned to his vessel a little after eight o'clock, he immediately sent up three rockets in the direction in which the *Alabama* was supposed to have gone. The *San Jacinto* at once ran under a full head of steam to the south side of the harbor and searched up and down with her crew at quarters until after midnight. At daybreak two of her boats were taken on board, one of which had spent the night in the southern side of the harbor and the other in the northern side. Nobody had seen anything of the *Alabama*.

People on shore solemnly assured the *San Jacinto*'s officers that the *Alabama* had not escaped but was hiding in some obscure part of the bay to await the departure of her enemy. The whole harbor was therefore explored by the *San Jacinto*'s boats, establishing the fact that beyond a doubt the *Alabama* was gone.

In a postscript to his report to the Navy department, Captain Ronckendorff says: "I could find out nothing of the future movements of the *Alabama*." Nor could anybody else. That was a secret which was kept locked in the breast of her commander. It was very rarely that the lieutenants in her own ward room knew where the vessel would be twenty-four hours ahead.

Capture of the *Ariel*

The next afternoon the *Alabama* ran down to the solitary little island of Blanquilla, near the coast of Venezuela, whither the *Agrippina* had preceded her. At the anchorage Captain Semmes was somewhat surprised to find an American whaling schooner. Some boilers had been set up on the island, and her crew were busily engaged in trying out oil from the carcass of a whale which had recently been captured. As the *Alabama* floated the United States flag, the captain of the whaler rowed out to her and volunteered to pilot the newcomer in, and expressed much satisfaction that the United States Navy Department had shown such a commendable determination to protect commerce in the Caribbean Sea.

After an inspection of the *Alabama*'s armament, he expressed the opinion that she was "just the ship to give the pirate Semmes fits." When

he was finally informed into whose hands he had fallen, his consternation was really pitiable. Semmes, however, was not disposed to stir up a
quarrel with even so weak a government as that of Venezuela, and mag-
nanimously informed the young skipper that he should consider the
island as a Venezuelan possession, notwithstanding the slight evidences
of occupation, and that the Marine league surrounding the island would
be respected as Venezuelan waters.

The Yankee master was detained on board the *Alabama* during her
stay as a precautionary measure. Some of the junior officers took delight
in tantalizing the enforced guest in the interim. A midshipman asked him
with great earnestness if "the old man" told him that he would not burn
his ship.

"Why to be sure he did," was the response.

And then followed doleful waggings of the head and the comforting
remark that it all looked very much like one of Semmes's grim jokes.

In the end the whaler was released and her master warned to get into
a Federal port at the earliest opportunity, and not permit himself to be
caught on the high seas, as he might not fare so well a second time.

The *Alabama* spent five days here coaling from the *Agrippina*. The
crew were allowed shore liberty in quarter watches, but as there were no
rum shops or dance houses on the island, the privilege was not greatly
appreciated by a large part of the rough sailors. Several of the boats were
rigged with sails, and the officers went fishing. Gunning for pelicans, plo-
vers, gulls, and sand-snipes was also a favorite pastime. Flocks of flamin-
goes waded in the lagoons around the island in search of food, or stood in
line like soldiers on the beach.

A few settlers from the mainland had taken up their residence on the
island and were cultivating bananas. The sailors helped themselves boun-
tifully to this fruit, and complaint having been made to Captain Semmes,
he squared the account with ship's rations.

A court-martial was appointed to consider the case of the incor-
rigible George Forrest, and he was condemned to be put ashore and left
on this island.

November 26th the *Alabama* left her anchorage at Blanquilla, and
on the 29th was coasting along the shore of Porto Rico. It was the hope

of Captain Semmes that he might capture a treasure steamer on her way north with gold from California. In the Mona Passage a Spanish schooner was boarded, which contained late Boston papers giving long accounts of the extensive preparations which were being made for a campaign in Texas, the conduct of which was to be placed in the hands of General Banks.

Captain Semmes had already heard of this proposed transfer of a northern army to the Texan coast, and had laid his plans to be in the Gulf of Mexico about the time it should arrive, which it was expected would be early in January. In the meantime he had something over a month to devote to other matters. The Spaniards were told that the *Alabama* was the United States steamer *Iroquois*. A few hours later another sail was sighted, and the *Alabama* having drawn nearer, it needed not the skill of Evans to pronounce her "Yankee." The stamp of New England was in her tapering royal and sky-sail masts and her snowy canvas. Newspapers were hastily put aside and attention concentrated on the chase.

Almost within sight of her destination the bark was overhauled and proved to be the *Parker Cooke*, of Boston, bound for San Domingo with provisions. Large quantities of butter, salt meats, crackers, and dried fruits were transferred to the *Alabama*, and at dusk the torch was applied to the prize.

That night the *Alabama's* officers had a bad scare, and the men were ordered to their guns. A large ship of war came suddenly upon them, and as the cruiser had her propeller up and no steam in her boilers, she would have been completely at the mercy of so powerful an adversary. The stranger, however, was evidently not Federal, and passed quickly by without paying the slightest attention to the *Alabama*, which was in plain view. Next day three vessels were boarded, but one showed Dutch papers and the others Spanish.

December 2nd the *Alabama* chased and overhauled a French bark, and her master's ignorance of international law came near costing him dearly. He paid no attention to a blank cartridge, and it was not until a solid shot was thrown between his masts and at no great distance above his people's heads that he consented to round to. When asked by the boarding officer why he had not stopped at the first summons, he replied that he was a Frenchman, and that France was not at war with anybody!

On the 5th the *Union*, of Baltimore, was captured, but she had a neutral cargo, and her captain having given a ransom bond and consented to receive on board the prisoners from the *Parker Cooke*, she was suffered to proceed on her voyage.

A sharp lookout was now kept for a steamer which it was expected would be on her way from the Isthmus of Panama to New York with a million dollars or upward of California gold. This money, if captured, would be lawful prize, and the portion of it which would go to officers and crew would be a welcome addition to the pay received from the Confederate government.

The *Alabama* held her post in the passage between Cuba and San Domingo from December 3rd to December 7th, but no steamer approached from the south. Many vessels were overhauled, but all were neutrals except the *Union*, which ran into the *Alabama*'s arms without the necessity of a chase. The 7th was Sunday, and while the captain was at breakfast and the crew preparing for the usual Sunday muster, the lookout raised his shout of "Sail-ho!"

"Where-away?" demanded the officer of the deck.

"Broad on the port bow, sir!" was the reply.

"What does she look like?"

"She is a large steamer, brig-rigged, sir."

Here was a steamer at last, but not in the expected quarter. This one was southbound, and visions of California gold vanished into air. Nevertheless, she might prove a good prize.

"All hands work ship," called the boatswain, and Lieutenant Kell, seizing his trumpet, directed the furling of sails and the lowering of the propeller. The firemen worked like beavers, and in twenty minutes a sailing vessel had been transformed into a steamer. At a distance of three or four miles the United States flag was run up, and the stranger responded with the same ensign. The rapidity with which the latter approached showed that she was swift, but it was soon ascertained that she carried no guns.

The *Alabama* ran down across her path as if to speak to her, but the stranger kept away a little and swept by within a stone's throw. The great packet-steamer had all her awnings set, and under these was a crowd of passengers of both sexes. Groups of soldiers were also seen and several officers in uniform. Many passengers with opera glasses could be seen curiously studying the construction and appointments of the false Union war ship.

As the *Alabama* passed the wake of the packet, she wheeled in pursuit, ran up the Confederate flag, and fired a blank cartridge. Instantly the state of amused curiosity on the stranger's deck gave way to panic. Ladies ran screaming below, and male passengers were by no means slow in keeping them company. Great clouds of black smoke poured from the smoke stacks of the fleeing monster, and her huge walking beam responded still more rapidly to the strain of her engines. A run of less than a mile convinced Captain Semmes that the stranger had the speed of him, and that if he wished to capture her he must resort to heroic measures.

The *Alabama* was yawed a little to enable the gunner to take accurate aim, and a hundred-pound shell splintered the foremast of the fugitive ten feet above the deck. Her master declined to expose his passengers to a second shot, and the stranger's engines were stopped, and she soon lay motionless, awaiting the approach of her captor.

The prize proved to be the California mail-steamer *Ariel*, Captain Jones, bound to the Isthmus of Panama with 532 passengers, mostly women and children, on board; a battalion of 145 United States Marines; and a number of naval officers, including Commander Sartori, who was on his way to the Pacific to take command of the United States sailing sloop *St. Marys*.

The boarding officer reported great consternation among the passengers. Many of them were hastily secreting articles of value, and the ladies were inclined to hysterics, not knowing to what indignities they might be subjected by the "pirates." At this juncture Lieutenant Armstrong was ordered to take the captain's gig and a boat's crew rigged out in white duck, and proceed on board arrayed in his best uniform and brightest smile, and endeavor to restore a feeling of security.

The young lieutenant found the most serious obstacle to the success of his mission in the person of the commander of the Marines, who strenuously objected to having his men considered as prisoners of war and put on parole. But the lieutenant had a clinching argument in the muzzles of the *Alabama*'s guns, then distant but a few yards, and the Marines finally stacked their arms and took the oath not to bear arms against the Confederacy until exchanged. Eight thousand dollars in United States treasury notes and $1,500 in silver were found in the safe, which Captain Jones admitted to be the property of the vessel's owner, and this was turned over to Captain Semmes. The boats' crews behaved very well, and none of the personal effects of the prisoners were seized.

The captain and engineers of the *Ariel* were sent on board the *Alabama*, and a number of the *Alabama*'s engineers took possession of the *Ariel*'s engines. Lieutenant Armstrong and Midshipman Sinclair, who acted as his executive officer, were not long in ingratiating themselves with the ladies, and when they finally left the prize two days later, nearly all the buttons on their coats had been given away as mementoes. They occupied respectively the head and foot of the long dining table. When champagne was brought in they proposed the health of Jefferson Davis, which they requested should be drunk standing. Their request was complied with amid considerable merriment, and then the Yankee girls retaliated by proposing the health of President Lincoln, which was drunk with a storm of hurrahs.

The next day after the capture of the *Ariel*, the prize crew was hastily withdrawn from her, bringing away certain small fixtures from the engines, which rendered them temporarily useless. The reason for this move was the appearance of another steamer on the horizon, which it was hoped would prove to be the treasure steamer for which the *Alabama* had been waiting for a week past.

Captain Semmes was doomed to another disappointment, however, for she was neutral. About eight o'clock the next evening, while in chase of a brig, which was afterward found to be from one of the German states, a valve casting broke in one of the *Alabama*'s engines, and the chief engineer reported that it would take at least twenty-four hours to repair the damage.

Captain Semmes had been extremely loath to release the *Ariel*. To get her into a Confederate port was, of course, impossible, and the *Alabama* could not possibly accommodate such an immense number of passengers, even for the short time necessary to run into the nearest neutral port. He was debating in his own mind whether it might not be possible to get his prize into Kingston, Jamaica, long enough to get his prisoners ashore, when the accident happened to the engine, and a boat sent to board the German brig brought back the information that there was yellow fever at Kingston. A bond for the value of the prize and her cargo was therefore exacted from Captain Jones, and the *Ariel* was suffered to proceed on her voyage.

FIGHT WITH THE *HATTERAS*

On the 5th of January, 1863, the *Alabama* left the Arcas Keys for her cruise to the northward. Full descriptions of the Banks expedition and its destination had appeared in the northern newspapers, and Captain Semmes was well supplied with information as to the character of the transport fleet and the time when it might be expected to arrive off Galveston. It was not likely that the transports would be accompanied by a great number of war vessels, as the Confederacy had no fleet in the Gulf, and the northern papers had reported the *Alabama* as well on her way to the coast of Brazil.

As there was only twelve feet of water on the bar, most of the transports would be obliged to anchor outside. A night attack—a quick dash— firebrands flung from deck to deck—and the fleet might be half destroyed before the gunboats could get up steam to pursue.

Semmes determined to run in by daylight far enough to get the bearings of the fleet, and then draw off and wait for darkness. He had permitted enough of his plan to leak through the ward room to the forecastle to put his people on their mettle, and the entire crew were eager for the fray.

On January 11th the man at the masthead was instructed to keep a lookout for a large fleet anchored near a lighthouse. His "Sail ho! Land ho!" came almost simultaneously, and the captain began to feel certain of his game. But later questioning brought the answer that there was no fleet of transports—only five steamers, which looked like vessels of war. Soon after, a shell thrown by one of the steamers was distinctly seen to burst over the city.

It could not be that the Federals would be firing upon a city which was in their own possession, and Semmes immediately came to the correct conclusion that Galveston had been recaptured by the Confederates. That the Banks expedition had been diverted to New Orleans, and would proceed toward Texas by way of the Red River, he could not know, but that it had not reached Galveston was sufficiently apparent.

The *Alabama's* prow was turned offshore again, and presently the lookout called down that one of the steamers was in pursuit. Commodore Bell, of the Federal fleet, had discovered the strange actions of the sail in the offing, and had suspected an intention of running the blockade.

The gunboat *Hatteras* was therefore signaled to go in chase of the intruder. The *Alabama* flew away under sail, but not so fast as to discourage her pursuer. The propeller was finally let down, and about twenty miles out she turned to meet the *Hatteras*. The engines on both vessels stopped at a distance of about a hundred yards, and the Federal hailed.

"What ship is that?"

"This is Her Britannic Majesty's ship *Petrel*," shouted Lieutenant Kell.

He then demanded the name of the pursuer. The first answer was not clearly heard. A second summons brought the reply:

"This is the United States ship—"

Again those on the *Alabama* failed to catch the name, and the people on the *Hatteras* seemed to be in a like predicament, for her officer shouted:

"I don't understand you."

"I don't understand *you*," rejoined Kell.

After a few moments' delay the *Hatteras* hailed again.

"If you please, I will send a boat on board of you."

"Certainly," was the reply, "we shall be happy to receive your boat."

Word was passed to the gunners that the signal to fire would be the word "Alabama." The creaking of the tackle as the boat was lowered was distinctly heard. Meanwhile the *Alabama's* engines were started and she was deftly maneuvered to get her into position for a raking fire. But Lieutenant Blake, of the *Hatteras*, was not to be caught napping, and as the boat cleared her side, the engines of the *Hatteras* were again started, giving her headway enough so that she could again present her port broadside. Seeing that further concealment was useless, Lieutenant Kell, at a word from his captain, placed the trumpet to his lips and shouted with all his lungs:

"This is the Confederate States steamer *Alabama*!"

Almost at the same instant, the whole starboard broadside was fired. At fifty yards there was little chance to miss, and the sharp clang of shot and shell against the *Hatteras*'s iron plates added to the din. The fire was immediately returned by the *Hatteras*, and both vessels sprang forward at full speed, leaving Master L. H. Partridge and his boat's crew making vain endeavors to regain their own deck.

Although the *Hatteras* was built of iron, she was not ironclad. Her plates had been made merely to resist the sea, not cannon shot, and the terrific pounding which the *Alabama*'s guns gave her was effective from the first.

Her walking beam was shot away, and great gaps appeared in her sides. Gunners on the *Alabama* reveled in the chance to revenge the long-suffered newspaper abuse.

"That's from 'the scum of England'!" "That stops your wind!" "That's a British pill for you to swallow!" were some of the expressions hurled at the *Hatteras* along with the shot and shell.

Meanwhile the *Alabama* was not escaping punishment entirely, although none of her wounds were of a serious nature. One shot through the stern passed through the lamp room, smashing everything within it. A shell striking a few feet abaft the foremast, ripped up the deck and lodged in the port bulwarks without exploding. A shot a few feet forward of the bridge tore up the deck. Two shells cut the main rigging and dropped into the coal bunkers, and one of these in exploding made a hole through the side. A shot demolished one of the boats and went completely through the smokestack, making the iron splinters fly like hail. Another shot struck the muzzle of a thirty-two-pounder gun and caused the truck to run back over a man's foot. There was no damage below the waterline.

The *Hatteras* was on fire in two places, and a shell broke the cylinder of her engine, thus making it impossible either to handle the vessel or to put out the fire. Finding his craft a helpless wreck, Lieutenant Blake ordered the magazine flooded to prevent an explosion and fired a lee gun in token of surrender.

To the inquiry from the *Alabama* whether he needed assistance, Lieutenant Blake gave an affirmative reply, and the *Alabama* lowered her boats. But they were hastily hoisted again when it was reported that a steamer was coming from Galveston. In this emergency the commander of the *Hatteras* ordered her port battery thrown overboard, and this proceeding doubtless kept her afloat during the few minutes needed for the *Alabama*'s boats to be again lowered and reach her side. Every man was taken off, and ten minutes later she went down bow foremost. The action lasted less than fifteen minutes.

Partridge and his boat's crew drew near as the battle closed, but the officer having satisfied himself that the *Hatteras* had been defeated, ordered his men to pull for Galveston. He was without a compass, but the night was clear and starlit, and the tired crew succeeded in reaching a Federal vessel near the city at daybreak.

Meanwhile Commodore Bell had heard the noise of the conflict, and had started out with two of his remaining ships to give assistance to the *Hatteras*. An all-night search revealed nothing, and returning next day, he discovered the tops of the masts of his unlucky consort projecting a few feet above the water.

BATTLE WITH THE *KEARSARGE*

On board the *Kearsarge* the long wait had bred doubts of the martial temper of Captain Semmes, and aside from the preparations already made, affairs had largely dropped back into the ordinary routine. Soon after ten o'clock the officer of the deck reported a steamer approaching from the city, but this was a frequent occurrence, and no attention was paid to the announcement.

The bell was tolling for religious services when loud shouts apprised the crew that the long-looked-for *Alabama* was in sight. Captain Winslow hastily laid aside his prayer book and seized his trumpet. The fires were piled high with coal and the prow was turned straight out to sea. The fight must be to the death, and the vanquished was not to be permitted to crawl within the protection of the Marine league.

Moreover, the French government had expressed a desire that the battle should take place at least six or seven miles from the coast. Ten, fifteen, twenty, twenty-five minutes passed. The *Alabama* kept straight on, and the *Kearsarge* continued her apparent flight.

Finally, at 10:50, when six or seven miles from shore, the *Kearsarge* wheeled and bore down upon her adversary. At a distance of a little over a mile the *Alabama* began the fight with her Blakely rifle, and at 10:57 she opened fire with her entire starboard broadside, which cut some of the *Kearsarge's* rigging but did no material damage. The latter crowded on all steam to get within closer range, but in two minutes a second broadside came hurtling about her.

This was quickly followed by a third, and then, deeming the danger from a raking fire too great to allow the ship to present her bow to the enemy any longer, Captain Winslow directed his vessel sheared, and fired his starboard battery. He then made an attempt to run under the *Alabama's* stern, which she frustrated by shearing, and thus the two ships were forced into a circular track round a common center, and the battle went on for an hour, the distance between them varying from a half to a quarter of a mile. During that time the vessels described seven complete circles.

At 11:15 a sixty-eight-pounder shell came through the bulwarks of the *Kearsarge*, exploding on the quarterdeck and badly wounding three of the crew of the after pivot gun. Two shots entered the ports of the thirty-two pounders, but injured no one. A shell exploded in the hammock nettings and set fire to the ship, but those detailed for fire service extinguished it in a short time, and so thorough was the discipline that the cannonade was not even interrupted.

A hundred-pounder shell from the *Alabama's* Blakely pivot gun entered near the stern and lodged in the sternpost. The vessel trembled from bowsprit to rudder at the shock. The shell failed to explode, however. Had it done so, the effect must have been serious and might have changed the result of the battle. A thirty-two-pounder shell entered forward and lodged under the forward pivot gun, tilting it out of range, but did not explode. A rifle shell struck the smokestack, broke through, and exploded inside, tearing a ragged hole three feet in diameter. Only two of the boats escaped damage.

As the battle progressed, it became evident that the terrible pounding of the two eleven-inch Dahlgrens was having a disastrous effect on the *Alabama*. The *Kearsarge* gunners had been instructed to aim the heavy guns somewhat below rather than above the waterline, and leave the deck fighting to the lighter weapons.

As the awful missiles opened great gaps in the enemy's side or bored her through and through, the deck of the *Kearsarge* rang with cheers. A seaman named William Gowin, with a badly shattered leg, dragged himself to the forward hatch, refusing to permit his comrades to leave their gun in order to assist him. Here he fainted, but reviving after being lowered to the care of the surgeon, waved his hand and joined feebly in the cheers which reached him from the deck.

"It is all right," he told the surgeon; "I am satisfied, for we are whipping the *Alabama*."

The situation on the *Alabama* was indeed getting serious. It is evident that Captain Semmes entered the fight expecting to win. On leaving the harbor the crew were called aft, and, mounting a gun carriage, he addressed them as follows:

Officers and seamen of the Alabama: *You have at length another opportunity of meeting the enemy—the first that has been presented to you since you sunk the* Hatteras. *In the meantime you have been all over the world, and it is not too much to say that you have destroyed and driven for protection under neutral flags one-half of the enemy's commerce, which, at the beginning of the war, covered every sea. This is an achievement of which you may well be proud; and a grateful country will not be unmindful of it. The name of your ship has become a household word wherever civilization extends. Shall that name be tarnished by defeat? The thing is impossible! Remember that you are in the English Channel, the theatre of so much of the naval glory of our race, and that the eyes of all Europe are at this moment upon you. The flag that floats over you is that of a young Republic, who bids defiance to her enemies, whenever and wherever found. Show the world that you know how to uphold it. Go to your quarters.*

As before stated, the "Persuader" began to speak at long range—more than a mile. But it was no peaceful merchantman that she had now to accost; no fleeing *Ariel*, vomiting black smoke in a vain effort to get beyond her range—no white winged *Starlight* or *Sea Bride*, piling sail on sail to reach the shelter of a neutral harbor.

The *Kearsarge* only raced toward her with still greater speed. At the third summons the *Kearsarge* yawed gracefully to port, and out of those frowning Dahlgrens blazed her answer. The *Alabama* staggered at the blow, and her creaking yards shook like branches in a tornado. Glass in hand, Captain Semmes stood upon the horseblack abreast the mizzen mast.

"Try solid shot," he shouted; "our shells strike her side and fall into the water."

A little later shells were tried again, and then shot and shell were alternated during the remainder of the battle. But no plan seemed to check the awful regularity of the *Kearsarge*'s after pivot gun. Captain Semmes offered a reward for the silencing of this gun, and at one time his entire battery was turned upon it, but although three of its men were wounded as stated, its fire was not interrupted.

"What is the matter with the Blakely gun?" was asked; "we don't seem to be doing her any harm."

At one time the after pivot gun of the *Alabama*, commanded by Lieutenant Wilson, had been run out to be fired, when a shell came through the port, mowing down the men and piling up a ghastly mass of human flesh. One of the thirty-two pounders had to be abandoned in order to fill up the crew of the gun. The deck was red with blood, and much effort was necessarily expended in getting the wounded below.

Water rushed into the *Alabama* through gaping holes in her sides, and she was visibly lower in the water. There was no concealing the fact that the vessel could not float any great length of time. Captain Semmes made one last attempt to reach the coast—or at least that saving Marine league, whose shelter he had denied to so many of his victims.

As the vessels were making their seventh circle, the forestaysail and two jibs were ordered set. The seaman who executed the order was struck while on the jib boom by a shell or solid shot and disemboweled. Nevertheless, he succeeded in struggling to the spar deck and ran shrieking to the port gangway, where he fell dead. The guns were pivoted to port, and the battle recommenced, with the *Alabama*'s head turned toward the shore.

The effort was a vain one.

Again the shells plowed through the *Alabama*'s hull, and the chief engineer came on deck to say that the water had put out his fires. Lieutenant Kell ran below and soon satisfied himself that the vessel could not float ten minutes. The flag was ordered hauled down and a white flag displayed over the stern. But the gunners were unable to realize that they were whipped. Semmes and Kell were immediately surrounded by excited seamen protesting against surrender. Even a statement of the condition of things belowdecks failed to convince all of them of the futility of further fighting. It is said that two of the junior officers, swearing that they would never surrender, rushed to the two port guns and reopened fire on the *Kearsarge*. At this point there is a flat contradiction in the statements of eyewitnesses.

Lieutenant Kell denies that there was any firing of the *Alabama*'s guns after the colors had been hauled down, and that her discipline would not have permitted it. Semmes and Kell both aver that the *Kearsarge* fired five shots into them after their flag had been hauled down.

When the firing had ceased, Master's Mate Fullam was sent to the *Kearsarge* with a boat's crew and a few of the wounded in the dinghy (the only boat entirely unharmed) to say that the *Alabama* was sinking and to ask for assistance in transferring the wounded. He told Captain Winslow that Captain Semmes had surrendered. But during the interval the *Alabama* was rapidly filling, and the wounded and boys who could not swim were hastily placed in two of the quarter boats, which were only partially injured, and sent to the *Kearsarge* in command of F. L. Galt, surgeon of the *Alabama*, and at that time also acting as paymaster.

The order was then given for every man to jump overboard with a spar and save himself as best he could. The sea was quite smooth, and the active young officers and men found no difficulty in keeping afloat. Captain Semmes had on a life preserver, and Lieutenant Kell supported himself on a grating. Assistant Surgeon Llewelyn, an Englishman, had tied some empty shell boxes around his waist, and although these prevented his body from sinking, he was unable to keep his head above water, never having learned to swim. One of the men swam to him a little later and found him dead.

The *Alabama* settled at the stern. The water entering the berth deck ports forced the air upward, and the huge hulk sighed like a living creature hunted to its death. The shattered mainmast broke and fell. The great guns and everything movable came thundering aft, increasing the weight at the stern, and, throwing her bow high in the air, she made her final plunge. The end of the jib boom was the last to disappear beneath the waters, and the career of the famous cruiser was ended forever.

The *Deerhound* having approached at the close of the battle, Captain Winslow hailed her and requested her owner, Mr. John Lancaster, to run down and assist in saving the survivors, which he hastened to do. Steaming in among the men struggling in the water, the boats of the *Deerhound* were dispatched to their assistance, and ropes were also thrown to them from the decks.

Master's Mate Fullam asked permission of Captain Winslow to take his boat and assist in the rescue, which was granted. Two French pilot boats also appeared on the scene and assisted in the work. One of these pilot boats took the men saved by it on board the *Kearsarge*, but the other, having rescued Second Lieutenant Armstrong and a number of seamen, went ashore.

Those taken to the *Kearsarge,* including the wounded, numbered seventy, among whom were several subordinate officers and Third Lieutenant Joseph D. Wilson. Captain Semmes had been slightly wounded in the arm and was pulled into one of the *Deerhound*'s boats in a thoroughly exhausted condition. Lieutenant Kell was rescued by the same boat. Fifth Lieutenant Sinclair and a sailor, having been picked up by one of the *Kearsarge*'s boats, quietly dropped overboard and reached one of the *Deerhound*'s boats in safety. The *Deerhound*, having picked up about forty officers and men, steamed rapidly away and landed them on the coast of England at Southampton.

NINE

Repelling the Chinese at Chipyong-ni

Leo Barron

FEBRUARY 14–15, 1951, 1732–0045 HOURS: ALONG THE LINE, G COMPANY, 23RD INFANTRY REGIMENT, MCGEE AND CURTIS HILLS

As the sun slipped behind the western ridgeline, the bushes and trees on Hill 397 began to stir as if they were alive. From his vantage point, Second Lieutenant Paul J. McGee saw tiny dots appear along the slopes of Hill 397. The platoon leader thought they looked like worker ants scampering down an anthill. He knew what was coming. His commander, Lieutenant Thomas Heath, also saw the coming invasion.

Harley Wilburn recalled what he witnessed that night. "We saw the Chinese coming from probably two miles south of George Company," said Wilburn. "And they were carrying torches of all things. I couldn't believe it, but there were so many of them, they weren't afraid of nothing. They came right across that flat ground carrying torches toward our position. You see thousands of lights coming at you like that at night and you're just a young nineteen- [or] twenty-year-old man, it really shakes you up."

At 1732 hours, the G Company commander requested that the battalion register their 81mm mortars in front of his position. Like McGee, Heath wanted to be ready. Several minutes later, the radio operators from 2nd Battalion reported to regiment "many gooks on [Hill] 397, firing on them now."

The forward observer for the 37th Field Artillery Battalion was Lieutenant William H. Gibson. He requested a fire mission, its target the saddle that connected Hill 397 with McGee Hill. Within minutes, twenty rounds of 105mm HE exploded on the spot. Corporal McCormack, the forward observer for the G Company 60mm mortars, directed his own fire mission on the same target. Despite the barrage, the Chinese kept streaming down the hill.

Around 1800 hours, the anticipated attack began. "There were more bugles and whistles," McGee later said. "And we thought we even heard something similar to drums. Some of the men heard digging, and we thought we could hear some of their machine guns that they pulled on carts. So we could tell that they were coming in force."

This attack was different for Paul L. Freeman, the regiment's commanding officer.

He later wrote:

> *This time, the Chinese had a plan. First, there was a heavy concentration of mortar and artillery fire which rained down on our position just at dark. This preparation lasted an hour and at seven o'clock the weird bugle calls rang out to the south. The enemy went to work again on the two roads leading into our position on each flank of the Second Battalion. Here the enemy concentrated his force. In column of companies he came down Hill 397 against G Company.*

Unlike the previous night, when 2nd Battalion faced large probing attacks along the length of its perimeter, the swarming Chinese targeted a particular spot along G Company's main line of resistance. Almost immediately, McGee knew he and his platoon were in for a long evening. "They hit us just about the full length of my whole platoon's position, plus the left flank of the First Platoon," he said. "They were coming in pretty steady, more of them, and they were firing more . . . they were standing—some of them even came at us running—and firing."

Heath heard the firing in 3rd Platoon's sector and alerted Colonel James W. Edwards that G Company was under attack. In response, the battalion commander requested a section of tanks from the regimental tank company to buttress the G Company lines.

Meanwhile, the enemy claimed its first casualty of the night. Within minutes of the opening fusillade, the light machine gunner attached to Corporal Eugene L. Ottesen's squad slumped over in his foxhole, wounded. McGee had positioned the machine gun to cover the eastern flank of his platoon on Curtis Hill. Without hesitation, Ottesen jumped behind the gun and opened fire while the platoon medic treated the wounded soldier.

The corporal from Minnesota operated the M1919 gun as if it were his primary weapon. Despite the stream of incoming direct fire from an enemy squad on Hill 397, Ottesen chugged away at the onrushing Chinese, who piled up in front of his machine-gun pit as their bodies crumpled onto the frozen ground. Wave after wave crashed against Ottesen's lead wall. For several hours, the men of 3rd Platoon battled the Chinese to a standstill, but they could not hold out forever. The enemy was far too numerous.

Lieutenant Heath had no reserves to plug the holes. Instead, he went to Baker Battery of the 503rd Field Artillery and asked for reinforcements. Since the enemy was too close for howitzers, the 155s of the 503rd were useless. Therefore, the gun crews pulling security on the gun line had little else to do. The battery commander agreed to lend Heath some of his artillerymen, but each time the G Company commander left with a group, they magically disappeared by the time Heath reached the main line. After the third attempt, Heath gave up. It was obvious to him that the gunners did not want to be infantrymen, even though their lives depended on it.

One man kept trying to recruit more men. Between 2100 and 2200 hours, Captain John A. Elledge, the liaison officer between the 37th Field Artillery and B Battery, 503rd Field Artillery, found a squad of eleven soldiers from the 503rd who were willing to fight. Moreover, they had a .50-caliber machine gun. Elledge led them to 1st Platoon's section of the G Company line, where five of the men and their squad leader set up their machine gun while the other five occupied foxholes around the crew-served weapon and acted as security for it.

While enemy infantry fixed the soldiers of 3rd Platoon, an enemy demolition unit crawled up the hill, using the dead space between 1st and 3rd Platoons, and closed within a few meters of 1st Platoon's eastern flank. There, the demolition team detonated several pole charges, which killed three US soldiers and a Korean volunteer. Worse, it meant the Chinese had taken out two foxholes and were now on the main line of resistance.

In a postwar interview, McGee described how the Chinese used the pole charges. "They had satchel charges attached to the ends of sticks or poles, and they'd push that pole right up to the edge of our holes. We stopped a lot of them, but once they got a satchel charge into a hole, it was too late. They were using grenades and small arms to try to keep the occupants of the foxholes down to where they could get close enough to deposit their satchel charges." The old platoon leader added, "When you put a satchel charge in on top of two men, you know there's really . . . nothing left."

After the earsplitting explosions, the communists did not waste any time. They immediately brought up a machine-gun team and occupied one of the captured foxholes. Within seconds, the enemy gunners opened fire on McGee's 3rd Platoon, cutting a swath across its flank. The first victim was one of McGee's BAR gunners, who stumbled into McGee's foxhole, where the medic bandaged his wounds. The lieutenant dropped his carbine and grabbed the automatic rifle from the wounded soldier.

Realizing that the machine-gun fire was emanating from 1st Platoon's area, McGee grabbed the field phone and rang up Lieutenant Heath, his commander. "Heath," he shouted into the receiver as tracers skipped past his foxhole, "is the 1st Platoon still up in position?"

After several seconds, the George Company commander replied, "Yes."

In fact, Heath had no inkling what was going on atop Schmitt Hill. When McGee had asked about 1st Platoon, the company commander called the 1st Platoon leader, Master Sergeant Emery S. Toth, who told him that his men were still in position. The problem was the platoon leader was not on the hill with his unit; his command post was behind the hill. Sergeant First Class Donald R. Schmitt, the platoon sergeant, was running the platoon atop the ridge; however, he was in a hole on the western side of the line. From his position, he could not have known that his eastern flank was gone. Lulled into a false sense of security, Schmitt told Sergeant Toth that his platoon was still in position. Toth then informed Heath that everything was under control. Unfortunately for G Company, 2nd Battalion, and the 23rd Infantry Regiment, he was wrong. It was now almost 2200 hours. The Chinese had breached the main line of resistance, and the only UN officer who knew about it was Lieutenant McGee.

Sergeant Billy Kluttz, McGee's platoon sergeant, also wanted to know what had happened to 1st Platoon. From his foxhole, he yelled, "Anyone from 1st Platoon?" McGee shouted out the same question.

No one answered. McGee rang up Heath and asked him again if 1st Platoon was still in position. Heath's answer was the same. Before the platoon leader from 3rd Platoon could find out what the situation was with Toth's platoon, he watched several CPVF soldiers duck into a hole on his western flank near his 2nd Squad. They were now behind Sergeant Franklin Querry's hole. McGee tried to phone the threatened squad leader, but enemy mortars had cut most of the communication wire to his squads.

Determined to alert his sergeant, he shouted to Querry, "There are four of them at the rear of your hole. Toss a grenade up and over."

Querry heard his lieutenant, but when he tried to lob his grenades, the enemy machine-gun team occupying the foxhole in 1st Platoon's area swung the barrel over and opened enfilade fire on Querry, pinning the sergeant in his hole.

Clearly, McGee's platoon was in danger. The Chinese were in a position to flank his entire platoon and roll up the rest of G Company. With few options, the platoon leader then tapped his runner, Private Cletis D. Inmon, and ordered him to open fire on the four infiltrators. Meanwhile, McGee emptied the magazine from his own recently acquired BAR. The deadly burst from the two guns killed the four CPVF soldiers instantly. The battle, though, was only beginning. It was now 2210 hours.

Meanwhile, Ottesen continued to fire away at the dark shapes charging up McGee Hill. According to McGee, the corporal's attention was fixated on the slope in front of his position. Therefore, he did not see the fifteen to twenty Chinese scrambling up the hill toward the saddle between Schmitt and McGee Hills. Luckily, the lieutenant saw them.

"About fifteen or twenty of them are coming up to your right front," warned McGee.

By the light of the half-moon, McGee saw Querry's hole, but he did not see Querry firing from it. He saw a bobbing head and realized his squad leader did not intend to expose himself to shoot at the approaching soldiers when an enemy machine gun was firing at him from his western flank. Once again, McGee and his runner, Private Inmon, raised their weapons and began to chip away at the oncoming Chinese mob.

Despite the furious fire from the lieutenant's BAR, the Chinese closed in on Querry's hole. Finally, they were within hand-grenade range, and several enemy infantry chucked some potato mashers at the sergeant's position. McGee yelled at the 2nd Squad leader, ordering him to toss his own grenades back at the Chinese.

Instead, the enemy grenades detonated, wounding the foxhole's occupants. Querry and another soldier climbed out of the hole and scrambled toward McGee and Inmon, screaming, "Lieutenant McGee, I'm hit! Lieutenant McGee, I'm hit!" They left a single private behind to face the Chinese alone. Within seconds, a satchel charge landed inside Querry's former home and exploded, obliterating the soldier.

The two survivors braved the enemy tracers and stampeded into McGee's hole, collapsing on top of the lieutenant and the runner. Querry had some shrapnel wounds from a grenade, but otherwise was unharmed. The other soldier, though, had a more severe injury. McGee was furious— with two bodies on top of him, he could not fire. "Get the hell out of here and get back with your squad!" he roared at his squad leader.

The officer's words spurred Querry to climb out of the foxhole and return to his unit. He had not gotten far when a bullet slammed into his shoulder, spinning him around. McGee shouted for a litter team. Within minutes, they arrived and evacuated Querry and the other injured soldier from 2nd Squad.

McGee and Inmon remained and continued to blaze away at the never-ending swarms of Chinese. However, soon McGee's BAR began to misfire. McGee later explained, "The ammunition we had been supplied with was mostly from the airdrop. The planes had to come in so low over those frozen rice paddies that when they dropped the ammo, the concussion of it hitting the ground had crimped some of the cartridges, and it was these cartridges that were jamming our weapons. About every fifteen rounds or so, the BAR would jam." But he had a solution: "I had a little penknife," he said, "which I'd use to eject the shell from my BAR when it jammed."

By 2300 hours, 3rd Platoon no longer had wire communications with the company. Facing annihilation, McGee ordered Private First Class John N. Martin to race back to the company command post and ask Lieutenant Heath for more men, ammunition, and litter bearers. The intrepid private dashed back toward the company headquarters, dodging random tracer rounds and mortar shells. When Martin arrived, he informed the commander about the situation on McGee Hill, and Heath secured fifteen men from the 503rd Field Artillery to send to 3rd Platoon as reinforcements. Around 2350 hours, Martin set out.

McGee saw Martin's group as they approached his position from the command post. When the men from the 503rd reached the crest of McGee Hill, Chinese soldiers opened fire, scattering them and leaving only three with Martin. They did not last long either. A mortar round exploded, killing one and injuring another. McGee never knew what happened to the third man. Undeterred, Martin returned to his foxhole.

The beleaguered platoon leader could only swear at his misfortune, but not for too long. The enemy did not give him the respite to recover his wits. Waiting for Martin to return, his BAR had become a liability after he dropped his penknife during the fighting; as a result, he had no way to eject the spent cartridges from the chamber. Fortunately, his carbine still worked, and with it he plinked away at the onrushing communist hordes.

At one point, McGee spotted a charging CPVF soldier who was only ten feet from his foxhole. The lieutenant raised his carbine and squeezed the trigger. THUNK! The bolt refused to close. The bitterly cold weather had frozen the oil inside the carbine, causing it to gum up the receiver. McGee had only moments before the enemy plunged a bayonet into his head. The officer shoved his palm against the charging handle. The brute force worked, and the bolt hit home. He fired four rounds at the enemy soldier, killing him.

Before McGee and Inmon could enjoy their good fortune, the enemy machine-gun team in 1st Platoon's sector discharged several bursts toward their foxhole. One round hit Inmon in the eye. He reeled back into the hole with his hands over his face. Inmon cried out: "I am hit in the face. I am hit in the face. I don't want my mother to see me this way. Get me back off the hill."

McGee could see that Inmon's wound was serious. He watched blood spurt out from between his runner's fingers, as if the injured private were plugging a hole in a dike with only his hands. The lieutenant spoke to him, "Lie down, I can't take you out now." He called over to his platoon sergeant for help. "Hey, Sergeant Kluttz," McGee shouted, "send the medic over. Inmon's been hit."

Shortly afterward, a medic appeared and bandaged Inmon's face. The lieutenant asked his runner if he could still fire his M1 Garand. Inmon replied that he could not. The platoon leader needed to keep Inmon in the fight to prevent him from panicking.

"Can you load the magazines for my carbine?" asked McGee.

Inmon nodded and said he would try. For twenty minutes, Inmon and the medic hunkered down in the foxhole while McGee blazed away at the enemy. When the lieutenant felt the enemy fire slacken, he ordered the medic to take the injured private back to the casualty collection point at the company command post.

Ten minutes after the medic evacuated Inmon, McGee noticed that Ottesen's machine gun was silent on Curtis Hill. "What happened to the machine gun? It stopped firing," he asked Sergeant Kluttz, who was still in the next hole.

Like McGee, Kluttz had no idea what had happened to Ottesen, but he did know that the Chinese were now between them and Corporal Raymond Bennett's 1st Squad, which occupied the eastern flank of the platoon. They realized that Ottesen's squad had ceased to exist. The platoon leader called Bennett on the phone (fortunately, the enemy mortars had not cut the line between him and Bennett's 1st Squad). When Bennett answered, McGee ordered him to send a couple of soldiers to plug the hole between his squad and the platoon leader's foxhole.

Signalmen had reestablished the communication between Heath and McGee. With enfilade fire now coming from both of his flanks, the platoon leader was convinced that the enemy occupied a portion of 1st Platoon's main line of resistance. He called his commander again and asked, "Heath, is the 1st Platoon still there?"

The acting G Company commander assured him that Schmitt was in control and 1st Platoon was still on the hill. After several minutes of arguing and another visit from Private Martin, McGee finally persuaded his commanding officer that the Chinese had breached the main line of resistance. In response, Heath called over to Fox Company and asked for reinforcements. Captain Tyrrell, the Fox Company commander, selected 2nd Squad, 3rd Platoon, under the command of Sergeant Kenneth G. Kelly, to head out. The time was now 0045 hours: It was already too late.

FEBRUARY 14, 2210 HOURS: MACHINE-GUN TEAM, H COMPANY

To keep other units from reinforcing the beleaguered G Company, the Chinese hit other sectors in 2nd Battalion's area of operations. At 2200 hours, CPVF units mounted a major assault up the draw that served as the boundary between F and E Companies. Waiting for them were four machine-gun teams from H Company, Seymour "Hoppy" Harris's team among them.

At first, Harris wondered if the Chinese would even come that night. Initially, all the action seemed to be to his left, but not to his front. "The only sounds are firefights taking place in the distance," he wrote in a letter. "Off to my left, I can hear the sound of automatic weapons and rifle fire. Green and red tracers arch through the sky like a 4th of July fireworks display at home. It would be beautiful, I think, if it weren't for the fact men were dying over there."

Earlier that evening, Corporal O'Shell had issued clear instructions to Harris, telling the replacement not to open fire until the first man had reached the barbed wire in front of his hole. Harris did not agree with his NCO's plan. He asked himself sardonically, "Why don't we just let them come into the bunkers with us?"

Shortly after 2200 hours, Harris thought he saw something in the wire. "I see the gooks coming, but at first it doesn't register on me. I look away," wrote Harris. "I thought, God, they look like ghosts. I must be going nuts! Then I slowly turn my head and look back up the draw. What I see makes my stomach do a backflip. Chinese! My God, the draw is full of them. They are about 100 yards from the wire. They come silently. Like little clowns. There is no chatter. The night is still as death. On and on they come. I wonder if anyone else sees them. My God, am I the only one who sees them?"

He kicked his companion and whispered, as if shouting under his breath, "Wake up! They're here!"

Groggy, but awake, his comrade asked, "Who's here?"

"The gooks! Who the hell do you think? Get the hell up, the ball's going to open!" replied Harris.

Alarmed, the other soldier peered over the edge of the foxhole. When he saw the oncoming Chinese horde, he started to mutter uncontrollably, "Oh, no! Holy Jesus, we've had it! Oh Jesus! Oh Jesus!" Instead of preparing for battle, the terror-stricken soldier burrowed into his sleeping bag, cocooning himself.

Disgusted, Harris raised his carbine and looked down the barrel of his weapon. "The gooks are nearly to the wire," he said. "I have been told to keep my carbine on semiautomatic, but I have my sights on three gooks who are rather close together, and without hardly thinking, I slip the selector lever forward, putting the weapon on full automatic."

It did not take long for a Chinese soldier to reach the first strands of barbed wire. On cue, Corporal O'Shell opened fire with his Garand, and Harris heard it thump. He inhaled one more time and squeezed his trigger.

Bedlam ensued. Harris described the scene:

It is like every weapon is wired together. They all go off at once. Tracers like laser beams streak out and I see them go clean through the gooks. I hear them scream, and go down like stalks of corn before a corn cutter. It is only seconds and the mortars start to rain in. And right behind them come the 105s, time fuse and point detonated. They turn the draw into an orange-gray hell. The noise is deafening beyond description. I am frozen, spellbound by the sight and sound of it. For a time I just kneel and stare at the horrible sight before me. Finally, I come to my senses and start to fire, although I cannot see a thing to fire at because of the smoke and flying debris. But the feel of the weapon jumping in my hands makes me feel better. By God, I'm doing something at least. It is 2210 hours.

After several minutes, the firing died down. The only sounds anyone could hear were the whimpers and murmurs from the wounded and dying Chinese soldiers. One of them sounded like a broken record. "Banzai, Banzai, Banzai!" he cried.

"Does anybody see that bastard?" asked a perturbed soldier.

According to Harris, the caterwauling ended several minutes later. Unfortunately, the communists were far from finished. Before he could catch his breath and relax, someone shouted, "Look sharp! Here comes them stupid shits again!"

"I look out the bunker and sure enough, here they come again," wrote Harris. "The draw is crawling with them. My God, I can't believe it. No one could be that stupid. Again, they are to the wire before O'Shell opens the ball. And it is a repeat performance."

But this time was different. Seconds after the gunfight resumed, a huge explosion rocked the earth; when the smoke cleared, a hole had appeared in the barbed wire. The enemy had detonated some type of Bangalore torpedo to clear a path through it. As if they had rehearsed it, the Chinese flooded into the gap. However, they failed to suppress the H Company machine guns before they attacked.

"Our machine guns pour their fire into this opening and soon it is clogged with dead gooks," explained Harris. Before he could celebrate the carnage, a nearby sapper opened fire. "I see a blue flash that seems to come out of the ground," he wrote. "It is a burp gun. The slugs rip up the dirt right in front of my face. I feel as if someone has stuck a lighted cigarette against my upper lip. I drop my carbine and in panic fall to the back of the bunker, pawing at my mouth. I cannot imagine what has happened. I can feel my lip swelling, but as far as I can see, there is only a little blood. My fingers keep catching onto something. Each time this happens it feels like a beesting."

Fortunately, the wound was superficial, and Harris continued to fight. In his mind, he did not have a choice. The Chinese seemed unstoppable.

February 14–15, 2100–0142 Hours:
Command Post, 23rd Infantry Regiment, Chipyong-ni

The staff of 23rd Infantry Regiment knew they were not going to sleep that night. They continued to operate the radios and phones, sending out information to the subordinate units while receiving reports from division. At 2100 hours, the regimental radio operator alerted the battalions. "British lead elements reached East/West Three-Six grid line," he began, "[British] are staying there overnight. Will not come up tonight but will come first light in the morning."

The operator added good news about the American relief column: "5th Cavalry passed thru them . . . cut toward the northwest. [5th Cavalry] will stay there overnight. Will not come tonight but will come up first light in the morning."

Major John H. Newell was the regiment's S4, or senior supply staff officer, for the 23rd Infantry. At 2130 hours, he informed the regiment that, despite the airdrops, the Tomahawks were short of 60mm and 81mm mortar ammunition. Even worse, the men did not have enough grenades—an essential weapon for night fighting. The messages confirmed that whatever they had on hand would have to last through the night.

At 2315 hours, both 2nd and 3rd Battalions reported receiving several rounds from a possible self-propelled gun. Five minutes later, the deluge intensified. The Tomahawk command post informed division that it was receiving "heavy" self-propelled, mortar, and small-arms fire. In addition, 2nd Battalion was under attack from Hill 397. By 2330 hours, the news coming in from Easy and Fox Companies indicated that the Chinese had concentrated their main attack against Colonel Edwards's battalion.

For another ninety minutes, the fighting seesawed back and forth along the southern side of the perimeter. By midnight, the Chinese 356th Regiment was a spent force. It had attempted to breach 2nd Battalion lines on two occasions, and with the exception of the penetration in G Company's western flank, it had failed. Unfortunately, the CPVF had more infantry. Following the 356th were the men of 1st Battalion, 115th Regiment. Shortly after midnight, they attacked.

The regiment had no clue that G Company was under tremendous strain. At 0050 hours, a Firefly dropped flares over Hill 397 to provide better targets for the machine gunners and mortar men, but it was not until 0142 hours that regiment received its first report that G Company was in trouble. At that moment, Colonel Freeman only knew that Heath's company was under heavy attack; he did not know that the Chinese already had penetrated his lines.

FEBRUARY 15, 0110–0130 HOURS:
ALONG THE LINE, E COMPANY, 23RD INFANTRY REGIMENT,
NANCE AND SAWYER HILLS

Elsewhere, the Chinese continued to probe along the length of 2nd Battalion's main line of resistance. At 0110 hours, a probing attack hit 2nd and 3rd Platoons. Shortly after, Captain Sawyer lost landline contact with 1st Platoon, and in response, he ordered his radioman, Douglas Graney, to fix the connection. Graney could not send his other linemen because they already were repairing the wire for 2nd and 3rd Platoons. With no one else available, he set out to complete the task himself.

"I grabbed a spool of wire and started down the hill toward the 1st Platoon," he wrote. "Heavy machine gun and rifle bullets slapped the frozen ground along our entire front. Chinese still trying to cut through our barbed wire were killed only to be replaced by more cutters. Boxcars flew overhead as I ran across the rice paddies. The flyboys launched flares by parachute that gave light to help us spot the enemy. I froze where I stood, as trained, when the light of a flare caught me in the open."

Tony Rego, a machine gunner in Easy Company, spotted Graney and shouted, "What the hell are you doing?"

"I'm pretending to be a tree," replied Graney.

"Trees don't grow in rice paddies. Get your ass out of there," yelled Rego.

Graney ducked into Rego's foxhole and waited for the flare to burn out. When it did, he climbed out of the hole and scampered over to the railroad embankment. There, he found Lieutenant Charles David-son, the 2nd Platoon leader. The lieutenant and several other soldiers, including a machine-gun team and a bazooka gunner, were firing into the railroad tunnel.

Graney asked the lieutenant, "I thought we boobie [*sic*] trapped the tunnel?"

Davidson nodded and replied, "We did. The gooks kept pushing their men to blow up all the traps we set. The Chinese must have a hundred dead soldiers in there. And still they come. But as long as we have ammo, we'll hold. Are you going up to the 1st Platoon with that wire?"

"Yeah," answered Graney.

"Watch yourself," warned Davidson. "The gooks are all over the place."

"Thanks. See you later," said Graney. He ran up Sawyer Hill to link up with 1st Platoon. After several minutes of bumbling in the dark, he found the 1st Platoon leader's foxhole and climbed in to check the wire. After reconnecting the field phone to the wire on the spool, he began to unwind it, trailing the new wire behind him as he walked back to his foxhole at the company command post.

Suddenly, the Chinese attacked again. "I reached the top of the hill near my foxhole as tracers and blasts from grenades erupted," wrote Graney. "The enemy launched another attack. It didn't last long. Our front quieted as Chinese, who were able to run, dashed back up the hills to our front. The moans of the wounded and dying Chinese lying in the blood-soaked snow could be heard across our entire front."

Though the attack had ended in front of Easy Company, Graney could hear the sounds of battle elsewhere. He wrote, "Machine gun and rifle fire from George Company's position continued. The Chinese had opened a hole through George's defenses."

At the time, he did not know how precarious the situation was west of his location. If George Company fell, then the rest of 2nd Battalion, including Easy Company, would be in grave danger.

FEBRUARY 15, 0045–0300 HOURS:
ALONG THE LINE, G COMPANY, 23RD INFANTRY REGIMENT,
McGEE AND CURTIS HILLS

Corporal Raymond Bennett stumbled into the darkness with a couple of his men. Thanks to McGee's warning, he knew the Chinese were somewhere out in front of him. Fortunately, his 1st Squad had beaten all comers, but now he needed to roll back the Chinese on his western flank or risk being overrun. Within minutes of leaving his hole, he found the enemy and even shot and killed one of the enemy buglers as he was sounding his second note.

The communists fought back. One of them hurled a grenade at Bennett's squad, and the subsequent explosion sent shrapnel everywhere. One piece blew a chunk off Bennett's hand. Before the squad leader could recover from the shock, another enemy soldier shot him in the shoulder, sending him staggering backward. Another grenade detonated, and this time a fragment hit him in the leg. Bennett, now seriously wounded, could not remain on the line. He hobbled down the hill toward the command post with another wounded soldier from 1st Squad, Private First Class Roy F. Benoit.

Meanwhile, Sergeant Kelly's squad from F Company arrived at 0100 hours and linked up with Sergeant Kluttz, who had recovered Ottesen's machine gun, which was still operable. The platoon sergeant led them past McGee's hole. Heath had ordered McGee to counterattack with Kluttz and the new squad to recapture the area on 1st Platoon's eastern flank. When the platoon sergeant was in position, he charged forward. Waiting for him were two Chinese soldiers with submachine guns. Kluttz killed them both, but not before they had wounded everyone in Kelly's squad. The platoon sergeant returned to his foxhole with the recaptured light machine gun.

When Kluttz walked past McGee's position, he told them that everyone in Kelly's squad was wounded. Despite the casualties, the platoon sergeant knew they had to stay on the hill for as long as possible: "McGee, we have to stop them."

Corporal Herbert Ziebell was one of the few men still alive on McGee Hill from 3rd Platoon. Like many of the soldiers, he was a replacement who had arrived in late January. Originally, he had been military police, but the 2nd Infantry Division did not need police—it needed infantry. The men at the replacement depot took away his carbine and gave him an M1 Garand, which he never had a chance to zero. "I couldn't hit nothing with that M-1, and I was hunting all my life," Ziebell later said.

Now, he was stuck in a foxhole with the Chinese swarming all around him. He quickly realized that engaging targets to his front would only mark his position for the enemy, so he held his fire. When the Chinese broke through on his west side, he banged away at them with his Garand.

"And when I shot I was pointing to the side of me," he said, "so they [the Chinese] saw that flash over on my right of my rifle. And the bullets were hitting over there first. And boy did I get down in the hole, my partner and me both. Well I didn't shoot for quite awhile, and they left me alone because they thought they got me."

At 0200 hours, G Company's main line of resistance disintegrated. Without receiving orders, 2nd Platoon, which held the eastern flank of G Company's line, pulled out. This unplanned movement unhinged Heath's entire battle position and meant disaster for McGee's platoon. McGee said the Chinese would "get in those holes and start assaulting. It got to the point where my positions were being hit from the front, right, flank, and the rear. They were hitting with grenades, small-arms fire, and machine-gun fire, and that's how I started losing my positions."

The platoon leader called over to Kluttz and asked him about the remnants of Bennett's 1st Squad. "I think that three or four are still left," his platoon sergeant replied.

Kluttz's machine gun was jamming. McGee heard it sputtering and shouted, "It looks like they have got us Kluttz."

The sergeant declared, "Let's kill as many of the sons-of-bitches as we can before they get us."

At 0215 hours, a round jammed in the chamber of Kluttz's M1919 machine gun, and he could not eject it. The platoon sergeant told his lieutenant, and McGee decided it was time to leave. "Let's try to get out," McGee said. "Let's throw what grenades we have left, fire what we can, and try to get back over the hill toward Bennett's squad."

The Chinese were now all over McGee and Curtis Hills, and the two survivors had to fight their way down the slope. After several minutes of searching, Kluttz and McGee found only two men left from their entire platoon: the runner, Private Martin, and Corporal Ziebell from 1st Squad. Sergeant Schmitt had withdrawn the remnants of 1st Platoon from its position. By 0300 hours, no one alive remained along G Company's section of the main line of resistance.

Lieutenant McGee wondered how he had survived the night when most of the soldiers in his platoon had not. In a postwar interview, he confessed, "All of my men stayed in their holes until they were killed or wounded."

Individual acts of heroism went unseen, but when the survivors returned the next day, they found many of their comrades still in their foxholes. Privates Burl J. Mace, Paul C. Baker, and Bruce M. Broyles were among those heroes. When the soldiers of George Company pulled out, they remained in their holes and fought to the death. The survivors found them the next morning, surrounded by piles of enemy bodies. Each received posthumous Silver Stars for their gallantry.

Like Mace, Baker, and Broyles, Corporal Hal McGovern chose to stay and fight, manning a machine gun in 1st Platoon. With the Chinese flooding past him, he ordered the men who were part of his team to withdraw to safety. Then he stood up in his hole and opened fire with his light machine gun, holding it like a rifle. His blistering fusillade delayed the Chinese so his comrades could escape, but he could not save himself. He died in his hole, where they found him the next day.

Private Paul Stamper was another hero who died trying to save his friends in G Company. For much of the fighting, Stamper ran around the battlefield, repairing signal wire so that the platoons could communicate with each other and the company. At one point, he ran across an open field, dodging incoming mortar rounds, to repair a break in the line. Once fixed, he came under fire from a nearby enemy machine gun. Without a second thought, he crawled toward the enemy soldiers. When he was close enough, he tossed a grenade at the machine-gun team, destroying it and the gunners. Unfortunately, another enemy soldier killed him shortly thereafter. G Company survivors found his body the next morning.

When Private Albert H. Enger saw an abandoned machine gun, he jumped into the foxhole and opened fire at the charging Chinese. For several minutes, he mowed down wave after wave. Eventually, like the others, he was overwhelmed and, like his compatriots, was found dead in his hole behind his machine gun.

Private Richard L. Svitck refused to leave his wounded comrades behind on the battlefield, several times carrying injured soldiers from Curtis Hill back to the aid station. He continued to return to the ridge even after the Chinese had captured some of the positions. Eventually his luck ran out, and the survivors found his body the next morning on the hill.

For their selfless service, the Army also awarded McGovern, Stamper, Enger, and Svitck posthumous Silver Stars.

Not all of the heroes were riflemen. Private Delmar Patton of Ohio was a mortar man serving as an ammo bearer for G Company's 60mm mortar section. When he saw the wounded men from the line platoons staggering down from the ridgeline, he grabbed his rifle and headed up the hill. Patton remained there and fought off the Chinese until he died; he was found in a hole the next day and, like Svitck, awarded a posthumous Silver Star.

However, not all of the Silver Stars were posthumous. Private First Class Harry L. Nace survived. When he reached the command post after the rest of G Company had withdrawn from its primary battle position, he discovered they had left two working .30-caliber machine guns on the hill and volunteered to retrieve them. Braving a deadly grazing fire, he crossed four hundred meters of open ground four times to bring back the two guns and all of their ammunition. During one of the trips, he was wounded when a rifle round hit him, but the wound did not prevent him from completing his mission. He saved the two weapons and prevented the Chinese from using them against their owners.

Private First Class William D. Gilleland was a platoon runner for G Company. At one point in the fighting, shrapnel from enemy mortar rounds cut one of the wires from the command post to his platoon. The young soldier from Iowa dashed out into the open and traced the wire to the break. When he found it, he immediately repaired it, even though mortar rounds were exploding everywhere around him. He then returned to his platoon. Shortly thereafter, he treated a wounded comrade and evacuated him off the front line, crossing the deadly open area between it and the aid station. Later, he carried .30-caliber ammunition across the same open space so that his platoon machine gun could keep firing.

Private First Class Pete Lucas Jr. was the gunner for one of G Company's 60mm mortars. When the line collapsed, he remained at his post and kept hanging rounds as the remnants of G Company streamed past him. When he felt a sting in his arm, he knew an unseen enemy soldier had shot him, but the fresh wound only slowed him down; it did not stop him. He continued to shoot his mortar until everyone had withdrawn from Curtis and McGee Hills.

Corporal Joe E. Halbrook was the section leader for one of G Company's 57mm recoilless rifle teams. He led his unit of Filipino-Americans and one Korean on a mission to neutralize some of the enemy mortars firing from the cemetery near the village of Masan. Braving the incoming rounds, he took one of the recoilless rifles and moved to a better firing position on Finn Hill in 2nd Platoon's sector. As he crept across the battlefield, he was under constant enemy fire. Despite the zipping tracers, he survived and loaded his weapon, firing it at one of the enemy mortar teams. His recoilless rifle shell shot through the air at a speed of 365 meters per second and detonated on contact, silencing it. "You'd see a fire from a mortar, and I'd fire at it," said Halbrook in a postwar interview. "I fired a lot of rounds. I don't know how many."

When the G Company line buckled, Halbrook refused to leave. He ordered his men to withdraw, but remained at his position to provide cover for them. With only hand grenades, his recoilless rifle, and his carbine, he held off the enemy until his men escaped. A few moments after the men withdrew, one of the attacking Chinese soldiers shot him, and the corporal realized it was time to go. He destroyed the recoilless rifle with a thermite grenade and left. Against the odds, Halbrook survived and later returned to duty.

Not all of the heroes were in G Company. Private First Class Leslie E. Alston was a jeep driver and part of the forward observer team for B Battery, 503rd Field Artillery Battalion. When the Chinese broke through the main line, Alston dashed through enemy fire to help replace inoperable machine guns while resupplying other soldiers with ammunition. He rescued several wounded comrades while under fire and carried them back to the battalion aid station.

Nace, Gilleland, Lucas, Halbrook, and Alston all received the Silver Star for their gallantry that night.

Sadly, the survivors never found Corporal Ottesen's remains. The Army initially listed him as missing in action, but later the adjutant changed his status to died-while-missing. His bravery, though, was not in doubt. The Army awarded him a Silver Star in absentia shortly after the battle. Kluttz and McGee also earned the Silver Star for their daring and courageous leadership of 3rd Platoon. Alas, McGee's fighting was far from finished.

FEBRUARY 15, 0020–0225 HOURS:
ALONG THE LINE, I COMPANY,
23RD INFANTRY REGIMENT, CHIPYONG-NI

Unbeknownst to Lieutenant McGee and the rest of G Company, the Chinese were attacking the UN perimeter at multiple locations simultaneously so that no one could reinforce the beleaguered soldiers of G Company. At 0020 hours, the communists struck K and I Companies.

Earl Becker was a recoilless rifleman in Item Company. "They'd come in big bunches," Becker said in a postwar interview, remembering the Chinese attacks at Chipyong-ni. "The first bunch had weapons, and if you killed them, then the second bunch would pick up their weapons. It was something else."

Item Company, like everyone else, was short on rifle bullets, mortar rounds, and hand grenades. George Collingsworth, a jeep driver, had spent much of the night carrying crates of small-arms ammunition from his trailer to the front line. "We had very little ammunition left," he said. "And if they ever knew that we didn't have the ammunition that [they thought] we had, [then] they would've just come in and slaughtered us because we would have never fought our way out after that."

By 0225 hours, the Chinese had captured several foxholes in the Item Company sector, and 3rd Battalion reported to the regiment that it was shifting two squads from King Company to plug the hole.

Attached to I Company were several heavy machine guns from M Company. These machine-gun teams were high-value targets for the Chinese sappers, and thus were the focus of several assaults. Sergeant First Class William S. Sitman was the team leader for one of the machine-gun sections. Born in 1923 and hailing from Altoona, Pennsylvania, like many NCOs he was a veteran of World War II. He had served in northwest Europe, where he had earned a Bronze Star for extinguishing a fire on an ammunition trailer. That morning, his machine-gun team overlooked a draw that was a likely avenue of approach for any would-be attacker. As a result, his gun crew was busy, slaughtering wave after wave of Chinese soldiers.

As the Chinese closed in, they began to lob hand grenades at Sitman's gun team. At one point, one knocked out his machine gun. With Sitman's gun out of action, the Chinese had an infiltration route into the northeast section of the 23rd Infantry's perimeter. In response, the I Company commander ordered Corporal John G. Larkin to replace Sitman's weapon with his own light machine gun.

After Larkin arrived, he set up his M1919 and resumed firing at the communist attackers. According to the corporal "the sergeant [Sitman] and his crew remained in the emplacement to give us security as there were several defilade approaches leading in."

With Larkin's machine gun chugging away, the Chinese threw themselves again at the position. Suddenly, Sitman shouted, "There's a grenade in our hole!" Without a second thought, the sergeant threw himself on top of the grenade and absorbed the subsequent blast. It killed him instantly, but the five other men in the foxhole lived. "Sergeant Sitman's heroic action, I feel sure, saved the lives of the other comrades in the emplacement and enabled us to deliver machine-gun fire from our position throughout the attack," Larkin said later.

Herb Drees was one of the soldiers who survived thanks to Sitman's actions. He recalled the incident, decades after the war. "When that grenade came in, there was a hell of an explosion. Sitman caught the blast, the whole darn thing in his groin area." Drees lifted Sitman out and called for help. When the medic arrived, he took one look at Sitman and said, "He's gone."

For his selfless act, the Army awarded Sitman the Medal of Honor. Thanks to him, the Chinese were unable to breach the I Company lines. Unfortunately, the communists had better luck along the southern edge of the perimeter.

FEBRUARY 15, 0315–0550 HOURS: COMMAND POST, G COMPANY, 23RD INFANTRY REGIMENT, RAMSBURG BOWL

The news of G Company's collapse was a thunderclap for the commander and staff of 2nd Battalion. At first, Colonel Edwards thought the soldiers of G Company had "panicked." In response, he alerted the regiment at 0315 hours and requested reinforcements. Meanwhile, his staff scrounged together elements from F Company's support platoon to seal the breach. Within two minutes of Edwards's request, Colonel Freeman authorized the commitment of one Ranger platoon to augment Edwards's reserves. With the additional combat power, Edwards ordered Second Lieutenant Robert W. Curtis, an Assistant S3 officer, to assume command of the composite force and recapture the old G Company positions.

Though he was a staff officer, Curtis was no slouch. He had earned a battlefield commission earlier in the war, and Edwards had wanted him to take a break from the line to receive additional training to help him become a better lieutenant. Now, with a new task and purpose from the battalion commander, the new lieutenant left for the G Company command post to meet up with the Ranger platoon.

Curtis remembered that night, writing, "As I walked down the road, I could hear enemy and friendly fire from all sides of the RCT perimeter and could see tracers crisscrossing the night sky. Frequently the whole area was eerily illuminated by enemy or friendly flares. I could hear the platoon of rangers coming up the road long before I could see them, and I could tell that they were extremely perturbed about something."

He was correct. The Ranger officers and men complained they were not the right force for the job because they did not have the best mix of weapons and men to hold a position after seizing it. First Lieutenant Alfred Herman, the Ranger company commander who had accompanied his platoon, thought defense was a job for regular infantry soldiers. According to Curtis, Herman was not complaining about the assault mission, but instead arguing against using his Rangers as part of a follow-on defensive operation.

The debate between Curtis and Herman continued until they reached the G Company command post. "On arriving at the CP," wrote Curtis, "I found the situation was desperate. There had been extremely high casualties. . . . Many of the key leaders were wounded and there was much confusion in the area. Lieutenant Heath was trying to complete a company reorganization and preparation for a counterattack."

According to Curtis, the last five hours of combat had reduced Heath's company to the size of a platoon. In addition to the remnants of George Company, Second Lieutenant Charles F. Heady had brought his 3rd Platoon from Fox Company to Heath's command post. However, his platoon was already down a squad, since it had given up its 2nd Squad earlier that morning to reinforce McGee's 3rd Platoon. Only the Ranger platoon was intact. In total, the composite force was three units from three different companies. After several minutes of discussion, the group decided that Curtis would assume command of the counterattack force since it was an ad hoc unit.

In addition to the platoons, Curtis had three George Company 60mm mortars, two tanks, and three of Heath's light machine guns at his disposal. (G Company's 2nd Platoon had pulled back but was still manning a sector on the main line.) Then, the Ranger platoon leader, Second Lieutenant Mayo Heath (no relation to the G Company commander), discovered that he had a date of rank that made him senior to Curtis. The Ranger company commander found that the rank issue made it impossible for him or his platoon leader to take orders from a junior officer. Lieutenant Herman declared that he would not move until he received a direct order from Colonel Freeman, because his company was the regimental reserve and not 2nd Battalion's reserve.

Realizing that no one had the authority to force Lieutenant Herman to move, Curtis called Colonel Edwards and informed him of the problem. The staff officer recalled the conversation in his postwar account: "I informed him [Herman] that since he was the senior commander on the ground he was welcome to take charge of all the forces in the area and lead the attack and that George Company and the platoon from Fox Company would follow his commands. I told him that I could put him in touch with Colonel Freeman, but all it would get him was an ass chewing for delaying attack."

When Edwards learned of the delay, he was furious. He ordered his battalion S2, Captain John H. Ramsburg, to "straighten out" the Ranger platoon leader, telling the captain, "Well, John, I guess you better go up and take command of that company and get that hill back."

Ramsburg left for G Company. Outside of the G Company command post, he ran into Lieutenant Curtis, whom he had known since August. The exasperated lieutenant said to him, "Christ, John, am I ever glad to see you. I can't do a damn thing with the Ranger company commander." It was now 0330 hours.

For the next ninety minutes, Ramsburg collected the disparate groups and organized them for a counterattack. According to Ramsburg, when he walked over to the shallow hill where the soldiers had gathered, he "found all the men mixed up, [and] decided they had to be sorted out and put into their own units."

First, Ramsburg sent Lieutenant McGee to find the G Company 60mm mortar teams. Then he sent Lieutenant Curtis to coordinate with Master Sergeant Andrew Reyna, who commanded the nearby section of tanks, and the three light machine-gun teams. He also told Curtis to scrounge up three radios so that the platoons could talk to each other and to him.

After several minutes, McGee returned with the mortar section. Captain Ramsburg directed the mortar crews to drop one round on the ridgeline so that he could adjust fire on the objective. In response, the crew plopped a mortar round in one of their tubes and then watched it detonate on the crest.

"That where you want them?" the section leader asked Ramsburg.

Ramsburg nodded. "That's exactly right," he said. "Now go ahead and sweep the crest of the hill in both directions. I want a five-minute concentration on that hill."

The section leader informed the captain that they were short on 60mm ammunition. Ramsburg responded, "Then fire all you have."

After several minutes, Curtis returned with three SCR-536 radios. Ramsburg allocated one to the Rangers, one to the F Company platoon, and one to himself. To coordinate with his battalion and regiment, Ramsburg then grabbed Harley Wilburn and his radio operator, Paul Fry, who was humping a SCR-300 radio. With command and control established, the S2 went over his plan one more time.

Ramsburg's scheme of maneuver was straightforward: The mortars would suppress the enemy on the hills, and as the teams expended their last rounds, the two platoons would advance. Heady's platoon, with twenty-eight men, would seize Curtis Hill in the east, while Heath's Ranger platoon, which had thirty-six men, would clear McGee Hill in the west. As the soldiers approached the objectives, the three light machine-gun teams would continue to suppress the enemy by firing over the heads of the two platoons. For additional combat power, Ramsburg had Lieutenant McGee and the last three soldiers from G Company's 3rd Platoon to augment Heady's platoon. According to Ramsburg, he wanted the tank crews to hold their fire because of the potential for fratricide (he did not have direct communication with the tanks, nor were they collocated with him).

At 0515 hours, the counterattack began. As planned, the mortars started thumping, and after several minutes Ramsburg ordered the three machine-gun teams to open fire on the ridge. This precipitated a response from the Chinese, who retaliated with their own mortars. Roughly a dozen shells exploded around the soldiers gathering in the assault position. Among the wounded were Lieutenant Heady, the F Company platoon leader, and five other men.

The Chinese barrage resulted in a brief period of bedlam. Lieutenant Herman thought the incoming projectiles were short rounds from G Company's 60mm mortars, and he began to yell at the mortar teams. Ramsburg knew they were from the Chinese and ordered Herman to secure the wounded and return with them to the battalion aid station. Disgusted with the operation, the Ranger commander left the area. With Herman finally gone, Ramsburg restarted the counterattack.

Several minutes after the argument, the mortar section informed the battalion S2 that they had three rounds left. It was the signal. Ramsburg shouted, "Okay, let's go, let's go!" He repeated the phrase on his radio.

Ramsburg described what happened next in an interview conducted several months after the battle. "On the order to move out, the men stood up and walked forward, firing toward the hill during [that] time. The snow through the gulley was knee deep in places, only six or eight inches deep on the side of the hill. The snow had a crust on it. The Rangers were doing a lot of yelling on the way up." Ramsburg marched up the ridge behind the two platoons.

Meanwhile, 3rd Platoon from F Company was climbing up Curtis Hill. According to Lieutenant Curtis, the Rangers were moving faster than the soldiers from F Company. He estimated that the Rangers would reach the top several minutes before the others. Ominously, the Chinese defenders had held their fire. Curtis walked over to speak with Ramsburg about the situation. When he reached him, "all hell broke loose along the entire attack line."

Leading the soldiers from F Company was Sergeant Cuillaula B. Martinez from Texas. When the machine guns and mortars blasted away at the advancing soldiers, the men from F Company sought cover wherever they could find it. As a result, the enemy pinned them down in the open. Martinez realized it would only be a matter of time before the incoming mortars would cause casualties. He stood up and charged ahead. Almost immediately, a shell fragment nicked him in the face. Undaunted, he kept running toward the crest of Curtis Hill. His courageous example inspired the men around him, who jumped up and joined him in the charge. Within minutes, they were almost to the top of Curtis Hill. But as he neared the top, Martinez suffered another wound and fell to the ground.

McGee was also scrambling up the ridge with Heady's platoon from Fox Company when the Chinese opened fire. Almost immediately, men started falling. On the eastern flank, it was even worse. The initial fusillade killed Lieutenant Heath, the Ranger platoon leader.

McGee later explained why the Chinese fire was so devastating:

> *One of the problems with the support fire that we did have was that the Chinese were on the reverse slope mostly. And our fire did not affect them because it was going over the ridge and beyond them; if the Chinese had been on the forward slope, there would have been more hits, more damage. As the rangers approached the crest of the hill, the Chinese would come up out of their holes and use their small-arms fire.*

"I could hear the Rangers shouting that they had taken their objective and needed litter bearers, medics, and more ammunition," Curtis later recalled. "Shortly after, the Rangers hollered that they needed help or they couldn't hold any longer."

Then, disaster struck. From the east, a single light machine gun left off a long burst of green tracers. Afterward, the gun ripped off several more short and steady bursts. Ramsburg thought the fire originated in the French sector, but according to Curtis, the source of the fire was forward of the French lines. Either way, the enfilade fire caused several more Ranger casualties.

When the tankers saw the tracers, they, too, thought it was a French machine gun, and blasted away with their own machine guns at the same target, which, unfortunately, were the Rangers on McGee Hill. Simultaneously, a Chinese machine-gun team that had occupied the former G Company positions on Finn Hill let loose on 3rd Platoon, F Company. The interlocking fire from all of the belt-fed weapons resulted in horrendous casualties for the Rangers and F Company. Among the fallen were the Ranger company's first sergeant and several other Ranger NCOs.

Ramsburg was livid. As Curtis recalled, "Captain Ramsburg hollered at me to go back and stop the damn tanks from firing into the Rangers. I ran back to the tanks as fast as I could, ordered them to cease firing and told them that we had taken the hill back and not to fire again unless given an order to fire."

Meanwhile, the Chinese continued to fight back. An unknown enemy soldier lobbed a grenade at Ramsburg. It exploded, spraying shrapnel and hitting him in the foot. The S2 never saw the grenade, and the blast stunned him. Initially, he thought he had shot himself in the foot with his submachine gun. Despite the agonizing pain, all he could think about was how he was going to explain his embarrassing injury to Colonel Edwards, the battalion commander.

As the S2 massaged his foot, Lieutenant Heath emerged from the darkness. "What happened to you?" he asked Ramsburg.

The ashamed captain explained his wound, but assured Heath that his condition was not serious. He told Heath that the Rangers needed reinforcements. Hearing this news, the G Company commander grabbed Ramsburg's SCR-536 radio, strapped it over his shoulder, and headed up the hill to assume control of the forces atop the ridge.

Unfortunately, Heath's attempt to regain control of the situation was short-lived. When he reached the crest of the ridge, Chinese soldiers saw him and opened fire. The G Company commander tried to reach for his carbine, but to his horror he had slung the radio over his weapon and could not disentangle his gun in time to shoot back at the enemy. Within seconds, the CPVF soldiers drew a bead on Heath and shot him in the chest. Before anyone could shoot back at them, they vanished in the swirling snow and darkness.

Moments later, a wounded US soldier found Heath lying on the ground. The unidentified soldier had only one working arm, his other hanging lifeless with only strips of flesh keeping it from falling off. He grabbed Heath's leg with his good arm and began to drag him down the hill. Midway, he met Captain Ramsburg limping up the slope.

"Where you going?" asked the S2 sternly. He then saw the soldier's arm and realized the GI was not deserting the battlefield. Next, he saw the wounded man on the ground and inquired, "Who's that you're dragging behind?"

The soldier answered that it was Lieutenant Heath. Ramsburg told him to head down the hill to the battalion aid station. Meanwhile, the S2 continued to stagger up the ridge. Moments later, he intercepted a small group of three or four Rangers. At first, he thought they were Chinese, hitting the deck and yelling, "Who are you?"

They replied they were the last Rangers on the hill. Even worse, they were withdrawing. They told the S2 that the Chinese were swarming everywhere along the ridge.

"What about F Company?" asked Ramsburg. They informed him they had not seen anyone from Fox Company on the ridge. Crestfallen, the S2 knew the counterattack had failed, and he returned with the Rangers to the G Company command post. On the way down, he met Lieutenant Curtis heading in the opposite direction and told him, "Get as many men as you can possibly gather up and get them on this hump to hold off the Chinese if they come over the hill."

Wilburn was still with Ramsburg and recalled a radio conversation between the S2 and Colonel Freeman. "He changed the channel on it to the headquarters [channel] to Colonel Freeman," said Wilburn. "And I heard him tell Colonel Freeman that we were in danger of not being able to get that hill back . . . and Colonel Freeman said 'don't fall back any further because if they get into this perimeter we're all going to be in trouble.'"

Meanwhile, Lieutenant Curtis kept climbing. "I continued on up the hill," he wrote. "And [I] encountered only wounded men coming down, assisting more seriously wounded soldiers. As I continued to the top I suddenly realized that the shouting in the Ranger area no longer came from on top of the hill but from the bottom of the hill near where I could just make out the silhouettes of the 155 howitzers. Also, little firing was occurring along the entire hill mass and I could hear only Chinese commands and I realized that I might be the only American left in the objective area."

Shortly after Ramsburg and Wilburn spoke with Curtis, Wilburn left the stricken S2 and continued up the slope to occupy his former foxhole on McGee Hill. He later recalled, "I jumped in on my foxhole, and when I jumped in, my feet went down like I had jumped on a mattress or something."

The forward observer asked himself, "What the hell is this here?" He felt around the base of his hole and discovered a field jacket. "I pulled on that cloth," he said. "And it was an arm of a redheaded kid that was with the Rangers [who] had been killed there. And the Chinese just threw dirt on him and stood on top of him and kept shooting."

After several minutes of waiting, Wilburn realized he was alone. No one else was coming to occupy the former G Company positions with him. Despite the bravery of the Rangers, the composite force had failed to recapture the hill. After hearing the word to pull back, Wilburn climbed out of his hole and returned to the G Company command post.

On the eastern side of McGee Hill, the survivors from F Company were falling back as well. Private First Class Clell E. Van Dorin volunteered to remain behind to provide covering fire so that his comrades could escape. With only his Garand, he held off the Chinese until his friends were safe and then returned to the G Company command post, wounded but alive.

After the platoon from Fox Company withdrew from the ridge, Sergeant First Class Clifford Logan found himself in a defilade position. From it, he saw a wounded soldier still on McGee Hill. Without a second thought, Logan raced back up the crest to evacuate him. Zigzagging through enemy tracers, Logan reached the injured soldier and pulled him off the hill. The sergeant from North Carolina made this hazardous trip several times until all of the wounded were off the ridge. For their bravery, the Army awarded both Van Dorin and Logan the Silver Star.

During the counterattack, the seemingly invulnerable Sergeant Kluttz had suffered a gunshot wound to the stomach, but fortunately survived. As a result, Paul McGee was the only leader from 3rd Platoon still in the fight; all the others were either dead or wounded. McGee later remarked matter-of-factly, "We were in a really bad situation."

West of McGee's position was Sergeant Reyna's tank section. There, the situation also was bleak. Colonel Freeman had originally positioned the tanks to block the road that served as the boundary between G Company and the French Battalion. Sergeant First Class Kenneth Paul Pitlick was a tank commander in the other M4. He recalled what happened that night after the Chinese captured the two hills, explaining how he was standing inside his turret when an unidentified sergeant ran past him and said, "They are breaking through on us! You've got to do—"

Pitlick interrupted the soldier, "I know it."

The tank commander climbed out of his tank and walked across the road. He found some soldiers huddled in the ditch that lined the road and saw another US soldier standing near them. At the time, he did not know that the unidentified soldier was a captain. Pitlick yelled at the officer, "You better get these men turned around. We are going to get wiped out."

"Yes, sir," the soldier said, adding, "I got [a] concussion."

Pitlick barked, "I don't care. Get them turned around and start—"

Before the tank commander could finish his sentence, he noticed an M16 half-track in the dark that had rolled on its side. "Look at that quad 50 laying there," said Pitlick. "It's turned over. Somebody has got to get that thing to work. You can hold off a battalion with that thing."

The captain and Pitlick bolted in two different directions to find a crew to help them rescue the stranded vehicle. When the sergeant returned to his tank, he told his crew, "There's nowhere to go. We're surrounded completely." He recalled, "I told them to pull back and I kept on firing until they got organized, you know, and then we pulled up and started opening up again."

Soon after the failed counterattack, Reyna's platoon leader, First Lieutenant Arthur J. Junot, arrived in his tank. Pitlick told his officer about the battle. It was still dark; however, there was enough light for Junot to scan the ridgeline in front of him. After doing so, he realized that nothing was between them and the enemy on the crest. Unbeknownst to the Chinese, the southern sector was wide open. The time was now 0550 hours.

FEBRUARY 15, 0605 HOURS: COMMAND POST, 2ND BATTALION

The failed counterattack stunned Colonel Edwards. Reports from the survivors indicated that a Chinese regiment occupied the old G Company positions. With this new information in hand, Edwards realized he needed more combat power if he wanted to throw the communists off the southern ridge. He informed Colonel Freeman of the situation, but the regimental commander had other problems beyond G Company. According to Freeman, 1st Battalion also was under attack, and, more important, his unit was running low on 81mm and 4.2-inch mortar ammunition. He could only allocate the rest of the Ranger company to 2nd Battalion.

Edwards acknowledged the order and began to gather his remaining forces for the next operation.

At 0605 hours, he contacted Captain Ramsburg, who was still at the George Company command post, telling him to prepare for the arrival of the rest of the Rangers. After he put down the phone, the battalion commander briefed his command post that he intended to organize and lead the next counterattack. Meanwhile, Lieutenant Curtis and the remnants from the composite force readied themselves for the next assault.

FEBRUARY 15, 0600–0645 HOURS: G COMPANY COMMAND POST

Lieutenant Curtis wondered where everyone had gone. "As I reached the CP area all firing had stopped and the whole area fell silent except for Chinese digging on the reverse slope of the hill, evidently improving the old George Company positions," he later wrote.

Inside the command post, the injured Captain Ramsburg argued with Lieutenant Herman, the Ranger company commander. According to Curtis, Herman felt the ground was not suitable for a defense. After much wrangling, an exasperated Ramsburg told the Ranger commander to leave and take his men with him.

When Ramsburg saw Curtis, he ordered him to find whomever he could and establish a new defensive line along the slight rise that ran in front of the G Company command post. Curtis left and searched the immediate area, finding a squad from F Company and several survivors from G Company. He also rounded up clerks and other support soldiers to add to the defense. All told, he counted twenty-five men on the line, including those who were slightly injured.

He realized that twenty-five men were not enough to stop a determined Chinese assault and asked Ramsburg for permission to grab a radio and head back up the hill to see if any survivors were still there. The S2 approved his request. Curtis left for the former G Company positions. As he approached the hill, Curtis ran into several artillerymen from the 503rd Field Artillery, whose howitzers were still in position. Amazed to see American soldiers in the area, Curtis asked if they intended to remain in position. The artillery officers assured him they were not going to abandon the howitzers.

Pleased that he had found more combat power, Curtis continued his search. He combed the base of the hill and found no survivors from G Company, nor from the earlier counterattack. After several minutes, he returned to the George Company command post. When he arrived, he heard a Chinese bugler. Seconds later, several enemy soldiers appeared on the crest of the hill. In response, the Americans opened fire, and the enemy disappeared.

After seeing the Chinese, Curtis and Ramsburg realized the wounded soldiers huddled around the G Company command post were sitting ducks. Curtis told Ramsburg to herd them back toward the battalion aid station. The S2 agreed and shouted, "Come on everyone, we are going back to establish a new defensive position."

Unfortunately, the radio operators and staff clerks thought Ramsburg's words were meant for them. They left with the wounded. Curtis tried to stop them, but they vanished in the darkness before he could reach them. The premature exodus meant Curtis now only had fifteen men in front of the G Company command post. Despite the miscommunication, he still had the one abandoned M16 half-track and the artillerymen from the 503rd. He reported his situation to Colonel Edwards and asked for reinforcements. The battalion commander replied that help was on the way.

"I found the squad leader from Fox Company," Curtis wrote, "and asked him to move all of the infantrymen left in the area into the far side of the road ditch and to extend the men south down the road toward the tanks as far as they could go and that the artillerymen would tie in with them and they would extend toward the Chinese. . . . He [the squad leader] asked me that if we were not going to make it that he would like to go back to Fox Company and go down with them. I promised him that he could go back to Fox Company as soon as we got help."

Curtis walked over to the gun line to coordinate with the cannon cockers of the 503rd Field Artillery. There, he met the battery commander and asked him, "Why don't you turn the 155s around and put some fire on that hill?" Curtis later revealed that his suggestion was in jest—he didn't think they could do it.

To Curtis's surprise, the battery commander replied, "Sure, we can do that."

Within several minutes, a crew had turned around one of the howitzers. A soldier pulled the lanyard, and the big gun boomed. They fired it six times, shooting white phosphorous rounds at the Chinese defenders. Curtis later wrote, "From where I was standing I knew that the rounds scared the hell out of the Chinese as they burst very close to their positions."

Not be outdone, one of Lieutenant Junot's tanks let loose with its main gun. "The rounds hit the frozen, icy road and reverberated down the valley," wrote Curtis. "The echo off the surrounding hills made a terrifying sound. I thought the Chinese would think that we had brought up a new type [of] weapon. After this demonstration of firepower the night grew silent."

FEBRUARY 15, 0645–0800 HOURS: BETWEEN FRENCH 1ST COMPANY AND G COMPANY

After Lieutenant Junot heard the howitzers from the 503rd Field Artillery thunder across the valley, a group of ten French soldiers approached his platoon of tanks and asked the tankers for grenades. The French allies had seen the failed counterattack, and this tiny group had decided to retake the hill themselves. It was also a matter of survival for the French: If they allowed the Chinese to occupy Schmitt Hill, the enemy would have enfilade fire on the entire French line. Wanting to help, Junot gave them some grenades. Captain Elledge, the artillery liaison officer, joined the group, armed with a BAR.

The small group climbed up Schmitt Hill. When they were within twenty meters of the crest, the Chinese retaliated. According to Junot, it was a "grenade fight." He ordered his tank driver to move his vehicle closer to the road so that they could engage targets on the back side of the hill. Repositioned, Junot engaged the enemy with all of his machine guns. Unfortunately, the Chinese were too far up the ridge, and Junot could not elevate his main 76mm cannon high enough to engage or hit them.

The Chinese emplaced a machine-gun team inside a culvert, opening fire on the attacking French. The culvert provided defilade for the gun team; therefore, Junot could not suppress it with his own guns. As a result, Elledge and the French had to withdraw back down the hill. The tank platoon leader later estimated they had killed about fourteen or fifteen enemy in total. It was now 0800 hours.

Sometime that morning, one of Junot's tanks had towed the M16 half-track out of the ditch. When Captain Elledge saw it, he decided to shoot the quad .50-caliber machine guns at the hill. The half-track was inoperable, but the onboard weapons system worked. According to Curtis, Elledge asked Ramsburg before he left whether he could expend all the ammunition on the half-track. Ramsburg approved Elledge's request, so Elledge climbed on board the damaged vehicle and opened fire with all four guns. The artillery officer wanted to use up all the ammunition and melt the barrels so the enemy could not capture it and use it against the UN forces.

At the time, Curtis did not know Elledge's plan; in fact, the M16 half-track was an essential part of Curtis's own overall defensive scheme. When he saw Elledge open fire, he was furious. "My first thought was to shoot the son of a bitch off the weapon," Curtis later wrote. "I jumped on the closest tank and laid the machine gun on the quad 50 intending to scare the gunner off the weapon."

However, he realized it was too late. "I saw that by firing the quad 50 [on] full automatic the barrels were red hot and were being burned out. They were glowing red in the darkness and seemed to be bending down."

Together with another soldier, Curtis ran over to the M16 after Elledge abandoned it. He discovered that the barrels on the quad .50-caliber machine guns had indeed melted. "When I found out the condition of the weapon I was mad as hell, as I had just lost the most important weapon we had to use against a massed Chinese attack," he later wrote. Fortunately, for Curtis and the other survivors, help was finally on the way.

February 15, 0803–0945 Hours:
Temporary 2nd Battalion Command Post

At 0803 hours, the Ranger company command post reported to regiment that it did not have the necessary combat power to execute a successful counterattack. Nine minutes later, Colonel Freeman committed Baker Company to retake the G Company positions and also designated his engineer company as an ad hoc reserve. At 0817 hours, the forward air controllers alerted 2nd Battalion that the next air strike would hit the G Company positions on McGee and Curtis Hills.

Colonel Edwards learned about the change in plan moments before leaving his permanent headquarters to assume command at a temporary command post atop Heath Ridge. Once he arrived at the new post, he consulted with First Lieutenant Carl F. Haberman, the mortar platoon leader, who assumed control of G Company after Lieutenant Heath's injury. Haberman listed what was left of his command. McGee had survived. Moreover, 2nd Platoon, which had assumed a new defensive position, was intact. However, other than the mortars, 2nd Platoon, and a handful of survivors, nothing else was left of G Company.

According to Colonel Edwards, the B Company commander, Captain Sherman W. Pratt, arrived at the makeshift forward command post to receive his instructions around 0945 hours. Edwards informed Pratt that he had attached several units to his company, including the remaining Ranger platoons, the tank platoon, and the recently arrived section of two M16 half-tracks. In addition, Pratt would have direct support from G Company's 60mm mortars, H Company's 81mm mortars, the remnants of G Company (including 2nd Platoon), and the forward observers for the artillery and mortars. He would have a ten-minute bombardment prior to the assault.

Edwards described the old G Company positions. "George Company's positions are just up there to the left and right of those points," the colonel said, pointing to McGee and Schmitt Hills. Seconds later, a mortar round exploded nearby, and an unseen man shrieked. Unflappable, Edwards continued his brief.

"Are there any of your men still in position atop the hill?" Pratt asked.

"No, there are only enemy troops there," replied Edwards.

Not convinced, Pratt countered, "I saw some bodies moving, I thought, a few moments ago."

"If you did, it has to be Chinks," said the colonel.

"And if we reach the top, there are emplacements in existence that we can drop into?" inquired Pratt.

According to the B Company commander, Edwards told him, "Piece of cake, Pratt. We had great positions up there. All your men have to do is ease back up the slope, rush quickly over the crest, and drop into our well prepared and protected positions."

Satisfied with his instructions, the battalion commander said farewell to Pratt, who left to conduct his own troop-leading procedures with his company. Edwards later wrote that he had "erred in issuing his order to the Commanding Officer of Company B. He [Edwards] should have issued definite detailed orders to the Company B Commander and should not have assumed that he was as expert as the 2nd Battalion rifle company commanders."

Like many Korean War officers, Pratt was a veteran of World War II. He had served in Europe and earned a Silver Star while fighting on the Rhine River in early 1945. Now he was a company commander whose job was to retake a hill.

According to Pratt, he had seen the G Company positions several days earlier. Since he was the reserve, Freeman had wanted him to check out all of the company battle positions in the regiment's perimeter so that he would know the ground in case he had to fight on it. He recalled that the G Company foxholes were not very deep because G Company did not have same the amount of preparation; it had to move because of the 155mm howitzer battery's arriving several days after everyone else had showed up at Chipyong-ni.

"I studied Edwards for a moment or so and glanced at my officers. We were reading each other's mind," Pratt later wrote. "We had been in these positions only a couple of days earlier before the big attack, and had found the positions wanting in many respects, as we had pointed out to the regimental S-3. I looked at Edwards again and tried to imagine what he was thinking."

The Baker Company commander reflected, "I realized that the 2nd Battalion's positions might have been improved since we last saw them, but I had the feeling that Edwards was being far from candid. I was tempted to ask him if the mission was such a piece of cake then why in hell didn't his own battalion reoccupy their own positions."

However, orders were orders. With his new task and purpose, Pratt conducted his troop-leading procedures. With him were his two platoon leaders, Second Lieutenant Maurice Fenderson of 1st Platoon and Lieutenant Richard S. Kotite of 3rd Platoon. Pratt did not have an officer in charge of 2nd Platoon because of the loss of its leader several days prior to Chipyong-ni, but he had picked up two replacement officers from headquarters: Second Lieutenant Herschel "Hawk" Chapman, a West Pointer, and Second Lieutenant Raymond Dupree.

"If the retaking of his positions was such a snap, Captain, why had the earlier counterattack under his command not succeeded?" Chapman asked Pratt. "Or why did he not make another effort?"

Pratt looked back at the new lieutenant and replied, "Hawk, my boy, you couldn't have said my thoughts more clearly."

Suddenly, machine-gun fire ripped through the area. One bullet slammed into the stock of Pratt's carbine, shattering it. Instinctively, the men hunkered down. Seconds later, the B Company commander heard Chapman groan.

"Are you hit, Chapman?" asked Pratt.

Chapman grimaced and said, "I think so, Captain."

"Where?" inquired the B Company commander.

The new lieutenant shrugged his shoulder and said, "My arm stings."

Pratt then noticed the rivulet of blood dripping down from Chapman's hand. "Are you dizzy, lad? Are you about to pass out?" he asked him.

"Not really," said Chapman.

The company commander leaned over and said, "Here, let me take a look at you." Even though he was not a medic, Pratt quickly surmised that the wound was superficial. Still, Chapman was injured.

"Make your way back and out of here when you can, Hawk," ordered Pratt. "Looks like you have the million-dollar wound—not serious but good enough to get you off the front lines."

Hawk shook his head. "No way, Captain," he declared. "I'm staying. If I withdraw with this slight wound I will be the laughing stock of my graduation class at the Academy. I would never live it down. Just give me an assignment and let's get on with it."

Impressed with the lieutenant's toughness, Pratt relented. "Okay fellow," the captain began. "If you feel that way, are you up to taking over the [2nd] platoon at this time? As you know, we have the platoon sergeant in charge and I'm sure he could use some help. I was going to wait a few days for you to get your feet better planted, but we have a bit of an urgency now, I think."

"Damned right, Captain. Thought you would never ask," replied Chapman.

Pratt smiled. "Then up and away. The platoon is just behind us. Find the platoon sergeant and let him know you're now in charge. I think he will welcome your arrival. Get ready to be committed. I'm sure we are going to have to commit the reserve platoon but [I] don't yet know just where. I'm going to send Ray Dupree along to help you or take over in case you get hit."

Pratt knew the situation was far from ideal. In a postwar interview with Thomas M. Ryan, another Eighth Army historian, Pratt said, "I didn't trust Edwards as far as I could throw one of our medium General Sherman tanks. I had seen his positions earlier and formed my own conclusions as to their unsuitability, which had now been confirmed, in my judgment, by his forced withdrawal from them."

Unfortunately, it was too late to do anything about it. B Company had a rendezvous with the Chinese, who were waiting for them.

FEBRUARY 15, 0945–1130 HOURS: B COMPANY

Pratt's company was already assembling on Heath Ridge when he returned from his meeting with Colonel Edwards. Pratt wanted his most experienced officers leading the attack, so he grabbed Lieutenants Kotite and Fenderson. The three climbed over the spur that served as the boundary between the Ranger and B Company assembly areas.

From there, Pratt explained his plan. First, mortars and artillery would pound Schmitt and McGee Hills while Junot's tanks provided suppressive fire on Schmitt Hill from the road. Pratt's own 60mm mortars would also provide indirect fire support for both platoons.

Fenderson's mission was to clear and seize Schmitt Hill, while Kotite's objective was to do the same with McGee Hill. The two assaults were supposed to be mutually supporting.

Pratt concluded his orders by saying, "Fendy, you and Kotite charge out. The time has come to bite the bullet." Both platoon leaders returned to their platoons and quickly briefed their soldiers on the upcoming operation.

Shortly after 1000 hours, the artillery and mortars initiated their bombardment. During the barrage, both platoons moved to their assault positions. Fenderson followed Junot's tanks down the road. When he neared his objective, his platoon left the highway and pushed up Schmitt Hill.

Junot ordered his tanks to drive up the hill. Initially, the tankers had some success, but eventually, the tank platoon leader found the ridge was too slippery because of the snow. His tank lost traction, sliding down the slope like an out-of-control sled. Sergeant Pitlick's tank also experienced problems negotiating its way up the hill and remained at the base of a nearby draw. In response to the American armor presence, the Chinese shot at Junot's tanks with recoilless rifles.

It was a slog for the infantry. Despite the preparatory bombardment, the enemy soldiers were firing back at the two platoons. Even before Kotite's platoon could reach the base of McGee Hill, it came under heavy flanking fire from Schmitt Hill. Consequently, his men had to move forward in short rushes, slowing their advance. Instead of two platoons hitting their objectives simultaneously, Fenderson's unit reached its hill first at 1015 hours, while Kotite's platoon took more than forty minutes to reach the base of its objective. The attack appeared disjointed and piecemeal.

Around 1115 hours, Kotite's platoon began its ascent of McGee Hill. In a letter written several months after the battle, Kotite described the final phase of the assault:

When we were about two-thirds of the way up, mortar[s] started coming in. We hit the ground and then I gave the signal to assault so we continued up to about five yards from the top and threw grenades then charged over the crest. The Chinese were on the reverse slope in holes. They had three machine guns that I saw myself as well as other riflemen, and they opened up. We pulled back about five yards below the crest and laid in the snow.

Kotite's platoon sergeant reported that Fenderson's men had pulled out, which meant 3rd Platoon now had an unsecured flank. Kotite's only option was to withdraw and reorganize for another attack. He ordered his men to fall back. When he reached the bottom of the hill, he went to look for Captain Pratt for further orders. The latest attempt to retake the G Company positions had failed—again.

FEBRUARY 15, 1105 HOURS: HELICOPTER LANDING ZONE, WEST SIDE OF CHIPYONG-NI

As Pratt's men labored up the snowy slopes of Schmitt and Curtis Hills, Colonel Edwards had left his command post to say goodbye to the injured Colonel Freeman, who was leaving on a helicopter that had touched down at the makeshift landing area behind the French lines. By his own admission, Edwards was not at his command post for thirty crucial minutes.

At 1105, the helicopter blades were spinning for takeoff. Freeman asked Edwards about the status of Pratt's counterattack. Edwards later admitted that he lied to Freeman, telling him "the Chinese penetration had been eliminated."

As justification for the lie, Edwards later wrote: "If the Regimental Commander had known that the situation was still very critical, he never would have left and would probably have been court-martialed by the Corps Commander."

As ordered, but against his better judgment, Colonel Paul Freeman boarded the chopper and left behind his beloved regiment. Several weeks later, he wrote a letter to the soldiers of 23rd Infantry. In it, he explained why he departed: "It is with deep disappointment and sincere regret that during your recent crisis at CHIPYONG-NI I was ordered evacuated. While my wound was slight, the Corps Commander wished me evacuated for other reasons. Although I protested, I was finally ordered out." He continued: "I want to say to you that there is no grander fighting regiment in all-the-world than the 23rd RCT. Your determination, courage, and ability was demonstrated magnificently during the recent action at CHIPYONG. I hated leaving without seeing the fight through to its successful conclusion. . . . I salute each of you and wish that I could shake every hand of the men who have so valiantly served."

His soldiers felt the same way about him.

February 15, Noontime: B Company

As Colonel Freeman's helicopter lifted off and flew away, the survivors of Pratt's failed attack streamed back toward their original assault positions, with the Chinese mortaring the assembly areas. Dewey R. Andersen, a mortar man in B Company, was a raw recruit, having arrived only a few days before the battle. Now he was in the thick of combat. According to Andersen, within an hour of the initial assault the Chinese had neutralized his B Company 60mm mortar with their own heavy mortars. Andersen was huddled in a foxhole while the incoming shells intermittently exploded around him.

Andersen's platoon sergeant ordered him to climb out of his foxhole and join him on the top of Heath Ridge, twenty feet above the private's foxhole. "Initially, I was reluctant to leave my foxhole," Andersen later explained in a postwar letter, "but he [the platoon sergeant] was insistent and I finally decided that I had better follow his orders. Within a couple of minutes, a mortar shell landed on the corner of the foxhole that I had left. Unfortunately, a BAR man and his Korean assistant had jumped in my hole when I left."

Nearby, Sergeant Joe R. Marez continued to hang rounds over his 60mm mortar tube. The Chinese counterbattery fire had already severely injured his ammunition bearer and assistant gunner, leaving him alone. He ordered both men to evacuate, but continued to operate the weapon even though he, too, was wounded. For several minutes, Marez fired his mortar, despite the incoming fire. He survived, and for his bravery the Army later awarded him the Silver Star.

Meanwhile, Lieutenant Kotite had linked up with Captain Pratt at the bottom of McGee Hill. There, Kotite learned that the first attack had shredded Fenderson's platoon. Pratt decided to combine the survivors of

1st Platoon with Kotite's 3rd Platoon for another try. The platoon leader returned to his men and readied for another assault. After several minutes of constant bazooka fire from the Chinese, he rethought the action, withdrawing his platoon back toward Heath Ridge. He wanted to discuss a new plan with the B Company commander.

By this point, Pratt had realized that Schmitt Hill was the decisive terrain. "Just as I was about to rise and go to the waiting reserve platoon, another shower of mortar rounds landed all around us," he wrote later. "Several men were knocked down, and I felt shell fragments tearing through my right pant leg and my waist area. I swore in annoyance. When I felt liquid running down my leg, I concluded I had been hit. Finally my luck had ended."

Clearly, Pratt thought he was wounded. "But the liquid running down my leg was cold," he wrote. "I remember wondering why my blood would be so cold. . . . I glanced anxiously down at my leg. To my chagrin and relief, I saw that the fragment had only torn the bottom out of my canteen and its cover. The water inside had doused my leg and clothing. But two of the men in the company headquarters were not so lucky. They lay bleeding to death from those rounds."

Pratt ordered his reserve platoon (the 2nd), under the command of Second Lieutenant "Hawk" Chapman, to assault the hill, using the same route Fenderson had used earlier. When Kotite arrived at the commander's location with his 3rd Platoon, Pratt added its combat power to Chapman's ongoing attack. He instructed his 3rd Platoon leader to approach the objective using the same route as Chapman's platoon, but told Kotite he would have to wait until after a planned airstrike on Schmitt Hill. Elsewhere, the battle raged.

FEBRUARY 15, 1200–1228 HOURS: TEMPORARY 2ND BATTALION COMMAND POST

Colonel Edwards returned from the helicopter landing area and, upon his arrival at his temporary command post on Heath Ridge, learned of Pratt's failure. He was livid. The battalion commander sat down with his staff and discussed what had happened. The Chinese were on the reverse slopes of Schmitt and McGee Hills, therefore making it nearly impossible to suppress the Chinese defenders with any direct fire.

Edwards looked out from his location, his eyes drawn to the Chipyong-ni–Kanhyon highway that bisected the perimeter and served as the boundary between the French Battalion and his command. He wondered if he could send a platoon of tanks down the road and past Schmitt Hill. If the tanks made it, the M4s would be on the back side of Schmitt, McGee, and Curtis Hills. From there, they would have enfilade fire on all the Chinese defensive positions. The biggest obstacles to his plan were the mines his men had laid on the road several days before to prevent the Chinese forces from using it. Now, these mines blocked his soldiers and tanks.

Resolved to try, he ordered Captain Perry Sager, his S3, to cobble together a task force of tanks and soldiers from the Pioneer and Ammunition (P&A) Squad to execute his plan. It was simple: The tanks would provide cover for the soldiers of the P&A Squad, who would disarm and remove the mines from the road. Edwards labeled this command Task Force S. Shortly after 1200 hours, Sager's force moved out, and by 1228 hours they reported that they were conducting the route clearance operation.

FEBRUARY 15, 1207–1238 HOURS: HEADQUARTERS, CHIPYONG-NI
Lieutenant Colonel John H. Chiles was finally in command. However, other than monitoring the radio and coordinating air support, he had little to do. The fate of the regiment was out of his hands because his predecessor, Colonel Freeman, had committed all of the reserves. As of 1236 hours, the only designated reserve remaining was the regimental staff. Fortunately, help was on the way.

At 1207 hours, division reported that 5th Cavalry was nine thousand yards south of the perimeter. Seventeen minutes later, the aerial observer confirmed that the relief column was approaching the lines, but moving slowly. Could the regiment hold out until they arrived?

The regimental radio operator called them at 1238 hours and pleaded, "Reach us as soon as possible. In any event reach us."

Airdrops were delivering much-needed supplies while close air support pounded the surrounding hills. However, Chinese mortars disrupted the supply recovery operations by plastering the landing area. The mortars targeted the regimental command post as well, resulting in several casualties. Even if the cavalry made it, the battle was far from finished.

February 15, 1200–1300 Hours: B Company, Schmitt Hill

Captain Pratt climbed up Schmitt Hill, following behind his reserve platoon. When he arrived near the crest, he learned of the horrendous casualties his company had sustained, including one of his platoon sergeants, Eugene L. Nabozny. Kotite's wounded platoon sergeant had led his men up the slope, and when he was near the top he launched an attack on the enemy's eastern flank. However, doing so exposed him and cost him his life. The advance bogged down near the top.

Warrant Officer Ralph E. Dusseau, the administrative officer for B Company, linked up with Pratt in a ravine on the side of the hill. "Captain," he began, "it looks like we got a real stalemate on our hands!"

Pratt replied, "It sure seems so, Dussy. What news from the platoons?"

"Our men are just short of the crest of the hill, and the enemy forces are just a few feet away, over the crest and near the top of the slope on the other side, or south side," said Dusseau.

"What are they doing?" asked Pratt.

"It's hairy, Captain. They mostly can't see each other, but they know each other are there. They're within a hand grenade's throwing distance and have been doing just that for over an hour," explained Dusseau.

Pratt later wrote about the tactical dilemma he faced. "The picture could hardly have been more grim. The platoons reported that each time they rose up to charge over the crest, enemy gunfire could cut them down in their tracks. The platoon leaders insisted that further efforts were simply suicidal, and wanted to know what to do."

Pratt's first idea was artillery. He asked his platoon leaders what they thought about an artillery barrage to suppress the Chinese defenders. They refused.

"You don't want artillery?" asked Pratt over the radio. He could not believe it.

His 1st Platoon leader, Second Lieutenant Maurice Fenderson, squawked back, "We don't think so. The enemy is so close to us that I fear any rounds aimed at them are sure to fall on us also."

Pratt wondered if tanks would work. Unbeknownst to him, Colonel Edwards already had ordered the tanks to push forward down the Chipyong-ni–Kanhyon highway. Several minutes later, the B Company commander watched the tanks rolling down the road past his position.

FEBRUARY 15, 1257–1512 HOURS: TANK COMPANY, ALONG THE KOKSU-RI–CHIPYONG-NI HIGHWAY

First Lieutenant Charles W. Hurlburt's 4th Platoon provided the bulk of the armor support for the route clearance operation. When the Chinese defenders saw the tanks rumbling down the highway, they opened fire with bazookas on the lead pair of tanks. Luckily, the first few rockets were ineffective. Still, the hidden antitank ambushes were enough to cause the two tanks to reverse gears and pull back toward their start positions. Without the tanks, the P&A Squad also had to withdraw. At 1257 hours, 2nd Battalion reported to the regiment that the clearance operation had hit a snag. "It looked like it was going to be a stalemate," Edwards later wrote in a letter to Colonel Freeman.

After Edwards's S3, Captain Sager, reported the issue, the battalion commander marched down to the assembly area to see him and solve the problem. Everyone was exhausted and few had slept. Tempers were high. The long night of battle had taken its toll on the officers and men. When Edwards arrived at the tanks, he spoke with Sager and Captain George E. Vontom, the executive officer for the tank company.

The Fort Benning schoolhouse answer for antitank ambush teams was infantry; after several minutes of discussing the situation, Edwards quickly realized it was their best option. The problem was the lack of infantry: The only available soldiers were the few Rangers left on Heath Ridge. Edwards spoke with Lieutenant Herman and told him he needed his Rangers to clear out the enemy ambush teams. Once again, the Ranger officer protested, insisting his men were not suited for that mission since they were "hit and run specialist[s]."

"I told him by God that now he was an infantryman and would do what I told him to or report to the rear under arrest," Edwards later wrote. With his back against the wall, the Ranger officer acquiesced and led his men toward Schmitt Hill.

Captain Vontom returned to his tanks, and Task Force S rolled out. Once again, the Chinese opened fire. Vontom, manning a .50-caliber machine gun on one of the tanks, blasted away at the CPVF defenders on Schmitt Hill while incoming tracers zipped by him. One round hit him in the heel, but he refused evacuation.

The P&A Squad went to work. Initially, the maelstrom of fire was too much for the clearance teams, but several men finally crept forward and began removing the mines. Corporals Ernest C. Lawson Jr. and George P. Munhall Jr. and Private First Class Keith C. Karschney were the first to clear a path through the minefields for the tanks. By 1512 hours, the M4s had inched past Schmitt Hill. For their contributions clearing the road, Vontom, Lawson, Munhall, and Karschney all received the Silver Star.

East of the highway, Pratt's two platoons made progress up Schmitt Hill from the north side. It was slow going. Close air support had saturated the hilltop at 1445 hours with napalm and it was danger-close. "At one point, some of the burning napalm bounced over the crest and was blazing throughout a Baker squad position," Pratt later wrote. "Some small amounts landed on the clothing of a couple of my men. Because of the heavy winter clothing, they were not burned on the skin, and the flames were doused. But they had a frightening experience from it and for some weeks afterward would not surrender their burnt clothing as they proudly showed off their 'battle scars.'"

By 1512 hours, the B Company soldiers had made some progress. Still, it was a knife fight. As Kotite described the combat, "We played catch with grenades . . . for a while and got an interpreter to tell them to surrender."

Despite the success of Baker Company and the tanks, the Chinese kept battling. Many of the UN soldiers wondered if the Chinese would ever quit. What the soldiers of the 23rd Infantry did not know yet was that the Chinese were close to the breaking point.

TEN

Breaking Out of Libby Prison

Isaac N. Johnston

The Battle of Chickamauga, one of the most stoutly contested of the war, may be said to have commenced on Friday, the 18th of September, 1863; but the heaviest fighting took place on Saturday and Sunday. We were outnumbered, as is well known; but, by the persistent courage of General Thomas and his brave associates, the enemy were foiled in their purpose— which was to retake Chattanooga—and the army saved from the disaster which at one time during the fight seemed inevitable. Bragg, it is true, claimed a glorious victory; but if battles are to be judged by their results, his victory was a fruitless one, the prize which was at stake remaining in our hands. True, we lost many brave men, and much of the material of war; but Chattanooga, the key of Georgia, was not wrested from our grasp; the valor of the troops, too, was never more nobly illustrated; for the stout men under Thomas stood unshaken on Mission Ridge as the wave-washed rock, against which the hitherto invincible legions of Long-street, like fierce billows, madly dashed themselves, to fall back, like those broken billows, in foam and spray.

Men fell upon that field whose names never will perish, and others, who still live, there gained immortal renown. There fell Lytle, the poet-hero; sweet was his lyre, and strong was his sword. There the modest yet brave Thomas displayed the qualities of a great general, firm and undismayed amid carnage and threatened disaster; and there Garfield, the gallant and the good, won richly-deserved honor.

But to my own story. I had been unwell for several days, but the excitement of the conflict aroused and sustained me. Late on the evening of Saturday our brigade was ordered to retreat, and, unable to keep up with the main body, I was overtaken and captured. I was taken in charge by two lieutenants, and regret that I did not learn their names or command, as they treated me with marked kindness, as brave men ever treat a conquered foe. They saw, moreover, by my appearance, that I was quite ill, and this doubtless excited their sympathy. Soon another lieutenant came up; he was a Georgian, and drunk; he took away my sword-belt and haversack. Being cautioned by the others to take care of my watch, I slipped it down my back unobserved by my Georgia friend, and saved it for the time being.

My captors conducted me about a mile and a half to the rear, and kept me there all night. We had to pass over the ground that had been fought over during the day; it was thickly strewed with the dead and wounded of both armies; their dead seemed to be in the proportion of three to our one. I saw General Bragg for the first time at a distance. The night was intensely cold for the season, and I suffered severely, having lost my blanket; moreover, I was exhausted from hunger, having eaten nothing for two days. I was fortunate enough, however, to meet with a prisoner of the 9th Indiana, who generously gave me a cup of coffee and a cracker, after which I felt greatly refreshed. This noble fellow also shared his scanty covering with me, and I trust he may ever find a friend as kind as he proved to me. By morning the number of prisoners was quite large, most of them nearly starved; the men guarding us were very kind, and said they would gladly give us food, but they were as destitute and as hungry as ourselves. To prove their sincerity they marched us to a sweet-potato patch, and all hands, prisoners and guards, in army phrase, "pitched in." We then made fires and roasted the potatoes, and often since have made a worse meal. We were then marched across the Chickamauga River to a white house, where we found another lot of prisoners collected; our names were taken, and every man was relieved of his haversack; they were taken by a Texas captain, who distributed them to his own men.

This was Sunday, the 20th. About ten o'clock in the morning the battle commenced again, and we prisoners were ordered into rank and marched in the direction of Ringgold. After an hour's march we were halted till about two in the afternoon, during which time there was another squad of prisoners marched to the rear and added to our number. During all this time the battle was raging furiously, and as the sound of the fierce conflict came to our ears there was the greatest anxiety on the part of our guard as well as ourselves. I had heard that Rosecrans had been heavily reinforced and, believing it to be true, was sanguine of success.

At two o'clock the captured officers, now numbering about one hundred and fifty, were ordered to fall in according to rank, non-commissioned officers and privates to follow. In this order we marched, stopping a few minutes to rest at the end of every hour, stimulated by the promise that we should draw rations as soon as we reached Ringgold. On our way we met one of Longstreet's brigades hurrying to the front; they were fine, soldierly-looking men, the very flower of the Confederate army, better drilled and equipped than any Southern troops I had seen, either at Shiloh or Stone River; they were confident, too, from their successes in Virginia; but they found their equals, at least, at Mission Ridge in the gallant men of the West. We reached Ringgold about nine o'clock at night, but failed to draw the promised rations, and were told if we would march four miles further we should come to the camp of a brigade of Longstreet's men, who were guarding a railroad station, and be sure to find the much-desired rations there. Many of us had been nearly worn out marching previous to the battle, and had passed through one day's fight; nevertheless, so hungry were we that we were glad to drag our weary limbs four miles further, and in that distance wade the Chickamauga three times, in the hope of finding food, fire, and rest.

When within a short distance of the camp, we were ordered to take rails from a fence to make fires to dry our clothes and make ourselves comfortable for the night. We were eager to avail ourselves of the liberty thus granted, and soon a column of men, about two thousand in number, each with from three to five rails on his shoulder, were marching on. About two o'clock in the morning, wet, dispirited, and weary, we reached camp, wincing somewhat under the burden of our rails, which grew heavier every step. Again we were doomed to disappointment; we found nothing there to relieve our hunger; so we kindled our fires, stretched ourselves near them, and strove to forget the pangs of hunger and the bitterness of captivity in sleep.

On the morning of the 21st we were marched to Tunnel Hill, a distance of five miles. We remained there till 2 p.m., in which interval the long-desired rations of corn meal and bacon were issued. We asked for time to bake our bread and divide the meat, and were assured that we should have the opportunity we desired. Men were detailed to bake the bread and cut up the bacon, and in imagination we saw the long-expected and welcome meal prepared; but scarcely were our fires lighted and the meat divided before we were again ordered into ranks, and obliged to leave nearly all our uncooked rations lying on the ground. To famishing men this was a severe trial; but orders were imperative, and with sad hearts we marched to the depot, where we found a train of cars awaiting our arrival. We got on board and reached Kingston, where we remained till morning. Here we met a brigade of Longstreet's men, who treated us with great kindness, many of them dividing their rations with us.

The same day we moved forward to Atlanta, which place we reached at 5 p.m. We found an immense crowd awaiting the arrival of the Yankees, and were stared at and criticized in a manner far from agreeable. Pity for our condition dwelt in the hearts of some, but they were forced to restrain any expression of sympathy; while those who came to jeer, and laugh, and to show their mean exultation, gratified their feelings to the fullest extent. Many citizens, both male and female, gratified their curiosity by calling to see us, doubtless expecting, from the reports they had heard, to see a race of beings far different from themselves. The next morning we were ordered to take the cars for Richmond.

Leaving Atlanta, we reached Augusta about twelve o'clock at night, and were marched to a churchyard, in which we camped till next morning. We were well treated by the citizens; many of them visited us, and showed us such kindness during our stay that we could not but conclude that many of them, at heart, were lovers of the Union still. Nor was this the only occasion, while passing through the South, that we discovered strong symptoms of a Union sentiment among the people; many have secretly cherished the sacred flame, and will yet welcome the army of the Union as their deliverers. Leaving Augusta, we crossed the Savannah River into

South Carolina, passed through Raleigh, Weldon, and Petersburg, and on the 29th of September, about seven o'clock in the evening, we reached the depot at Richmond, and were marched to our Libby home.

During our trip from Chickamauga to Richmond the weather was clear and beautiful, but the nights were cold, and many of us, having lost our blankets, suffered much; for, in addition to the want of our usual covering, we were hungry nearly all the time. Many of the cities and towns through which we passed presented a pleasing appearance; but the country, for the most part, had a desolate look; few men were to be seen, save such as were too old for service, and the farming operations bore marks of neither care nor skill.

The officer who had the prisoners in charge was kind and gentlemanly, and rendered our situation as agreeable as was possible under the circumstances; that we suffered for food was no fault of his, and when we were turned over to the authorities at Richmond we parted from him with a feeling akin to regret.

All the private soldiers were sent to Belle Isle, a place which has become infamous on account of the cruel treatment to which they were subjected; but the officers had quarters assigned them in Libby Prison. This now world-famous building presents none of the outward characteristics of a prison, having been used in peaceful days as a warehouse; but none of the castles and dungeons of Europe, century old though they be, have a stranger or sadder history than this. There many a heart has been wrung, many a spirit broken, many a noble soul has there breathed out its last sigh, and hundreds who yet survive will shrink in their dreams, or shudder in their waking moments, when faithful memory brings back the scenes enacted within its fearful walls. The building is of brick, with a front of near one hundred and forty feet, and one hundred feet deep.

It is divided into nine rooms; the ceilings are low, and ventilation imperfect; the windows are barred, through which the windings of the James River and the tents of Belle Isle may be seen. Its immediate surroundings are far from being agreeable; the sentinels pacing the streets constantly are unpleasant reminders that your stay is not a matter of choice; and were it so, few would choose it long as a boardinghouse.

In this building were crowded about one thousand officers of nearly every grade, not one of whom was permitted to go out till exchanged or released by death. To men accustomed to an active life this mode of existence soon became exceedingly irksome, and innumerable methods were soon devised to make the hours pass less wearily. A penknife was made to do the duty of a complete set of tools, and it was marvelous to see the wonders achieved by that single instrument. Bone-work of strange device, and carving most elaborate, chessmen, spoons, pipes, all manner of articles, useful and ornamental, were fashioned by its aid alone. If a man's early education had been neglected, ample opportunities were now afforded to become a proficient scholar. The higher branches of learning had their professor; the languages, ancient and modern, were taught; mathematics received much attention; morals and religion were cared for in Bible classes, while the ornamental branches, such as dancing, vocal music, and sword exercise, had had their teachers and pupils. Indeed, few colleges in the land could boast of a faculty so large in number or varied in accomplishments, and none, certainly, could compare in the number of pupils.

But truth must be told; the minds of many of those grown-up, and, in some instances, gray-headed pupils, were not always with their books; their minds, when children, wandered from the page before them to the green fields, to streams abounding in fish, or pleasant for bathing; or to orchards, with fruit most inviting; but now the mind wandered in one direction—home. Others were deeply engaged in the mysteries of "poker" and "seven-up," and betting ran high; but they were bets involving neither loss or gain, and the winner of countless sums would often borrow a teaspoon full of salt or a pinch of pepper. Games of chess were played, which, judging from the wary and deliberate manner of the players, and the interest displayed by lookers-on, were as intricate and important as a military campaign; nor were the sports of children—jack-straws and mumble-peg—wanting; every device, serious and silly, was employed to hasten the slow hours along. But amid all these various occupations, there was one that took the precedence and absorbed all others—that was planning an escape. The exploits of Jack Sheppard, Baron Trenck, and the hero of Monte Cristo were seriously considered, and plans superior to theirs concocted, some of them characterized by skill and cunning, others by the energy of despair.

One of these was as follows: After the arrival of the Chickamauga prisoners, a plot was made which embraced the escape of all confined in Libby, and the release of all the prisoners in and about Richmond. The leader in this enterprise was a man of cool purpose and great daring; and success, I doubt not, would have attended the effort had it not been that we had traitors in our midst who put the rebel authorities on the alert only a few days before the attempt was to have been made.

Our first plan of escape being thwarted, no time was lost in devising another, which, after many delays and interruptions of a very discouraging character, was finally crowned with success. Captain Hamilton, of the 12th Kentucky Cavalry, was the author of the plan, which he confided to Major Fitzsimmons, of the 30th Indiana, Captain Gallagher, of the 2nd Ohio, and a third person, whose name it would not be prudent to mention, as he was recaptured. I greatly regret to pass him by with this brief allusion, as he had a very prominent part in the work from the beginning, and deserves far more credit than I have language to express. As this, however, is one of the most wonderful escapes on record, when its complete history is written he will not be forgotten. John Morgan's escape from the Ohio Penitentiary has been thought to have suggested our plan, and to have equaled it in ingenuity and risk. His difficulties, however, ended when he emerged from the tunnel by which he escaped, while ours may be said to have only begun when we reached the free air, and every step till we reached the Union lines was fraught with great danger.

After Captain Hamilton's plans had been entrusted to and adopted by the gentlemen above named, a solemn pledge was taken to reveal them to none others, and at an early date in December 1863, the work was begun.

In order to reach a perfect understanding of it, a more minute description of the building is necessary. It is not far from one hundred and forty feet by one hundred and ten, three stories high, and divided into three departments by heavy brick walls. The divisions were occupied as follows: The two upper east rooms by the Potomac officers, the two middle upper rooms by those captured at Chickamauga, the two west upper rooms by the officers of Colonel Streight's and General Milroy's command; the lower room of the east division was used as a hospital, the lower middle room for a cook and dining-room, and the lower west is divided into several apartments which were occupied by the rebel officers in command. There is also a cellar under each of these divisions; the east cellar was used for commissary stores, such as meal, turnips, fodder, and straw—the latter article was of vast benefit in effecting our escape. The rear and darker part of the middle cellar was cut up into cells, to which were consigned those of our number who were guilty of infractions of the rules of prison—dungeons dark and horrible beyond description. The portion of it in front was used as a workshop, and the west cellar was used for cooking the rations of private soldiers who were confined in other buildings, and as quarters for some negro captives who were kept to do the drudgery of the prison.

As the plan was to dig out, it became necessary to find a way into the east cellar, from which to begin our tunnel, which was accomplished as follows. Near the north end of the dining room was a fireplace, around which three large cooking stoves were arranged. In this fireplace the work began. The bricks were skillfully taken out, and through this aperture a descent to the east cellar was effected. This part of the work was entrusted to Captains Hamilton and Gallagher, who were both housebuilders, and in their hands it was a perfect success. The only tools used were pocket-knives; consequently their progress was slow, and fifteen nights elapsed before the place was reached where the tunnel was to begin. The stoves mentioned above aided greatly in the prosecution of the work, screening the operators from observation. Immediately in front of them the prisoners had a dancing party nearly every night, and the light of their tallow candles made the stoves throw a dark shadow over the entrance to the newly-opened way to the cellar, and the mirth of the dancers drowned any slight noise that might be made by the working party. Considerable skill was necessary in order to reach the cellar after the opening was made; and on one occasion one of the party stuck fast, and was released only by great efforts on the part of his associates. Poor fellow! Though fortunate enough to escape detection in this instance, and afterward to reach the free air, he was recaptured and taken back to a confinement more intolerable than before.

The cellar being reached, a thorough examination was made in order to decide upon a route which would be most favorable for our escape; and it was determined to make an attempt in the rear of a cook-room which was in the southeast corner of the cellar. The plan was to dig down and pass under the foundation, then change the direction and work parallel with the wall to a large sewer that passes down Canal Street, and from thence make our escape. The attempt was accordingly made; but it was soon discovered that the building rested upon ponderous oak timbers, below which they could not penetrate. Determined to succeed, they began the seemingly hopeless task of cutting through these; pocketknives and saws made out of case-knives were the only available tools; and when this, after much hard labor, was effected, they were met by an unforeseen and still more serious difficulty. Water began to flow into the tunnel; a depth below the level of the canal had been reached, and sadly they were compelled to abandon the undertaking. A second effort was made; a tunnel was started in the rear of the cook-room mentioned above, intended to strike a small sewer which started from the southeast corner, and passing through the outer wall to the large sewer in front. Some sixteen or eighteen feet brought the tunnel under a brick furnace, in which were built several large kettles used in making soup for prisoners. This partially caved in, and fear of discovery caused this route to be abandoned.

With a determination to succeed, which no difficulty could weaken or disappointment overcome, another attempt, far more difficult than the preceding, was made. A portion of the stone floor of the cook-room was taken up, and the place supplied by a neatly-fitting board, which could be easily removed; and through this the working party descended every night. The plan was to escape by the sewer leading from the kitchen, but it was not large enough for a man to pass through; but as the route seemed preferable to any other, it was determined to remove the plank with which it was lined; and this out of the way, the tunnel or aperture would be sufficiently large. The old knives and saws were called for, and the work of removing the plank was continued for several days with flattering success, till it was concluded that another hour's work would enable us to enter the large sewer in front, into which this led, and thus escape. So strong was the conviction that the work would be completed in a little time, that all who knew the work was going on made preparation to escape on the night of the 26th of January.

After working on the night of the 25th, two men were left down in the cellar to cover up all traces of the work during the day, and as soon as it was dark to complete the work—to go into the large sewer, explore it, and have everything ready by eight or nine o'clock, at which time the bricks would be removed from the hole leading into the cellar, which had to be placed carefully in their original position every night, from the beginning to the completion of the work. When the last brick was removed, a rope ladder, which had been prepared for the occasion, was passed down and made fast to a bar of iron, placed across the front of the fireplace. Now came long moments of breathless silence and agonizing suspense, all waiting for the assurance from one of the men below that all was ready. He came at last; but, alas! his first whisper was, "bad news, bad news"; and bad news, indeed, it proved. It was found that the remaining portion of the plank to be removed was oak, two inches thick, and impossible to be removed by the tools which had heretofore been used; moreover, the water was rapidly finding its way into the tunnel, and all the labor expended had been in vain. The feelings of that little band who can describe!—from hopes almost as bright as reality they were suddenly plunged into the depths of despair.

Nearly all the work above mentioned was performed by Captains Hamilton and Gallagher, Major Fitzsimmons, and another officer. As a natural consequence, they were worn out by excessive labor, anxiety, and loss of sleep, that being the thirty-ninth night of unremitting toil. They were, however, still unconquered in spirit, and declared that another attempt must be made as soon as they were sufficiently recruited to enter upon it. Noble fellows! Hard had they toiled for liberty, and it came at last.

While the party last named were resting, there were others not inactive. Captain Clark, of the 73rd Illinois, Major McDonald, of the 100th Ohio, Captain Lucas, of the 5th Kentucky, Lieutenant Fislar, of the 7th Indiana Battery, and myself proposed to the originators of the plan of escape that we would commence at some other point, and push on the work till they were sufficiently recruited to unite with us. This meeting with their approval, on the following night Major McDonald and Captain Clark went down and commenced operations.

The plan was to begin a new tunnel in the cellar on the east side, near the northeast corner of the building. The first thing to be done was to make a hole through the brick wall, which they effected in one day and night. This was done by picking the cement from between the bricks with a penknife, and then breaking them out with an old ax. This, of course, made considerable noise, and was calculated to arrest the attention of the guards; but it happened, providentially, as it seemed to us, that just at that time the authorities of the prison determined to place iron grates in all the windows, to render the escape of the Yankees impossible. This was accompanied by great noise; and while they were thus engaged our boys thumped away with a will, and made their way through the wall without exciting the least suspicion. The night after the breach was made, Lieutenant Fislar and myself went down to work; but having nothing but a small penknife, our progress was, of necessity, very slow. In spite of all difficulties, however, we made an excavation of about two feet, and felt that we were that much nearer freedom. We remained in the cellar all the next day, and at night were relieved by two others; and thus the work was continued from night to night, till its completion. One of our number remained in the cellar every day to remove all signs of the previous night's work, and to replace the bricks in the cavity made in the wall, to avoid discovery, as some of the prison officials or laborers came into the cellar every day, either bringing in or taking out forage or commissary stores.

I have been asked a thousand times how we contrived to hide such a quantity of earth as the digging of a tunnel of that size would dislodge. There was a large pile of straw stored in the cellar for hospital use; in this we made a wide and deep opening, extending to the ground; in this the loose dirt was closely packed, and then nicely covered with straw.

As the work progressed from night to night, and our hopes increased with the length of our tunnel, the number of laborers was increased, till the working party numbered fourteen. This was the more necessary, as the work of removing the loose dirt increased with every foot we advanced. I have often been asked how we managed to get the dirt out of the tunnel, which was too narrow to permit a man to turn round in it. As the whole process was somewhat novel, one in all probability never attempted before, I will describe it for the benefit of the readers.

Our dirt-car was a wooden spittoon, with holes through each end opposite each other, through which ropes were passed; one of these ropes was used by the one engaged in digging, to draw the empty spittoon from the entrance to the place where he was at work; and when he had loosened earth enough to fill it, he gave a signal to the one at the mouth of the tunnel by jerking the rope, and he drew the loaded box out, and the miner recovered it by pulling the rope attached to the end of the box nearest him; thus it was kept traveling backward and forward till wagonloads of earth were removed. After penetrating some distance the task became very painful; it was impossible to breathe the air of the tunnel for many minutes together; the miner, however, would dig as long as his strength would allow, or till his candle was extinguished by the foul air; he would then make his way out, and another would take his place—a place narrow, dark, and damp, and more like a grave than any place can be short of a man's last narrow home.

As the work approached completion the difficulty of breathing in the tunnel was greatly increased, and four persons were necessary to keep the work moving; one would go in and dig awhile, then when he came out nearly exhausted another would enter and fill the spittoon, a third would draw it to the mouth of the tunnel, a fourth would then empty the contents into a large box provided for the purpose, and when it was full, take it to the straw pile and carefully conceal it, as before stated. This labor, too, it must be remembered, was not only extremely difficult in itself, and especially so when the imperfect tools and means of removing the earth are taken into the account; but in addition to this was the constant anxiety lest the attempt we were making should be discovered. Moreover, the fact that all previous attempts had failed was calculated at times to fill our minds with fears lest some unforeseen obstacle should occur to prevent the success of our enterprise. On the other hand, however, the hard fare and confinement of our prison, the monotony of which had become unendurable, and the possibility of escape at last roused us up to exertions almost superhuman. Under any other circumstances the work would have been deemed impossible; but there are no impossibilities to men with liberty as the result of their labors.

Before the work was completed, those who had been engaged in the previous attempt had recovered from their exhaustion, and were able to take part in this, which, in the end, proved successful. But what is to be most regretted is, that though all of them regained the liberty for which they so patiently toiled, one of them was recaptured—the one, too, who, of all others, the rest confidently believed would escape, if escape were in the power of man. What he has since suffered we can only conjecture; but the disappointment must have been most sad to his great heart—to have gained the free air, and almost in sight of the flag of the Union—to be recaptured and borne back to a captivity more hopeless than before.

I have also been asked frequently since my escape, how it was possible for a man to be left down in the cellar every day without being discovered. Such a thing seems strange; but the entire work was a marvelous one, and this was a necessary part of it; and though the officers, or other persons employed about the prison, visited the cellar every day, yet for fifty-one days one or another of our company was down there without being discovered. The duty of the one left there was to remove all traces of the work of the previous night, as soon as it became light enough to do so; he would then conceal himself for the day in the straw, of which there was a large quantity there, and but for which our undertaking must have been discovered nearly as soon as begun. To account for the absence of those persons required some ingenuity, as two of our number were sometimes on duty at once in the cellar. This was managed as follows: The officers were drawn up in four ranks, and the clerk counted them from right to left; one, two, or three, as the case might be, would change their places so as to be counted twice; the number being all right, the clerk was deceived.

This, however, was suddenly brought to an end. Some of the officers had succeeded in obtaining citizens' clothes, and passed them guards without suspicion and escaped; one or two also escaped by disguising themselves in the Confederate uniform. After this we were all collected into the two east rooms, and required to answer to our names.

About the time the change was made Major McDonald and Lieutenant McKee were on duty in the cellar, and failed to answer to their names;

this caused quite a stir, and for some time it was thought that they had escaped by a trick similar to that of the others. The next day they were reported by someone as being present—perhaps the clerk, who knew that the major, particularly, would bear watching. The consequence was they were both called down to the office to render to Major Turner the reasons for their absence on the previous day. The lieutenant, with an air of perfect innocence, stated that, feeling quite unwell, he had wrapped himself up in his blanket, had fallen asleep, did not hear the order for roll-call, and was overlooked. His excuse was deemed valid, and he was immediately sent back to his quarters. The major was not so fortunate; the fact is, he was regarded as a suspicious character, and in consequence had a severer ordeal to pass. The question, "Major, your reason for non-attendance at roll-call yesterday," was put quite laconically. Said he, "I happened to be in Colonel Streight's room, and failed to get back in time."

"In Colonel Streight's room, indeed! How did you get in there, sir?"

That I may be understood better, it is necessary to state that some time previous some of the officers of Colonel Streight's command had given much trouble to the authorities of the prison by being in our room at roll-call; and, in order to prevent a similar occurrence, had nailed up the door between the rooms occupied by the Chickamauga officers and those captured with Colonel Streight. The door had not been nailed up half an hour before some quick-witted fellow sawed the door completely in two below the lock, extracted the nails, placed some benches near the door so as to conceal the crack, and we were thus able to pass in and out at pleasure. The occupants of the other room took good care that the traces of the saw should be concealed on their side, and thus free intercourse was kept between both rooms without being suspected.

The major, with great seeming candor, explained the trick which accounted for his presence in the forbidden room; and the next question was, "How did it happen that the officer of the day and the clerk did not see you there when they came in to see if that room was cleared before commencing to call the roll?" This would have been a poser to many—not so to the major, who readily replied, that, being in the wrong room, not wishing to be found there, and being compelled to disclose the means by which he entered, he had climbed up on the plate or girder that passed through the room; "and when the search for me began," said he, "I laid there close to the timber for ten hours, and would have melted, drop by drop, before I would discover myself, and subject the officers in that room to censure, and cause all intercourse between the two rooms to be cut off."

His questioners seemed rather to doubt his excuse, ingenious though it was; but as they were ignorant of the true state of the case, and he reaffirmed his story so positively, he was dismissed to his quarters with a reprimand and an admonition.

The day after this occurred it was my turn to stand guard in the cellar. At quite an early hour the roll was called, and there being no one willing to run the risk of answering for me, my absence was discovered. There were several, it is true, who would willingly have answered for me, but they were so well known, and somewhat suspected, which would have rendered it dangerous to them, and of no benefit to me. The fact of my absence made it necessary for the calling of the roll several times in succession; all the officers were kept in rank, confined in one room, till three o'clock in the afternoon, and diligent search was made for me in every room in the building; and it was finally concluded that I had made my escape. At night, when the working party came down, they informed me of what had taken place; and upon consultation it was thought best that I should remain down in the cellar till the tunnel was completed. To remain in this cold, dark, and loathsome place was most revolting to my feelings; but the fear of being handcuffed and put in the dungeon if I returned to my room, and the hope of gaining my liberty shortly, induced me to stay. After agreeing to stay down, it was suggested that I might with safety go up to my quarters after lights were out, and sleep till four o'clock in the morning, and go down again when the working party came up. I did so; but the first night I was seen, either by some traitor or very careless prisoner not acquainted with our secret, who stated at roll-call the next morning that I was in the house, as he had seen me go to bed the night before— which was really the case. The result was that the roll was called several times, and another careful search for me was instituted. Great excitement prevailed through the prison; those of our own men who knew nothing of the plan of escape, and the place of my concealment, thought that I was hiding in some of the rooms, and thought it very wrong in me to do so; they even said that I ought to come out of my hiding-place and give myself up, as they, though innocent, were suffering on my account. On the contrary, those who knew where I was declared that it was impossible that I could be in the building, after the strict search that had been made for me; and as others were known to have made their escape recently, it was more than likely that I had done the same.

This was corroborated by Lieutenant Fislar, who improvised a story to fit the case. He said that he was my messmate and sleeping-companion—which was true; but that I had been missing from my usual place for some time, and he had no doubt but that I had escaped. He said, moreover, that two of my cousins were among our guards—that I had been courting their favor for some time, and that they had finally furnished me with a rebel uniform—that I had made a wooden sword, a tin scabbard, and a belt out of a piece of oil-cloth, and that they had eventually passed me out as a rebel officer.

This story was taken up and so stoutly confirmed by all who knew where I was, that the point was yielded by most of the opposite view, though a few still contended that I must be in the prison still.

All this was related to me by the working party when they came down at night, and I then resolved to make my appearance at my quarters no more. This resolution I have kept faithfully. I never saw my room again, and never desire to do so, unless it be as the bearer of freedom to those who are pining there still.

The cellar was now my home. I was fed by my companions, who nightly brought me down a portion of their own scanty fare. Had I been discovered by the authorities of the prison it would have gone hard with me; and knowing this, the greatest sympathy was manifested by my associates, who felt that this danger was incurred not less for their advantage than my own.

Everything moved on as well as could be expected. I had plenty of company—little of it, however, agreeable, as it consisted of rebels, rats, and other vermin. With the former I had no communication whatever; whenever they made their appearance I leaped quickly into a hole I had prepared in the straw, and pulled the hole in after me, or nearly so, at least, by drawing the straw over me so thickly that I could scarcely breathe. The rats gave me no annoyance, save when making more noise than usual, they startled me by making the impression that my two-legged enemies were near; the remaining nuisance, which shall be nameless, was one which all prisoners will ever remember with loathing, and from which there was neither respite nor escape.

The night of the 7th of February came, and it was thought that our tunnel was long enough to reach the inside of a tobacco-shed on the opposite side of the street, under which it passed. We made our calculation in the following manner: Captain Gallagher had obtained permission to go to a building across the street, where the boxes sent from the North to the prisoners were stored, to obtain some of the perishable articles; and while crossing the street he measured the distance, as accurately as possible, by stepping it both ways, and came to the conclusion that fifty-two or fifty-three feet would bring us to the shed. On measuring the tunnel it was found to be fifty-three feet long, and we fondly hoped that our labors were ended, with the exception of a few feet upward to the light. So confident were we that the work could be completed in an hour or two, that we had our rations already prepared in our haversacks, fully expecting to begin going out at nine o'clock—nay, we even went so far as to communicate the success of our plan to many who had not been partakers in the labor or the secret of the undertaking, but whom we invited to become the companions of our flight. When all were thus expectant, all thinking that the long-wished-for hour had come, Captain Randell, of the 2nd Ohio, was appointed to open up the way to light and liberty.

It was agreed that the mining party, who had labored so faithfully, should go out first, and that our friends should follow; and we stood anxiously awaiting the return of Captain Randell with the news that the way was open. There are times when minutes seem lengthened into hours—this was one of them. The suspense began to be painful; it seemed as if we could hear the beatings of each other's hearts, as well as feel the throbbings of our own, and the unspoken question on every lip was, Will he succeed? At length he emerged from the tunnel, and, in answer to the question, "What success?" in an excited tone and manner he replied, "All is lost!" We gathered round him, and when he became somewhat calmer he spoke as follows: "I have made an opening, but a large stone which lay on the surface fell into the tunnel, making considerable noise; the hole, too, was on the outside of the shed, and within a few feet of the sentinel who was on guard; he heard the noise, and called the attention of the other sentinel to it; the light from the hospital shone upon the side of the shed; I could see both the guards walking toward the spot; I have no doubt they have discovered the tunnel, and perhaps will soon be in here to arrest us."

Imagine, if you can, our feelings; our bright hopes so suddenly crushed, and everyone in expectation that the guard would soon be upon us. Great excitement prevailed, yet no one was able to suggest how to act in this sudden and unexpected emergency.

Amid all the excitement, however, incident to such an occasion, there was much sympathy felt in my behalf. I had been missing for some time, and was supposed to have made my escape; to be discovered now, as seemed inevitable, would be proof that I had much to do with the attempt to escape, and would subject me, at the very least, to the dungeon and handcuffs. In a few moments the cellar was nearly cleared, most of the party returning to their quarters in the different rooms above; but Major McDonald and Captain Hamilton remained with me, determined, if they could not aid me, at least to share the same fate. Noble, self-sacrificing men! Their conduct proved that disinterested friendship and high, chivalrous feeling have not yet departed.

After all was quiet, the major determined to go upstairs and make what discoveries he could. He soon returned, saying he had been up to the upper east room, from which he could see the sentinels very distinctly; and, from all appearances, he concluded that they had not discovered the hole. I advised him to go into the tunnel and examine the breach, and stop it up if possible, as it was not at the right place to render our escape at all likely, being outside of the shed instead of inside, as was intended, and within a few feet of the guard. If the hole could not be stopped, of course it exposed us to certain discovery in the morning; and I proposed to go in and enlarge it, and, great as was the risk, try to make my escape at all hazards; for if I should fail, I would rather be caught in the attempt than wait to be found in the cellar or my quarters. When the major returned he reported favorably, saying that the breach might be repaired. An old pair of pantaloons were procured and stuffed full of earth; some dirt, too, was put on the outside of them, so that the cloth could not be seen, and thus excite suspicion. These were forced into the aperture, and earth pressed in beneath; and he returned greatly elated with the hope that all danger was past, and that in one or two more nights our labors would be crowned with success.

After a few minutes' consultation it was agreed that I should remain in the cellar till the next night. All the next day a close watch was kept, by some of our number in the east room, on the guards who were stationed near the place where our tunnel ended. There was no token, however, that any discovery had been made, and the next night the mining operations were resumed, and between two and three o'clock in the morning an opening was made to the free air, this time inside of the shed, at the very point we desired, at a distance of fifty-seven feet from the point of starting. The tunnel was about two feet wide by two feet and a half deep; it was arched above; and Lieutenant Davy, who is a practical miner, declared that it was done in a workmanlike manner. We found a very hard, compact sand all along the route; the loose earth was disposed of as I have before stated, till within about ten feet of the end, when it was strewn along the entire length, thus reducing very considerably the size of the passage. Near the terminus it was rather a close fit for a large man, and when I was passing through I stuck fast, and had to call on Major Fitzsimmons to pull me out of a very tight place.

The principal tool used in this work was a chisel, which was found among some rubbish in the cellar, a handle for which was made from a piece of stove-wood.

When the surface was reached there was too little of the night remaining to effect our escape; two of our number, however, passed out and explored the lot, and planned the course to be taken after emerging from the tunnel. The shed in which our labors terminated fronted the canal; between them was a brick building, through the center of which there was a passage into the lot, closed by a gate; and the route fixed upon was through this passage. The question then arose, who shall go out first? Some thought that I was entitled to that honor, as I had been confined so long in the cellar, and had incurred more risk than the rest. Others thought that, though to go out first might be esteemed the post of honor, it was also the post of danger, as the first would run more risk than those who should follow. It was finally agreed that I should be the fifth to pass out, and that Lieutenant Fislar should be my partner in flight. Then arose the question, how the aperture through the surface should be concealed till the next night; for should anyone go into the shed during the day, as was most probable, our plan might yet be frustrated. A piece of plank was found, and Captain Hamilton dispatched with it to the outer end of the tunnel, over which he placed it, being careful, however, to bury it just below the surface, and to cover it with dry earth. He soon returned, having successfully accomplished his task; and all retired to their quarters, leaving me in the cellar to cover up all traces of their work—cheered by the thought that with night would come liberty.

It came at last—the last night, the night of release; and the working party was assembled in the cellar for the last time. There was a shade of sadness on many a brow; for we were about to go forth two by two, to separate to meet again—when? Perhaps never! The party consisted of:

Colonel Rose, 77th Pennsylvania Infantry
Major Fitzsimmons, 30th Indiana Infantry
Captain Hamilton, 12th Kentucky Cavalry
Captain Gallagher, 2nd Ohio Volunteer Infantry
Captain Clark, 79th Illinois Volunteer Infantry
Captain Lucas, 5th Kentucky Volunteer Infantry
Major McDonald, 100th Ohio Volunteer Infantry
Captain Randell, 2nd Ohio Volunteer Infantry
Captain Johnston, 6th Kentucky Volunteer Infantry
Lieutenant Fislar, 7th Indiana Battery
Lieutenant Simpson, 10th Indiana Infantry
Lieutenant Mitchell, 79th Illinois Infantry
Lieutenant Davy, 77th Pennsylvania Infantry
Lieutenant Sterling, 29th Indiana Infantry
Lieutenant Foster, 30th Indiana Infantry

It was agreed that ten minutes should elapse after the first two passed out before the second couple should start. Lieutenant Fislar and myself were the third couple. After emerging from the tunnel we faced to the right, and passed across the lot to the passage through the brick building, already described, into the street; and in doing so we passed within forty feet of the sentinels. We were not observed, and you may be sure we did not linger, and soon we were out of sight of the hated place.

One hundred and nine persons thus escaped from eight o'clock at night to three in the morning, notwithstanding that the night was clear and beautiful, and all had to pass between two gas lights; of these, however, only about one-half succeeded in reaching the Federal lines.

As my comrade and myself were passing through the city, two ladies, who were standing at the gate of a house which stood back from the street, observed us; one of them remarked to the other that we looked like Yankees. We did not stop to undeceive them, and met with no further trouble till the city limits were passed. We then changed our course and traveled northeast, and soon came to the rebel camps, which stretched round a great portion of the city. We were excited, of course, and bewildered for the first hour, not knowing whether we were in the path of safety or danger. All at once I became perfectly composed, and told my comrade to follow me and I would conduct him safe through. I then started due north, taking the North Star for my guide, changing my course only when we came near any of the camps, sufficiently to avoid them. After traveling three or four miles we saw another camp ahead, and thinking that the camps possibly did not connect, we determined to attempt to pass between them. As we approached, however, we found out our mistake—the camps were connected by a chain of sentinels, and this chain must be passed before escape became even probable.

We advanced cautiously, and when we reached a small ravine we could hear the sentinel, on his beat, on the other side. We saw his fire, too, which we, of course, avoided; and at one time only a few small bushes were between us and the guard; the wind, however, was blowing briskly, causing quite a rustling among the dry leaves, and we succeeded in getting by safely. We moved on rapidly, and soon came near the cavalry pickets; these we passed without difficulty. After continuing our course north for some time, we changed to northeast and passed over four lines of the rebel defenses. It was our intention to strike the Chickahominy above the railroad bridge; but, to our surprise, we struck the railroad on the Richmond side.

We then traveled down the road about a mile, and as day began to dawn we left the road a short distance to find a hiding-place, expecting that with the coming of light there would be a keen search made for us. The rebel fortifications were near; in front of them all the timber had been felled, and among this timber was our hiding-place the first day—all the safer, too, no doubt, for being within a few hundred yards of the rebel guns. The weather was excessively cold; we had walked during the night over bad roads, through mud and water, and our pantaloons were frozen stiff up to our knees. We did not dare to make a fire so near the rebel camp, for fear of discovery; but our suffering was greatly lessened by the thought that we were free.

As soon as it was light enough to see, we made the rather unpleasant discovery that there was a picket-guard not more than one hundred and fifty yards from the place where we had taken refuge; and soon two working parties came out from the fortifications and began to cut cordwood. These two parties, with the picket-guard, formed a triangle—the wood-choppers on each side, the guards in front—so that we were obliged, half frozen though we were, to lay very close to the ground till kind and merciful Night, who kindly lends her mantle to escaped prisoners, should come.

This, the first day of our escape, was a long one, full of anxiety and fears, lest, after all our toils, we should be retaken and subjected to a captivity far worse than we had experienced before. About sundown the working party withdrew, and soon after nightfall we resumed our journey, again toward the North Star. We had scarcely got fairly started before our ears were saluted by the tramp of horses and the clank of sabers; we immediately left the road and lay down behind some brushwood. It proved to be a scouting party, perhaps in pursuit of us; but we let them pass unchallenged.

We continued our course till we reached the Chickahominy River; going up the stream a short distance, we found a log across it, passed over and kept our course for several miles, then changed our course north-east, and traveled till nearly daylight. We camped for the day by the side of a swamp, under a large pine-tree, near the foot of which was a thick cedar bush, whose shade we found most welcome, as it afforded us concealment and shelter from the bleak wind. The night had been very cold, and having crossed several swamps in our journey, our feet were wet, and our clothes frozen, as, indeed, was the case, day and night, till we reached the Union lines.

On the night of the 11th we traveled east, and crossed the railroad about half-past eight o'clock; we also crossed the main road from Richmond to Williamsburg, and two or three other roads, all leading into the main road from the Chickahominy, and just before day went into a hiding-place near one of these roads. As soon as it was light we saw that our place of rest was not well chosen; that scouts, or anyone in pursuit of us, could come close upon us before we could see them; we therefore sought another place, from which we could see to a considerable distance in every direction.

We were careful to shun everything in the shape of a man, whether black or white; but after traveling through swamps and thickets, on the fourth night we came to a path along which a negro man was passing; we stopped him and asked a number of questions and were convinced, from his answers, that he was a friend and might be trusted. We then told him our condition, and asked him if he could give us something to eat. He said that he was not near home, or he would do so cheerfully; but pointing to a house in the distance, to which he said he was going, assured us that friends lived there, and if we would go with him our wants should be supplied. He said the people who lived there were Union folks, and that we need not fear; but we had suffered so much that we did not feel inclined to trust strangers; however, I asked him to go to the house and see if any rebel soldiers were there. This he did readily, and soon returned, telling us to come on, that the way was clear, and supper, such as they had, would soon be prepared for us. I then asked him if he would stand guard while we went in, as I was still fearful of being retaken. He agreed to do so. We then entered the house, found a good fire, and some friendly faces; and the inmates set about preparing supper for us with all speed. We happened to have a little coffee with us, the very thing of which they seemed most in need. We added this to their store, and soon we had the first good meal we had taken for months before us, and a cheery cup of hot coffee, which made it seem a feast. After the meal was ended, being fully satisfied that the people were friends, and our black friend outside faithful, we rested awhile, which we certainly needed, if ever men did, and gave to our kind entertainers all that we could—our heart-felt thanks. When we were ready to start, the faithful negro sentinel, who had stood guard for us, offered to be our guide, and conducted us about four miles on our journey; he advised us to cross to the north side of the road, as we should meet with fewer swamps, and consequently make better progress.

We then traveled on till daylight, and stopped, as usual, for the day; but our clothes were so wet and frozen that we were obliged to travel on to keep from being perfectly benumbed with cold. We had not traveled any in the daytime before, and began to think that we were out of danger; still, we kept a vigilant watch, but met with no interruption, and we gradually became bolder. About sundown we saw before us a negro chopping wood; and as he was directly in our line of march, and our adventure of the previous night had given us confidence in those having black skins, we walked directly toward him, intending to inquire about the roads, the position of the rebel pickets, the movements of scouting parties, and other matters of interest. Judge of our surprise, however, when we came within a few paces of him, to find a white man with him, seated at the foot of a tree! It was too late to change our course, as he evidently saw us; so we went up to him and inquired how far it was to Barnesville, a small town we had passed a few miles back. He answered us civilly, and we asked several other questions, which he replied to satisfactorily. He gave us to understand, however, that he recognized us as Union soldiers. We told him that was not the case, but that we were Confederate scouts in disguise, and asked him if he had, during the past few days, seen any Yankees in that vicinity. He said that he had not, and insisted that we were Federal soldiers ourselves. At length I told him we were, and that we had escaped from Libby Prison. He protested that he was glad to see us, had heard of the escape of the Libby prisoners, but did not credit it—but must believe it now, as he had the living witnesses before him. He talked freely with us, saying, among other things, that he was a citizen, and had taken no part whatever in the war, and even expressed the wish that we might make our escape.

I told him that I expected, as soon as we were gone, that he would go to the nearest picket-post and inform his rebel friends what course we had taken. He declared that he had no such intention, and repeated the wish that we might have a safe journey. I then asked him if he knew of any pickets near. He replied there were none nearer than Burnt Ordinary, which was some miles distant, and that he had not seen a Confederate soldier for three weeks—in fact, that they seldom came in that direction. The truth was, as we soon discovered, there was a picket-post not more than half a mile from the place where we stood. This he well knew, and did his utmost to betray us into their hands. He advised us to follow a certain path, by doing which he said we should avoid a swamp that it was difficult and dangerous to cross, and even went with us a short distance to see that we did not take the wrong path. I could not, however, resist the conviction that he was treacherous, and did all I could to impress him with a salutary fear, telling him that if he informed on us, there was a certain General Butler, of whom he had doubtless heard, who had a way of finding such things out; and if anything happened to us he would doubtless send out a detachment that would destroy everything that he had. If, however, he conducted himself as a quiet, peaceable citizen, he and his property would be respected. He assured us that no harm should come to us through him, shook hands with us, and wished us again a safe journey.

We had not gone over a hundred yards when, happening to look back, I saw our friend traveling at a pace quite unnecessary for one so friendly, and the whole matter flashed on my mind. I turned to my comrade and said, "We are gone up; that scoundrel, I feel certain, has gone to report us to the nearest picket-guard!"

So well assured did I feel of his treachery, that I proposed that we should change our course from south to east, which we did immediately—and then almost too late. We had not pursued our new course more than half a mile when we heard voices of men talking in a low yet earnest tone; we stopped and listened; it was even as I had suspected—the professed friend, from whom we had recently parted, had gone to the nearest pickets, informed the rebels who we were, and how we might be intercepted;

and the officer was now placing his men on the road near where we were expected to cross, and we were now within fifteen or twenty paces of them—they, aware of our coming, wary and watchful. It was a moment of fearful suspense; we were screened from view, however, by the bushes; and our only chance was to change our course; we started, but the rustling of the dry leaves beneath our feet betrayed us, and we were sternly ordered to come out of the brush.

We hesitated, and the order was repeated in fierce, quick tones, which were accompanied by a volley of musketry. On this we came out at a double-quick, but in a direction opposite to that which we were thus rudely invited—in other words, we broke away and ran for life. With a shout our enemies joined in the pursuit, and pressed us so closely that I was obliged to throw away my overcoat, and Lieutenant Fislar lost his cap. On came our pursuers, nearer and nearer, till, at length, in order to save ourselves, we had to take refuge in a large swamp. Orders were given to surround it, and we could hear men on every side calling to each other, and giving direction how to prevent our escape—and all this when liberty was almost in our grasp; for we were then but three miles from the Federal lines.

While thus lying concealed in the swamp, our reflections were not of the most agreeable character. We had almost reached the reward of much toil and suffering; we had even begun to think and talk of home and the loved ones there; and now, by the baseness of one of our fellow-beings, to lose the prize almost in our grasp, was too painful a thought to be calmly endured. We contrasted the duplicity—nay, almost perjury, of the civilized white man who had betrayed us into the power of our enemies, with the fidelity of the African slave who had proved so kind and true, and felt that under the dark skin beat the nobler heart. The one, of our own race, in violation of promises the most solemn, would have given us back to a fate worse than death; the other, of another and despised race, did all in his power to restore us to freedom and home.

Thus encircled by our enemies, our only hope of escape lay in crossing the swamp in front of us, which was a most perilous undertaking, as all who have any acquaintance with the swamps of the Chickahominy well know. The remembrance of the prison we had left, and the fear of one even worse if retaken, urged us on; and, after many difficulties, our efforts were at last successful. We attempted to cross four or five times before we were able to do so, and more than once we were ready to despair. In one of our attempts I stepped from a log and went down into mud waist-deep; every motion I made only served to carry me down still lower; but my true friend Fislar was at hand, and saved me from a horrible fate. He came to the end of the log, and I roused every energy and threw myself toward him; he was just able to reach my hand, which was eagerly stretched out to him, and he drew me exhausted from the mire.

Never can I forget that kind, generous friend—a truer man to country and friends does not live; the trials through which we passed only served to develop his noble nature, and he will ever seem dear as a brother to me. He is a noble specimen of a man, physically; has dark hair, brown eyes, and light complexion—is six feet high, well-proportioned, and has an agreeable face—is possessed of fine natural abilities, is twenty-three years of age, brave, active, and daring, ready for any emergency—and, to crown all, has as noble a heart as ever beat in human breast; and, for friend and companion, at home or abroad, in prosperity or adversity, there is no one that I have ever known that I would prefer to him.

Being exhausted by our journey through a swamp, which would have been deemed impassable had we not been urged on by hopes before and fears behind, we stopped for a time to gather strength for new efforts, hoping before sunrise to be beyond the reach of successful pursuit. Again we began our march, and near midnight we saw the picket-fires near Burnt Ordinary, but supposed them to be those of the rebels, as we had been told by the man who had betrayed us, that the rebels had a picket-guard at that place, which was true; but that evening, before we reached there, the Union cavalry had driven them away, and the fires we saw were those of our own pickets. Our narrow escape had rendered us very cautious; and having every reason to believe that the fires in sight were those of the enemy, we passed around them at what we thought a safe distance, and then struck out for Williamsburg, then, as we afterward learned, about twelve miles distant. We had not gone far before we were halted. Inquiring of the sentinel who he was, and where we were, he informed us that he belonged to the 11th Pennsylvania Cavalry, which was under General Butler's command. As we had tried to play Confederate ourselves, we were not certain but that this might be one of them trying to play Yankee. After questioning him very closely, and being fully satisfied that he was "all right," we advanced. When we got up to him he told us that he and his comrades had been sent out on that advanced post in order to meet and aid prisoners who were said to have escaped from Libby Prison; and, added he, "I guess you are some of them." We told him we were, and he expressed great pleasure at meeting with us, and we felt what words never can express—a joy which can never be felt save by those who, after privations and anxieties like ours, feel that they are safe at last.

The next morning, having been furnished with horse, sword, and pistol, I moved forward with the column, which was composed of picked men from three companies of the 11th Pennsylvania Cavalry. My position was in front with the captain—every man with eager eyes on the lookout for the late inmates of Libby. We had not advanced more than two miles before we saw two men emerge from a thicket and regard us anxiously; they were immediately recognized as escaped prisoners; but oh! What emotions filled my heart when I saw and knew the well-known forms and faces of Major Fitzsimmons and Captain Gallagher, of the old working party—companions in suffering, and soon to be partakers of joy such as mine! Spurring my horse in advance of the rest, and swinging my hat and cheering as I went, I hastened to meet my old companions—and seldom is so much joy pressed into a few brief moments as was ours when we met; we wept, we laughed, we shouted aloud in our joy, and warmer, gladder greetings will never be exchanged till we meet in the land where there are no partings. Our men came up and welcomed the fugitives warmly—not a man in the band who was not willing to dismount and let the wearied ones ride; and together we rode in search of others whom we doubted not were near; and during the day eleven more were added to our number— each one of them increasing our joy. I have known hours in my captivity when I have almost lost faith in man; but that day my faith in humanity was restored.

During the day we had several skirmishes with the rebel scouts, and captured a few horses and accouterments, and returned the same evening to Williamsburg, when another detachment was sent out on a mission similar to that in which we had been engaged; and I need not say they bore with them our warmest wishes for their success.

We were all furnished with transportation to Yorktown. From thence we went by boat to Fortress Monroe, and were conducted by General Wistar to headquarters, and introduced to General Butler, who expressed the greatest pleasure at our escape, and only regretted that some of our number had again fallen into the hands of the enemy. We had, of course, to go over the story of our treatment while in the hands of the rebels, and our perils on the way to the Union lines; and were made to feel the contrast by the attention bestowed upon us. Every heart seemed full of sympathy, and every tongue had a kind word. For ourselves, words were powerless to express the gratitude we felt for such constant kindness. Many had mourned us as dead, and our return was like the grave giving up those it had once claimed as its own; and we were unutterably glad to be under the old flag and at home once more.

Sources

"Benedict Arnold's Navy" from *The Major Operations of the Navies.* Alfred Thayer Mahan. London: Sampson, Low. Marston & Company Limited. 1912.

"Breaking Out of Libby Prison" from *Four Months in Libby and The Campaign Against Atlanta.* I. N. Johnston. Cincinnati: E. P. Thompson. 1864.

"Capturing San Juan Hill with the Rough Riders" from *The Rough Riders.* Theodore Roosevelt. New York: Charles Scribner's Sons. 1899.

"Doolittle Hits Tokyo" from *The Greatest Air Aces Stories Ever Told.* Colonel Robert Barr Smith and Laurence J. Yadon. Lanham, MD: The Lyons Press, an imprint of The Rowman & Littlefield Publishing Group, Inc. 2017.

"How the *Merrimac* Was Sunk in Cuba" from *Historic Adventures: Tales from American History.* Rupert S. Holland. Philadelphia: George W. Jacobs. 1913.

"Omaha Beach: Following General Cota" from *D-Day Genera: How Dutch Cota Saved Omaha Beach on June 6, 1944.* Noel F. Mehlo Jr. Lanham, MD: Stackpole Books, an imprint of The Rowman & Littlefield Publishing Group, Inc. 2021

"Raiding Union Commerce with Rafael Semmes" from *Cruise and Captures of the* Alabama. Albert M. Goodrich. Minneapolis: The H.W. Wilson Company. 1906.

"Repelling the Chinese at Chipyong-ni" from *High Tide in the Korean War: How an Outnumbered American Regiment Defeated the Chinese at the Battle of Chipyong-ni.* Leo Barron. Lanham, MD: Stackpole

Books, an imprint of The Rowman & Littlefield Publishing Group, Inc. 2015.

"Supplying the Embattled Marines at Khe Sanh" from *The Battle for Khe Sanh*. Captain Moyers S. Shore II. Washington, DC: History and Museums Division Headquarters, US Marine Corps. 1969.

"Taking Mount Suribachi" from *Closing In: Marines in the Seizure of Iwo Jima*. Joseph H. Alexander. Marines in World War II Commemorative Series. Washington, DC: US Marine Corps Historical Center. 1994.